MW01242817

FAITH
(APPLIED)

SURVIVOR

**8 PRINCIPLES FOR ACTIVATING
THE MIRACLE MAKING
POWER OF THE UNIVERSE**

NLV Industries
4325 Glencoe Avenue
Unit 11594
Marina del Rey, CA 90295

213-293-6025 Direct
www.WinWithFaith.com

Cover Design: Brent Emmett Mandolph II
Book Layout: Brent Emmett Mandolph II

ISBN-13: 978-1537140490
ISBN-10: 1537140493
BISAC: Self-Help / Spiritual

Table of Contents

Table of Contents

Introduction to Faith Applied   5

— **The Great TV Incident**

Faith Applied Principle #1   19

— **Accept the challenge**

Faith Applied Principle #2   33

— **Set the goal and a firm deadline to do what
must be done to achieve the challenge**

Faith Applied Principle #3   49

— **Position yourself for success**

Faith Applied Principle #4   75

— **Stay out of the Loser Clique**

Faith Applied Principle #5   101

— **Ask everyone who might help**

Faith Applied Principle #6   163

— **Don't waste time on people and situations
that don't help you get your goal**

Faith Applied Principle #7   193

— **Delay Judgment**

Faith Applied Principle #8   245

— **Work up to and through the deadline**

Epilogue   287

— **The Multiple Myeloma Incident**

Faith Applied Resources   333

— **Your Guiding Principles**
— **Faith Applied Project Planner**
— **A Personal Message for the Reader**
— **A Special Offer for the Reader**

"God is real! God is still here! Through the power of FAITH, God is still performing miracles for men and women today! And, if you will let me teach you how to APPLY the FAITH that already lives inside of you, He will surely begin to work His miracles for you too!"

If there is a core message that I want for you to take away from this book, that is it. To that end, it seems to me like a great place to start this book is by telling you what it is, why I'm writing it now and *what's in it for you if you will invest the time to truly read it – or even better, study it.* So that you know, this is information that I have known and used for many years now. It is wisdom that was passed to me personally from the *Creator* Himself. It was passed to me on the battlefield of life. It is not something that I read in someone else's book and then put into use.

I have certainly read books on the subject of faith. I have, of course, read about faith and the importance of it in the bible. But for some reason, the wisdom of those lessons has always gone right over my head. In that truth, I know that I am not alone. I don't know why it is that we human beings struggle with this life altering wisdom. But it seems that we just do.

I do know that to the degree that we struggle to grasp this powerful wisdom, we can tend to struggle in our lives. For there are some places in life where nothing else can do what faith can. Having it at those moments can make all the difference in the world.

I have certainly had my share of these incidents and I have been on both sides of the outcome. Thankfully at some point I was handed this wisdom to take into life's battles, especially the ones that matter the most.

Before this chapter comes to an end, I hope you'll see how this wisdom and faith power has served me. More importantly, I hope you will see how it can serve you too. But first, I feel it necessary to share that while I have had this wisdom for some time, I am almost embarrassed to admit that I haven't always lived by it, nowhere near so.

My tendency has been to pull it out when I had no other choice. That was usually when my back was up against the wall in some crisis that was beyond my natural ability to handle.

At other times, I would pull out this wisdom in times when the outcome was inconsequential in my life – when the outcome, good or bad, would have no real impact on my personal well-being.

All in all, through these moments in my past I never got an inkling that I should use this God-given faith formula as a guiding force in my life – as a way to create the lifestyle that I desired or to capture the goals and dreams that I had set out for myself.

This despite the fact that over many years, when I did employ this formula toward some purpose in my life, it always produced positive results for me, it always led to my receiving whatever I needed or hoped to receive.

At the same time, while I wasn't employing it in the most meaningful way, I always had a gnawing feeling that through the use of this God-given formula, my faith was being developed for some bigger purpose. I just had a gut level awareness that both these inconsequential events and the crises where I was wielding the power of this faith formula were actually a training ground for some yet to come, big event – one where my having the ability to successfully apply faith would be vital.

In the end, I could have never been more right in that thinking, as that greater purpose showed up nearly 17 years to the day after I had first been given the formula for faith. It showed up in the form of a medical diagnosis that would have floored most people – cancer. I will relate this story in greater detail later, but let's just say for now that I went from being a normally healthy guy to a person literally battling for my life and my ability to even stand and walk.

In between these two points on the calendar of my life, I have had many other chances to see the power of this faith formula in action. In just relating the stories of a few of those occasions, this book really could write itself and serve as a reminder of the power that each of us has available to us for living a victorious life, no matter what comes our way.

That is one of the reasons why I am writing this book; to keep this formula before me from now on. So that instead of just pulling it out in a jam, I can start to live by it on a regular basis and go on to build my dream life. In fact, in the aftermath of my using the formula to overcome the cancer that I was stricken with, I made a commitment to myself that I would make this faith formula a guiding force in my life.

I literally said to myself,

> *"Once I beat this, once I recover from this, once I am back on my feet and I have my life back, I am living the rest of my life by FAITH."*

In that moment, I committed to staying aware of and using this formula to walk by the power of faith for the rest of my days on this earth.

When I got home and up on my feet, I dug my notes on this wisdom and formula out and begin to organize what God had given me into a guidebook that I could live by and share with others. As I did so, I got a perfect chance to immediately use the formula to capture a few small victories beyond saving my life and prove to myself yet again that it truly does work. I am now writing this book about these and other successes I've had using this wisdom to stay reminded it works and get clear on how it was used in those moments.

Another reason for this writing is my desire to share these principles with people like you that may be in need of them. If you have picked up this book, you must have a desire to understand how faith works and to get the power of it flowing in your life. I don't believe that you would have picked it up for any other reason.

Perhaps you are like me in that you have struggled to understand how faith works and you need a simplistic formula to help you apply faith to your life. It is my hope that this text can be that simplistic guidebook that you can easily understand and apply to your life. Or, perhaps you are just starting to try to understand faith and you know nothing at all about how or why it works. Whichever the case, I hope this work will be of great help and value to you.

Most importantly, I want it to be a quick reference on the subject of faith; a place where you can come to to get the kind of wisdom that will produce reliable results. Even when I didn't fully know by name what principles I was employing, whenever I operated from a base of this formula, it always produced reliable results for me.

Now I hope that by giving you a thorough knowledge of the world's first practical faith formula, by teaching you it's 8 principles by name, you will be able to do even greater things with this wisdom in your life.

Explaining the 8 principles of *FAITH (APPLIED)*, proving to you that they are real and that they will work for you is simple. There was a singular incident that served as the origin of my awareness of these principles and it perfectly exemplifies the miracle-making power that is activated when they are put to proper use. Let me now relate that story to you so you too can clearly see the power of *FAITH (APPLIED)!*

July 30th, 1995

I could not ever begin to understand why on this particular day the *Creator* of this universe chose to impart such a valuable piece of wisdom to me. Neither could I have known why he chose such an inconsequential event at my job to be the delivery point for this wisdom. I am sure that these were principles that I had not thought about or toyed with in any way before.

I am also sure that by the end of this day, I'd been given my own private demonstration of 8 working principles of faith; principles that when applied could activate the miracle producing power of this universe. By the end of this day, I had witnessed the power that comes from putting these principles together and using this faith formula to work towards what might otherwise be seen as an impossible task.

On July 30th, 1995, I was a regular Joe working in a dead end retail sales job and struggling to make ends meet. My wife and I had one son, Brandon who was 3 and a half years old. And, we had just had our second son, Bryant 25 days prior.

I was the main breadwinner, and given that my wife was recovering from giving birth to our son, the only income earner in the house at the time. While my income covered the basic bills, it was scarcely enough to take care of my family in the manner that I desired to. Thus, extra money was greatly needed and desired.

As much as I'd like to believe that I would have done just about anything that was presented to me – so long as it was legally, morally and ethically fine to do, that just was not true. I had had opportunities to earn extra income in the past from things that involved things like direct/personal sales or network marketing.

As great as these things were for others, despite signing up, I just could not seem to get any value out of them for my family. Like most people like me, I was more seeking something that would allow me to trade some of my time for money. I wanted to work extra hours for more hourly pay. But I couldn't seem to find anything like that back then.

On this particular day, I got another one of those chances to earn extra income that had been of no financial value to me in times past. It came to me in the form of a special offer from my employer.

Not only was it the kind of offer that yielded me nothing in the past, but it was even more doubtful that I could successfully undertake this task this time around because it would require me to do in one day, what I had only previously been able to do with nearly a full month of effort.

To be exact, I needed to do in one work day, what it took me the previous 29 work days to do. And, to make matters worse, this particular day was the shortest of all possible work days to achieve this task.

The offer was this, hit a special sales quota that management laid out that morning and receive a $1,000 bonus for doing so. Now to put this in perfect context, a $1,000 bonus would be like nearly doubling my income for the month.

As attractive and exciting as that offer was, as much as I would have loved to receive such a bonus at that time, what I'd have to do to receive it was just a bit too far-fetched. You see, for me to hit the sales target that was laid out before me, I would have had to end the day with sales of $16,000 for the month.

To do that, I would have had to double my sales output for the month in just one day – as in, on this day, I had only managed to bring in sales of about $8,000. Now to get this $1,000 bonus, I would have to sale another $8,000 worth of merchandise in just one 8 hour day.

I would imagine that you can see the problem with even believing that I could accept this offer, let alone achieve the task. Well it is up against that backdrop that this story plays out. For some reason still unknown to me, on that day I did accept the offer and what followed in the ensuing 8 hours, through the guidance of the *Creator* was a master course in how FAITH works when it is properly APPLIED.

By the days end, by the gift of a power far greater than my own, I had achieved the goal of doubling my sales and was one of only a few members of the sales staff who earned the $1,000 bonus. And, getting to that end result was a day filled with drama, learning and ultimately nothing short of miraculous. The story begins like this.

The Great TV Incident

The day began like any other month end day at this job, with my boss, *Mr. Kahane* complaining about how poor a month we were having. He talked about how this was the last real selling day of the month and how if things didn't get better, management would eventually want him to let some people go.

Then he went around the room and asked each one of us in sales what it would take for us to raise our numbers. There were a lot of great sounding answers, but nothing that he could see that anyone would really put into practice.

By the end of this meeting, he was questioning whether or not we as a sales staff could raise our numbers. In his words, he could see in the eyes of some of us that we just were going through the motions.

He said, if that were the case, he along with ownership would start handing out pink slips. By the end of this meeting he had made up his mind, something needed to be done to see where this group stood.

He excused himself from the meeting for a moment to phone the owner of the company. When he returned, he did so with an offer that was part too good to be true and part too high to reach, even if it were true.

He said,

"Listening to you guys talk this morning, I have decided that it is time for the rubber to meet the road. It is time for me to determine who wants to sale and make real money and who just wants to stick around and collect an hourly check. So here is what the owner and I have agreed to. Each person, in each department in the store who hits the special quota set out for their department will receive a $1,000 bonus. No matter where you are as we start the day, whether you are close to hitting the quota or far away, if you are at the quota at the end of the day, $1,000 is yours!"

That was the offer. For me, as I mentioned before, as I listened to this offer being laid out I immediately realized that I was only about half way to the special quota that sales people in my department were expected to bring in and that it would all but take a miracle for me to earn that bonus.

There was no advance warning that this offer was coming down. It had been born out of the back and forth between the sales staff and management from the morning meeting. Thus I had no prior knowledge that my morning would start with this dilemma. So as that offer gets laid out, the first thing I had to do was make a split second decision as to where I stood on the matter.

Again, this was a Sunday, the shortest selling day of the week. Also, it was Sunday the 30th – the last real selling day of the month, just a one day challenge. In structuring it this way, it was almost like they were putting the offer on the table, but designing it in a way that was not likely to give us a real chance to achieve it. And, with these facts going against me, I somehow found the faith inside myself to believe that I could do it and quietly set out to achieve it.

8 hours later, to even my shock, I had the goal in my hand. In fact, I was the only person in my department and one of only a few in the overall store to achieve the goal, and this despite the fact that there were others who were way closer to the goal at the beginning of the day than I was.

I am purposely sparing you the overall details of how I did it because the details make up the 8 principles of this faith formula. In the coming chapters I will lay out each of these 8 principles in full detail and tell you exactly how it related to the events of that day. But for now I must tell you how the day and my quest for this goal ended in dramatic and miraculous fashion.

"Tell me about this $2,000 TV!"

It should really go without saying that this was a really tough task to achieve. Trying to do the equivalent of 29 previous days of selling in 1 day required a ton of focus, effort and FAITH. Even though I was managing to make some sales, there were many times throughout this day when I privately wondered what I had signed myself up for. However through it all, I just kept pushing.

As I reached the point where 7 hours and 40 minutes of this 8 hour work day had ticked off, despite my best efforts, I still found myself in need of $4,000 in sales to hit the quota and earn the $1,000 bonus. At that point, with just 20 minutes of selling time left, it would have been perfectly reasonable for me to give up. After all, I had given it my best shot.

That is when the miraculous happened. Just when the other salespeople in the department started to wrap it up and prepare to close the store and go home, in walks a gentleman asking about a $2,000 TV. Guess who was right there to help him? Me!

As I begin to explain the features of this 36 inch TV, the thought occurred to me that even if I could get him to buy it,

I'd likely still be $2,000 short of what I needed to hit the quota. However through it all, I just kept pushing.

I did my job. I showed him all the features and got him really excited about buying this TV. Then it occurred to me that we had talked up the final 20 minutes of the selling day. The store was now closing and he still had not said he would buy it. However through it all, I just kept pushing.

Eventually I said,

"Sir, this really is a great set. As you can see, we are closing up now and I don't know if you are really seriously interested in buying this set, but now is the time to make a decision if you want to do it today."

To which he said,

"Well I am very serious, in fact, I was going to ask you do you have 2 of them that I could buy?"

Did you hear that? Did it hit you like it hit me when I first heard it? I thought my ears were deceiving me. As the clock hit zero, did he just say he needed 2 of them or $4,000 worth of TV's – the exact amount I needed to sale to hit my quota? I repeated it back to him and he said I had heard him right.

A quick check of inventory revealed that we had the sets. Could it be that I achieved this unachievable goal? I still didn't have the goal officially so I just kept my cool. I came back and told him that I had them.

He said,

"Great! Now I just need to go get the money."

In my mind I wanted to scream,

"There it is, I knew it was too good to be true."

However through it all, I just kept pushing. I ask him what did that mean and he explained that he had to return to his business to get the funds. He said it was a local trip. The store was already closing while this is all playing out. So I went to my manager and ask if we could let this guy back in and do this deal if he indeed came back. The manager said *"yes"*, so long as he made it back within 30 minutes of us closing. I relayed this condition to the gentlemen and he was on his way.

After he left the store, in my mind I definitely wanted to scream, *"I knew it was too good to be true."* When some of my fellow sales mates got wind of what was going on, they made sure that they said it for me. However even through this, I just kept pushing mentally, I kept believing in my mind.

Each minute that he was gone felt like an eternity. Part of me wanted to believe. Part of me wanted to get excited. Part of me even wanted to start spending the $1,000 bonus in my mind, but the goal was not in hand. Plus another part of me wanted to believe like my comrades that it wasn't going to happen.

Even though my department was way in the back of the store and I had duties to carry out back there before I could go home, I couldn't bring myself to leave the area around the front door. I wanted to make sure that if this gentleman did come back, there was no way that we'd miss him or fail to let him in.

As it turned out, I didn't have to wait for long. As unlikely as it all was, this gentleman reappeared. He had come back like he said he would. It was now about 25 minutes past closing. In keeping with the condition that my manager had put on his return, he made it back with only 5 minutes to spare.

We let him in and he produced from his pocket a bankroll, the size of which I had never seen – $5,000 in cash money. He bought those 2 TV's, the service warranty for each, plus he paid us to deliver them. In so doing, he capped off the best and clearly the most miraculous selling day that I had ever had up to that point in my career.

The check that resulted from that unbelievable day (Payroll + Bonus – taxes) would go on to represent the most money that I had ever made at one time in my life – $1,800 and made for a fun shopping spree for my wife and I.

When it was all said and done, I became a little darling to the management at my job. Even though they had no clue of the role *FAITH(APPLIED)* had played in this achievement, they used me and the story of the results that I achieved on this day as proof that our numbers could be raised, if that was what we were trying to do.

While ownership never set this type of special quota or made this type of bonus offer again, and I never sold this amount of merchandise at that job again, it still showed me that I was capable of way more than I had been doing.

Yet as I worked through this day, as powerful and miraculous as these events were, I had no awareness of the principles or the formula that I am now able to share with you. It took a little while longer before the **Creator** unveiled the 8 principles and their larger truth to me. In fact, it was in looking back a month later, after the shock and disbelief had just about worn off that the **Creator** showed me what was truly behind this accomplishment.

8 Principles for Activating the Miracle-Making Power of the Universe

I can now say that what the **Creator** eventually revealed to me was a practical formula for how the force known as *FAITH* could be activated to produce miraculous results in the affairs of my life.

The benefits of activating this force are almost beyond words. However I feel that it is of the utmost importance to tell the reader that the power of this force is that it is an aid that helps you to achieve things in your life that you could never achieve otherwise.

When tapped into this wisdom I have brought to bear power that was beyond my own power and strength. This force brought to bear senses, or a level of senses that were beyond my normal level of awareness. I could see things in my consciousness that I normally couldn't see. I could perceive things that I normally did not perceive. Ideals came to me with greater clarity. Clear instructions came as to how to solve long pressing problems. It was like I all of the sudden had a sixth sense.

If money was what I needed, I would be led to a place where I would find the money I needed, literally. If it were say $100 I needed, I am talking about being led to a place where I would find the $100 that I needed in the form of a $100 bill lying on the ground as I drove down the street in my car. Finding money in this way has happened to me on so many occasions that my family knows to take me serious when I say I see some money lying at the curb as we drive.

When plugged into this wisdom, human angels would appear to do for me what I couldn't do for myself. In moments of great crisis, these angels would do or open a path for me to do, what it seemed like would never get done. In simple words, when plugged into this wisdom, I am literally talking about the mountain moving effortlessly – I am talking about the cares of this world becoming light.

And, it was in the aftermath of this work incident that the 8 principles of this formula for activating the miracle-making power of this universe were revealed to me by name for the first time. It was also the first time that I was shown that success achieved by the use of this 8 principle recipe, in a moment of crisis or in pursuit of a goal, was no random occurrence.

Since that day, the ***Creator*** continued to use my business and work life to further my awareness of these 8 principles. And, in my personal life, He took me through many incidents where I had to use this faith recipe to achieve what could easily have been considered to be the *"Impossible."* Each of those occasions have always helped to bolster my belief in the validity of this wisdom.

In writing this book, I have chosen to present much of this wisdom through the sharing of some of the tales from the business and work events that the ***Creator*** used to teach me these 8 faith principles. As you read these tales, don't make the mistake of thinking that this work is not about you mastering the lessons of ***FAITH (APPLIED)***.

Falling into the trap of such thinking would be a huge mistake. Instead, as you read make the effort to translate these stories and the lessons that they convey into their broader context and then relate them to the affairs of your life.

If you must question why the text seems to rest against a work/business backdrop, simply stay mindful of the fact that that is where the ***Creator*** himself chose to deliver much of this wisdom to me. And, it was also a large part of the proving ground He used to validate the principles and perfectly drill them into me.

So let it go at that and stay focused on the points that are being conveyed. Doing this would be of great benefit to you. If anything, take to heart the fact that these principles and this formula have application in all settings; as in they will work in your professional life, just as surely as they have perfect application in the affairs of your everyday life.

For me, now having used them to overcome cancer, I have committed the rest of my life to living by them in all areas of my life and to sharing them with all who will hear and embrace them as well.

So what do you think would be the first thing that must be done to call into action the miracle-making power known as *FAITH*? Well here is what the spirit of **God** showed me. To activate the miracle-making power of the universe, you must first:

Accept the challenge

What is the challenge that you are confronted with in trying to meet this crisis or achieve your goal? Can you identify it? Is it one main barrier, or can it be broken up into multiple smaller parts? Whatever the case, even if you can't identify what it is, don't think about what sounds realistic or doable for you. Just accept the challenge as it is. Be open minded and believe that it can be done, that you can do it and hold this in your mind and thoughts intensely from that point on. Most importantly, during the undertaking do not see or entertain, for even one second, any other outcome for yourself other than the one you desired when accepting the challenge. That is the starting point of FAITH(APPLIED).

On July 30th, 1995, the most logical thing for me to do would have been to see it as too great a challenge to achieve the task that management had set before me, no matter how nice a $1,000 bonus would have been. And, if I had taken that attitude and position, no one would have considered me wrong to think that way. After all, I needed to do in 1 day, what it had taken me 29 other days to do. Again, it was one of the shortest days of the selling week.

On that day, as it related to my ability to successfully achieve that goal, all of the indicators pointed toward it being impossible. Normally that is exactly how I would have saw it. But on that day, something inside of me, something instinctive, told me to just accept the challenge for what it was at face value.

Once I had done that, I simply put the matter to rest and did not ever question whether it could be done again. Little did I know at that time, that seemingly simple decision started me on the path to an understanding that would literally save my life.

Make no bones about it, it was a stark difference from the response of many of my co-workers on that day. Many couldn't wait until the meeting was over to spew their negative attitudes.

Most of those who were negative were even closer to quota than I was when this offer was placed before us. But instead of *accepting the challenge* to go after this $1,000 bonus, they declined. And, once they took this stance, they made every excuse under the sun for why they could not achieve this task.

They painted their gloomy forecast of what the day ahead held for us in terms of customer flow and sales. They pointed out that this was a Sunday, the shortest selling day of the week. They questioned the motives of management, *"Why had they waited until this one day to make such an offer?"* They called it, *"a deck stacked against us."*

For my part, I just sat quietly and let them speak, choosing to add nothing to their roundtable of negativity. Without a doubt, once the doors opened for the day, their attitude became their actions; or I should say their inaction. They performed exactly like they predicted they would.

On the other hand, in *accepting the challenge* quietly to myself, I chose to just go with the flow of things and see where the day would take me. I didn't consider how far away from the goal I was. I didn't try to forecast what the day would hold in terms of customer traffic.

I didn't care that it was a Sunday. I didn't question the motives of management. All I heard was that they were putting some money on the table for anyone that wanted to go get it. Beyond that, I didn't add a bunch of thought to the equation.

Most of all, I didn't try to judge something that hadn't had a chance to happen yet. Without me realizing it at that moment, that little act, one that was a bit uncommon for me then was the first step to me calling up a spiritual force that could do things that I couldn't do in the physical.

Because I didn't judge the challenge, I tapped into a spiritual force that was not bound by what my co-workers saw as the immovable barriers to our success. Just quietly *accepting the challenge* was the first step to what I would later come to learn was the power of *FAITH (APPLIED)*.

There have been many times throughout my life when I did the same thing when confronted with a seemingly unachievable task. Especially in times when I was dealing with something that simply had to be done – something where failure was not an option. Having done this many times, I can truly attest to the fact that this is an essential component to applying faith in your affairs.

There simply is no way to even begin applying faith without developing the ability to *accept a challenging circumstance*. I have heard it said that one of the things that people who overcome crisis or people who do great things have in common is the ability to *accept a challenge* and to approach it from the standpoint of,

"What if the impossible can be done?"

When the underdog sports team manages to beat the highly favored opponent, we invariably find out that the underdog team had no problem *accepting the challenge* and embodying a spirit of,

"What if the impossible can be done?
What if we can do what no one thinks we can do?"

That is a far cry from doing what most of us do when confronted by challenging tasks. We have all just about been conditioned to give up before we ever even consider whether or not the task is possible.

We draw on our own limited wisdom. We draw on our own limited connections. Or, we draw on our own past record of low achievement and it appears that there is just no way for us to successfully rise to the challenge placed before us.

I certainly could have done that on this day. As well as, several other times that I was in similar situations. Looking from the vantage point of our physical eyes or from our past failed or limited endeavors, we just can't see where the results we desire will come from. And, many of us have never been made aware of the truth that we don't have to know where we will get a result when we commit to getting it.

I have read many books and taken many courses before that taught that you should not worry so much about where your results will come from when you are trying to achieve a task. They all say that the universe will deliver it to you. But until I got a hold of these principles, that thinking has always felt unnatural to me.

In fact, it took me years to get it. But I have found this to be profoundly true. You don't have to know where it is coming from! You just have to know it is out here! And, that you can get it! In fact, more often than not, we really don't have a clue as to where our results will come from.

For example, I have had many instances in business where the prospective client that I thought would do a deal with me, declined to take my proposal. Yet, the proposal that I submitted to a seemingly uninterested or unqualified prospect, became a closed deal. I have had this truth play out in my life on many occasions.

Because of this, one of the mottos that I now live by is this,

"I don't have to know where my results will come from;
I just have to be in motion."

I literally use this thinking when I am engaged in trying to solve an impossible problem or complete a duanting business project. I will usually say this slogan to myself over and over while engaged in the project. I use this thinking to release myself from the burden of trying to know who will do what.

The challenge with trying to know or even guess who will help you solve a problem or do business with you is that we get demoralized when we are wrong. From that place we usually give up on ourselves, or the project, or on finding a solution to our problem before the real answer can come along. And, often, if we had just ridden the cycle out to the end of the time allotted, the answer would have come along.

Sometimes you just don't know where your results will come from. Other times you are just wrong about who it will be. Actually, in my experience, more often than not that is the truth. But none of that matters so long as you get the result.

Usually we don't care who does the deal or who helps us solve the problem – we just want the result. So learning how to just stay open and keep moving is critical to success. You just keep moving and leave the *"Who"* to the **Creator**.

The Great Jay Knott Incident

To begin with, the faith answer sent from the **Creator** is often foreign to us anyway. The closest I have come to having a clue as to when something was the right answer or was being offered to me by the guidance of **God**, is when it doesn't feel like the one to me.

As in, there have been many instances in my faith walk when the spirit was pulling me in a direction that felt totally illogical to me, but it turned out to be the answer to my prayer and exactly what I was standing in faith for.

I remember a time when my family needed to move from our apartment and find a new place to live. My wife and I were a young couple, with a couple of small children at the time. Like many young couples, our family was not financially stable yet.

Back then, due to the high cost of daycare, my wife stayed at home with the kids and I worked in professional sales. And we didn't have any real family support. Going home to someone in the family was not an option and would not be a solution to our problem.

Despite my sincerest efforts in my sales job, we were struggling financially and struggling to keep a roof over our heads. After falling behind on rent, the landlord became impatient with our situation and just asked us to move.

As life would have it, the timing of this was all bad. If we were struggling to pay where we lived, there was no doubt that moving would be an even bigger challenge. Moving would cost even more with the upfront outlay of rent and deposits (Both rent and utilities), plus moving fees.

Is it any surprise that we didn't have money for all of this? Something had to come through for us or we were out on the streets. You talk about having to **accept the challenge**. This was one of the biggest challenges I had seen in my life at the time. It was certainly the biggest I had faced as a young husband and father.

We had been given 30 days to get out of our current place and into a new place. And, it seems like those days flew by without any improvement in our situation. In fact, as the clock ticked down we had no real prospects for a new place and no real improvement to our money situation. Truthfully, all we had was prayer. And, I can't say that I really believed that that would do anything for us.

Before long, we were at the deadline day for us to have rounded up a new place and the money to move into it. I remember it like it was yesterday. It was a Monday morning. On that morning, I arose early, if I had slept at all the night before. I prepared for the day like any other work day – although I felt like the clock was ticking toward our doom.

I left the house not feeling like I had any real sense of direction for the day. As far as I was concerned, it was just a matter of hours before we'd meet our doom and nothing I did that day would make any difference. It would all just be too little, too late.

As I drove around the city, really just passing time, a sudden urge came over me to go to the pawn shop and take out a loan on my work pager (Pager! – How long ago was that?) and my little micro-cassette recorder.

My first thought when this idea entered my mind was disbelief. For starters, the pager was not mines. It was issued to me by the company whose copiers I sold. It was how they got in touch with me if my boss (The company owner) or a client needed to speak to me.

Secondly, these items combined could have been worth no more than $10 or $15 bucks. So I thought that this was just a useless or desperate thought from me; or what I like to call an RST = **R**andom **S**tupid **T**hought. So I shrugged it off and just kept drifting around without any real direction.

But it came back again and this time, a second thought came with it that suggested that this was a word from **God** himself. My reaction this time was one bordering on anger. I angrily thought to myself that this can't be **God**. I thought what would **God** have to do with a Pawn Shop?

To me, this wasn't the best and I associated **God** with the best. I guess I had the impression that if **God** brought a solution to your problems, it would be in the form of a spectacular, heavenly, rainbow like presentation.

That didn't sound like the pawn shop to me then and if I thought about it, it probably wouldn't sound like a pawn shop to me today. So once again, I shrugged it off.

When I say that money was a problem for us back then, I mean literally. So much so that I was driving around that day, trying to find a solution to my situation on a tank of gas that wasn't going to take me too far, if something didn't give soon. All odds were seriously against me.

The thought came back a third time. This time, it came with a third thought that told me what to do once I got the cash. It told me to put the money in the gas tank and go to my other office in the valley – about 25 or 30 miles from where I was at the time.

As I mentioned earlier, I had a second income source at the time; one of those part time business opportunities that you join when you need extra money. Although at that time I had never made any real consistent money with that business, I had managed to sell a few copiers to some of the brokers in the business.

So with this thought, I felt the spirit was telling me to go to that office and try to sale this broker who hadn't accepted my proposal in the past. In fact, he never really took the time to seriously meet with me.

His wife had heard me out. Some of their broker buddies and higher ups had bought from me. But this guy had responded coldly to my proposal in the past, at best.

Once again, I thought you have got to be kidding me, **God**. This can't be the answer you have in mind. As far as I could see from past experience with this joker, there was nothing there. Once again, I shrugged it off and just kept going in a big circle.

As you might guess, eventually gas began to become an issue. The low fuel light was on and I knew that I didn't have much longer to be driving around going nowhere. Just then the thought came back a fourth time,

"Go pawn the pager and the micro-cassette recorder, get some gas and go to your office in the valley."

It had been about 3 hours or so since the original thought had entered my mind. Finally, with no other real prospects for a solution, I yielded. I went to a pawn shop that I was familiar with and pawned the pager and the micro-cassette recorder and got $10 just like I had thought I would.

I put the money in the gas tank and headed for the valley, believing that I was being led to go see this guy who had not been interested before. I knew he'd be there, or at least I thought he would, because the brokers had a Monday morning managers meeting and they were all required to be there.

I arrived at the office just as the meeting was wrapping up. I went looking for this guy but I was not seeing him. It appeared that he was not there. I looked real good. But after a while, it became clear that he was not there for some reason.

As you might imagine, I began to have the thought that I was right, that there was nothing here. I was just starting to think about how bad my situation was and how I had just been going in circles without any real direction. But then the real reason why I was led to come to this place appeared.

"Hey Brent, where's my copier?"

Before I could get too down on myself, out of the back comes a gentlemen that I had only briefly spoke to in the past. I had only verbally made a proposal to him to buy a machine from me.

In theory, he was less successful than the guy that I thought I was being led to come see. But he too had just opened his own office. He remembered I sold copiers and wanted to get one from me, right on the spot.

You talk about tears of joy!!! I told him hang on, ran to my car and got a sales contract. I came back in and tearfully wrote up his sale, all the while thinking about how **God** had just delivered.

That one sale paid me nearly $2,500 and single handedly solved our moving issue. But it only came true because I yielded to the urging of the spirit of **God**.

As I said, nothing about this process made sense to me in the natural. If I were to have followed my own judgments about the matter, we were doomed. It was simply too late and virtually impossible for us to do something about our plight.

There is also another truth that I have learned by going through moments like this and being urged to some action by the spirit of **God**. It is this,

*"You won't know what **God** is trying to do for you unless you get obedient in following the urging of the spirit and go through to the other side."*

Had I continued to reject this thought and just went home, I would have never known that there was someone else looking to buy from me.

All of my rationalizations would have made perfect sense TO ME. And, my failure would have been justified TO ME. But I am not **God**. What **God** can do through our **FAITH (APPLIED)** is much greater than what you or I can do.

I have literally seen this truth many times over. But only because I went through to the other side, did I get to see that there was something that only the spirit of **God** could see.

Remember I said that using these principles brings to your aid powers that you don't normally have. Remember I said that it can move the mountain or summons human angels to your aid? Wouldn't you say that that story is an example of that?

To tell you how the story ends, I got paid out from this sale, found a great apartment and signed a 12 month lease on it. The only thing was we had to wait a week to move in. So we ended up going out of town and spending a week with my mother-in-law (A week was about all we could do, believe me).

The great thing was that we showed up with no issues. We already had the keys to our new place. And, we had a pocket full of money. Plus, I moved my family out of the place that we had to vacate with time to spare.

So our visit became a mini-vacation instead of us looking for someone to put us up for a time. We needed to find a solution to this problem and by ***accepting the challenge*** and applying FAITH, **God** delivered. And, in a miraculous fashion at that.

I would be remiss if I did not point out what I believe is another faith activating principle that you should have picked up on from that story. Namely, the need to learn when not to even listen to you when you are engaged in a faith project.

I am sure you noted that it took the urging of the spirit of **God** four attempts to get me to act on the guidance that was being given to me. I don't know whether to call it normal, comical or sad, but that has been a fairly consistent theme with me and faith, especially when I was new to using it.

I almost never moved to action the first time the spirit showed me something. I would hear the guidance clearly. I knew who the guidance was coming from, as in, I knew that the thought didn't come from me.

But I guess you could say that I doubted the rightfulness of the guidance. And, thus, I was slow to act on it. However, in the end, that guidance was always 1000% accurate.

Over the years, I have learned to be a bit quicker to act on that kind of urging from the spirit of *God*. But to this day I still am not perfect and have my moments where it takes me a minute to get it.

The good news is that *God* gives me a minute to get it, as these urgings will generally keep coming so long as I don't give it a final denial. In the end, acting on that guidance usually means knowing when not to listen to myself, let alone others around me.

As that story perfectly illustrated, the directions that I was given were so far from where I would have thought a solution was going to come from. Not to mention, what I thought *God* would have instructed me to do.

If I didn't have the ability to go beyond my own narrow minded thinking and just let the spirit lead, I would have never achieved what I was led to achieve. Keep that in mind as you employ the tool of **FAITH** in your life.

Again, it is a spirit and a power beyond you and your understanding so don't try to understand it. Just enjoy the fact that you have access to a spirit and a power that can see and do what you can't.

Let me give you another quick example of what it means to *Accept the Challenge!* When I fell ill, even before I knew what I had, I made up my mind that I would beat it. I will explain more in detail later about my battle with a serious illness. But, right now as it relates to this principle, I must share this truth.

When I was first taken to the hospital I thought that I was having a heart attack. Under that circumstance, I thought that there wasn't much that I could do. But once that was clearly not the case I begin to reformulate my thinking on the situation.

As the doctors ran their test to find out exactly what was wrong with me, I preemptively made up my mind that I was going to beat whatever it is that they were going to come back and tell me they found.

Ultimately, they came back and told me that I had cancer. Even worse, how it attacked me was by putting a growth on and eroding some of the bones near my spine. As a result, I eventually realized that I couldn't sit up, stand or much less walk. In fact, I was completely bedridden for just about the first 6 months of this health crisis.

As a matter of fact, I had no control over my upper body and had to be physically moved by nurses or my family, if I needed to be moved. Making matters worse, if I was moved wrong, my body would go into a long, painful spasm.

When I say that my health and mobility was in question, I mean literally. So I had to not only stare down cancer. But I also had to stare down this circumstance that had for all intent and purposes, made me paralyzed in my core.

Still I carried this attitude that,

"I would beat whatever they tell me I have!"

I carried this attitude with me all the while I was in the hospital and all while I was going through treatments.

To even my main doctor's amazement, by way of this attitude, I have always responded well to the treatments and had a pretty swift recovery from this very serious attack on my health and mobility.

He always tells me that he can't understand why that is. I have tried to get him to understand that it is due to the power of faith; a power that was activated when I **accepted the challenge** that this illness brought and made up my mind that I would beat it.

From this place, it was easy for me to be upbeat and optimistic about my ability to overcome this challenge and recover. As a result, I have consistently been told that I am one of the most upbeat people that you will ever encounter that is facing such a predicament.

Even when I was in the hospital, all of the medical staff that worked on me expressed a joy in having me as their patient because of my positive outlook and pleasant demeanor. I have managed to maintain that upbeat spirit because of my understanding of the power of faith.

When people ask me how I am doing, my normal response is, *"I am doing excellent!"* When hearing that, most people pause to ask me how that is, especially if they know about my situation. What I always explain to those people is that,

"I have had the right set of wrong circumstances."

By this I mean to convey the truth that because of my faith walk, I not only know what a real problem looks like. But, I also know the power that you and I have to overcome any challenge that comes our way. *Accepting the challenges* that come your way just as I did here is the first step to igniting that power.

Are you starting to get the picture of what it means to *Accept the Challenge?* I hope so because one of the things that I hope to do here is to keep my explanation of these principles as brief as possible.

While I may need to get a little wordy to give you a clear understanding of how to apply some of the principles that we will be covering here, I still want to pen just enough to get you to get the point and no more.

In the end, I want to make this a work that you can read, digest and get into practice fast. Isn't that usually what our challenges require anyway? Isn't that also what we usually want in a plan to help us go out and achieve our goals and dreams? That's what I want this work to be for you – a fast reference that you can easily integrate into the battlefield of life.

Besides, when these principles were delivered to me, or whenever the spirit of *God* is showing something to me, those things are always shown to me in a flash of vision or a quick thought. There are never a ton of words or a wide span of time involved in these messages being delivered to me. It has always been about *"the picture equaling a thousand words."*

So when it comes to the word count here, I want to keep that *"as little as needed"* flow going. For the record, that is so not how I am in person. I can tend to be long winded in my communication style, but not here. Wherever possible, I'll aim to be brief. If a principle does run on the long side, know that it is a point of importance in this ***FAITH (APPLIED)*** formula.

Now that's not to say that the shorter principles are of less importance. Each principle is a key component of the ***FAITH (APPLIED)*** formula. It's just to say that I will spend more time on the points and principles that require me to do so.

So now that you have considered these key aspects of what it means to ***Accept the Challenge*** that is ahead of you, let's look at the second step in activating the miracle-making power of the universe:

Set the goal and a firm deadline to do what must be done to achieve the challenge

What is the goal that you are confronted with in trying to meet this crisis or achieve your dream? Are you clear about what that goal is? Is it one main goal, or can it be broken up into multiple smaller goals? Is it laid out in the form of the tasks that must be achieved in order to get the goal? Is there a specific timeframe within which you need to achieve this goal? The circumstance driven goal will usually include a specific timetable for which completion is required, and for that matter, a consequence for failing to achieve the desired result. If your goal does not have a specific timeframe for completion and consequence for failure, give it both of these. Then be prepared mentally to stick to them, no matter what the outcome.

On July 30th, 1995, I was confronted with a pretty big goal in trying to grab this $1,000 bonus that had been set out before me. As I've previously related, I needed to sale another $8,000 in merchandise to be exact.

On this day, I instinctively knew that I needed to start out by getting clear on exactly what the goal was, down to the penny. And, as the day went by and sales were made, I kept myself updated with where I stood in relationship to the amount that I needed to bring this goal home.

All throughout the day, I kept peeking at the computer terminal to see what I had brought in and what I still needed to bring in. For starters, doing this helped me to feel a sense of progress. I wasn't just standing still. I was actually moving ahead with each minute or each hour that I worked, with each customer that I helped.

At the end of the day, I know that giving myself this feeling of progress was very important. It certainly beat out allowing myself to feel as if nothing was being done. It kept me feeling like while I wasn't where I ultimately hoped to be, I certainly wasn't where I had started out.

The way I see it, a lot of why we fail to achieve the goals that we set out before ourselves is because of the two things that I just touched on. One, we don't know exactly what we want. Two, we don't keep ourselves informed of the progress that we are making. As a result, we allow ourselves to get demoralized and dejected in the process.

But of all the things related to goal setting that I think we struggle with the most is not being accurate about what our needs are. Basically, we set our goals too low; we don't step up and ask for all of the things that make the goal come true. It is like we are afraid that the order will be too big. It is like we are afraid that we are asking for something that we don't really deserve. It is like we don't want to own up to the real tab for our goal because it might offend the *Creator*.

Again I could have done that on this day. I could have believed that I could do some smaller number. But to step up and have the audacity to believe that I could go after such a big task took real nerve.

I can't say that I would have normally taken such courageous action. But for some reason on this day that was exactly what I did – placed the order, not judge whether it was too big an order to place.

"You can get whatever you want," if you can believe!

Perhaps you and I would always operate that way when we set our goals if we were confident that we were going to get whatever we order from the *Creator*. And, perhaps we would be more confident that the *Creator* will give us whatever we order if we would only come to realize that what we desire is there for the taking.

It is like when I first started selling copiers. The company that I worked for had a *Monthly Quota Dinner* for all the sales people who had brought in their monthly numbers. This was truly one of the great perks of working for that company. They would take us to some expensive, high class restaurant and let us get whatever we wanted to eat and drink on the company's dime.

Usually these were the kind of places that you and I would never go if we were paying. It was not only a great night of food and drink, but it was also a great night of camaraderie and fun. The first time I qualified to partake in this dinner, I had a hard time believing how generous the company was to us.

As the night began, I had noticed that the senior sales reps seemed to be hitting the bar pretty hard during the reception before dinner. But I just assumed that they were spending their own money, so I just had water. And, I don't mean the fancy bottled water that we all drink these days. I mean the kind that flowed straight from the restaurant's tap.

Once we moved to the dining room, all of the first time reps were seated at the head of the table, near the branch manager. As the menus were passed around, I again noticed that the senior reps were ordering up a storm. As I studied the menu, from right to left, price before item, I was blown away with the price tags that were listed for these delectable sounding dishes.

I was having a hard time choosing what to order because I was having a hard time dislodging the old way of handling a restaurant menu from my head. If I was paying, I would not have even been in this place.

Sensing my angst, the branch manager eventually leaned in and said, *"You can get whatever you want."* To which I thought,

"Did he really just say that I can get whatever I want?"

To ears that were new to all of this, I just couldn't believe what I was hearing. Even though as I looked around the dining room that we were in, that is exactly what the senior reps appeared to be doing.

I studied the menu for a bit longer until I found something that I perceived to be reasonable and I just ordered that. I gave no regard to whether or not it was what I wanted or whether or not I'd actually like it. I just did what I thought was the right and polite thing to do.

I got that meal, ate it, enjoyed it and graciously thanked my manager for the treat. I did the same thing with my dinner bar tab. In fact, if I could have did like we did when we went out as a family and drank out of one big cup, I probably would have. The sad thing was that in taking this attitude, I only cheated myself.

By the end of the night, I realized that the senior reps were doing exactly as I had been instructed to do, but failed to believe and do. They were ordering whatever they wanted to eat and whatever they wanted to drink. They were not only ordering whatever they wanted, they were ordering as much of it as they wanted.

In fact, they were even ordering some of it to take home. And when it came to dessert, they were not only ordering what they wanted; they were ordering whole orders of it, as in, *"Give me that whole Cheesecake to go!"* For that matter, so were the managers, and here I was holding back for fear that I would be looked upon as being greedy and impolite.

That is exactly what many of us are doing with the **Creator**. We are holding back on our order when we set our goals. We are trying to be polite when we should be stepping up and requesting exactly what we want.

I eventually found out that our branch manager was given a large monthly slush fund to pay for these events. And, corporate gave the branch manager this money with the expectation that it would be generously spent on those sales reps that performed their monthly sales duties as expected.

So in holding back, I only cheated myself. I had done my job and here I was forgoing my just reward, even though I had been told to get whatever I wanted.

I believe that many of us function in this same manner when dealing with the **Creator** of the universe. We fail to partake in the unlimited supply of resources that he has made available for us to have to meet our needs and wants.

I believe that the biggest way we fail to do this is in failing to ask for what we actually need and/or want. And, from my use of the principles that I am sharing with you now, I can tell you that the **Creator** doesn't even ask you and I to perform as expected. As in, these principles have worked for me in many instances when spiritually I wasn't exactly being the best practitioner of my faith.

In fact, I think that it is important to point out that these principles will work for anyone who applies them. No matter what your current religious standing or affiliations are.

For sure, I have sat in those churches and heard those sermons where some supposed religious leader has preached that our ability to get the help that we need from the **Creator** is based upon our level of religiosity.

But I must tell you now that this book and this **FAITH (APPLIED)** philosophy is not about that. This is simply about you and I learning to follow the 8 step formula that the **Creator** himself passed to me. From the vantage point of my experience on this subject, he simply asks you and I to learn how to believe and have faith that our needs will be met by him.

In our failing to do this, perhaps that is where we are failing to perform as expected. But if only we could grab this concept, we would be more powerful than anything that could ever come our way to separate us from our needs and desires.

So that it is clear, whenever I qualified for the quota dinners with that company, I never made the mistake of not asking for what I wanted again. Having gotten the message that I was only cheating myself, when I did qualify for these events from that point forward, I went crazy.

To be sure, by the time I went on the last quota dinner before I left that company, I was a completely different person. By then, I had come to understand that you should always step boldly when requesting things that are there for the taking.

The last event that I qualified for was held at the world famous *Lawry's Restaurant* in *Beverly Hills, California*. This is the same place where the Rose Bowl teams go each year for the Beef Bowl. At this event, you have the players from the two respective teams competing to see who can put away the most Prime Rib, the signature dish of Lawry's.

Well it would be safe to say that when we went there, I had my own private Beef Bowl. I also had my own private Bar Bowl. And, I had my own private Cheesecake Bowl. Believe me when I say that I asked for whatever I wanted and I thoroughly enjoyed myself in the process.

I happen to know that my bar tab alone was upwards of $250. If the drink is still there, they have this brandy that is kept in a glass display case behind the bar. Each shot went for about $80 back then. I had three of them, as did, a few of the other senior reps. Put tax and tip on top of that and you are past $280 easily.

I created just as robust a tab at the dinner table. Now before you think that there is something wrong with that picture, remember they said, *"Get whatever you want,"* right?

I have eventually learned to be the same way when setting my goals and making those request known to the **Creator**. To activate the miracle-making power of the universe, we must stop thinking in terms of our limits and just put it all in the order. There is simply no way to get what you need if you don't ask.

Plus, I believe the very mindset of limits is part of what sets us up for failure; probably because it naturally puts us in a doubtful space. After all, how do you know that you still didn't ask for too much? I think you can see how that approach would be filled with doubt.

By contrast, when you are all believing, it is logically easier to believe in it all. From this frame, it should be easy to be free from doubt. Does that make sense?

I'll trust that the illustration above has perfectly driven the point home. So now that you have that, let's take a minute to talk about how specifically to *set the goal*.

Set your goal in the form of the task that must be completed to achieve the goal.

One of the truths that I believe these principles have taught me is that you not only get what you believe and focus on, but in large part, *YOU GET WHAT YOU DO.*

Because of this, you must find a way to put your goals into a basic plan of action so that the very essence of having your goals is going after them, or walking them down. Setting your goal in the form of successive tasks is the simplest way that I found to do that.

Back on that day in 1995 when I was first shown these 8 principles, I started the day clearly mindful of the things that needed to be done to achieve the end goal of reaching quota. From that start, I tried as best as I could to give myself tasks to accomplish for each hour that went by.

This served as a way to keep myself focused on the bigger goal. It also helped me to think of the bigger goal as a series of smaller tasks, as a way to break it up into little bite-sized pieces. It is like the saying that I heard years ago,

"Inch by inch, it's a cinch!"

Over the years I have found that taking this same mentality into planning for your goal and pursuing your faith project is a vital key to achieving success through the 8 principles of *FAITH (APPLIED)*.

Here is an example of a moving project that I undertook and worked purely on faith. In starting out, I was confronted with the challenges of trying to move with limited funds and credit that was considered weak for the community that I was trying to move into.

The upscale waterfront community that I was attempting to move into usually required you to have a much higher credit score than I had at that time. It also required its residents to shell out way more in the way of move in cost than I cared to offer up.

Still thinking that this backdrop would be a great place to go about the process of restoring myself to health, I chose to undertake the faith project of moving there. Once I made that decision, I also gave myself the challenge of a limited time table to pull it all together. When all of my planning was said and done, the task list looked like the one listed below.

The Great Beach House Project

Task to be completed to achieve this goal:

Task 1. Lock in Marina property on Friday, February 8th, 2013

Task 2. Line up move–in monies for Sunday, February 10th, 2013

Move-in Special available - 1 Month Free Rent @ $2,315.00

Prorate Credit available - $63.96 per day (Credited for March)

Deposit Check Credit   - $350.00

Cash on Hand   - $3,800.00

Total Move-in cost out of pocket - $156.49, for February 10th, 2013

Task 3. Schedule moving truck for Monday, February 11th, 2013

Estimated cost   - $100.00 ($50.00 per day x 2)

Task 4. Buy Rental Insurance on Monday, February 11th, 2013

Task 5. Sign lease on Monday, February 11th, 2013

Task 6. Get keys on Monday, February 11th, 2013

Task 7. Move-in on Monday, February 11th, 2013

I focused my energy on achieving these seven task and at the end of the project, I was able to secure a great home in *Marina Del Rey, California*, overlooking the Pacific Ocean. The property was newly rebuilt and offered many great amenities. It was truly a great place for me to rehab and recover from cancer.

At the end of the day, I was able to meet the challenges of a weak credit score, limited move-in monies and limited closing time that made this move a faith project for me in the first place.

Achieving this success was yet another measure of proof that these principles work when they are simply worked. And, it was also proof that even against great odds, the *Creator* will deliver as long as we set clear goals for what we want.

Setting goals for my healing and restoration –
The Four Fundamental Truths of My Recovery

Operating from this mentality works no matter what the goal is that is being sought. When I first got home from the hospital, even before I could get out of the bed I assessed my situation and begin to set goals and tasks to help me firmly regain both my health and my physical mobility. I created a project called, *The Four Fundamental Truths of My Recovery.*

Instead of focusing on where I was in this challenging moment, I used this project to focus myself on the distance that I needed to travel to get back to the level of health and mobility that I enjoyed before cancer interrupted my life. I also used it to keep myself clear on the physical and mental things that I needed to do to make the journey back to health.

Over the course of the project, the written version of this list of goals has taken on many different focuses and tones, obviously reflecting my physical condition and the corresponding physical challenges in the moment.

The good news is that it has continually led me to new levels of physical, mental and emotional well-being. The example that I list below reflects the outcome of my most recent checkups. These checkups involve me being checked from head to toe, i.e., blood work, MRI's and P.E.T. scans.

All of these test combined serve both as an early warning system and scientific confirmation for my doctors of exactly where I stand in relationship to my medical recovery from cancer.

While I may be content to draw my own confirmation of my recovery from my faith, these men and women of medicine prefer to get theirs from the sciences that they have been schooled in, and, that's just fine by me.

If anything, the great reports that they get back only serve to confirm the faithfulness of **God** in keeping his promise to heal me and bolster my willingness to stand in faith in the face of such a serious issue.

Planned with an eye out towards both my medical and physical condition and recovery goals, the written project looks like this:

SURVIVOR

The 4 Fundamental Truths of My Recovery
(To be read aloud and visualized daily)

1. – As a result of the medicines, treatments and nutritional support that I've received, this disease is placed into permanent remission, any & all growths, both new ones and those that were housed in my body have now stopped, shrunk and have disappeared from my body. (100% true as of March 21st, 2014 – per Dr. Farjami.)

(I am free of pain, presence and bodily constriction – free to enjoy my normal range of motion and mobility – I can sleep comfortably on my sides and my stomach without stressing my back, I can carry out my field marketing activities and my field recruiting and client meetings without stressing my feet and legs. (85% true as of March 21st, 2014)

2. – As my bones were being cleansed of this disease, new stronger bones were quickly growing back and taking the place of the disease-weakened bones that once existed. (100% true as of February 1st, 2014 – per Dr. Farjami.)

(I am free of the risk of breaking bones, injuring myself or causing paralysis of any kind, especially through the carrying out of my basic daily activities, sleeping on my sides or through engaging in light weight lifting / toning exercises.)

3. – Physically, I have regained near complete bodily strength, I have fluidity in and normal functional use of my lower body – i.e., my legs, the soles of my feet and my knee joints. I am now working to regain full functional use of my full core, i.e., my back & stomach muscles.

Overall, I am healthy and while I must be careful not to put stress or strain on my feet or my back, I must avoid pandering to them and being needlessly inactive because of them.

(I can stand & walk comfortably & normally without causing my feet pain the next day, I am free to resume my ideal daily regimen and part-time work schedule. I can also ramp up my full muscular rehabilitation/toning & my weight loss program. (90% true as of March 21st, 2014)

4. – I have now fully reversed the condition of neuropathy and regained normal nerve sensation, feeling and function in my hands and feet. The soles of my feet, the front of my feet & toes, my hands are all back to normal. My back & sides are free of pain, discomfort and spasms. With all things considered, I feel normal in all ways from head to toe and all places in between. (80% true as of March 21st, 2014)

(I am fully restored to the level of health, wellness and personal mobility that I enjoyed before being stricken with this disease. Now being fully healed, I am off of all medications and treatments. I have suffered no lasting or lingering side effects from taking the medications and going through the treatments that were used to heal me and make me whole again. (75% true as of March 21st, 2014)

To GOD be the glory for my Recovery & Restoration!!!

In Jesus name, AMEN!!! **Last revised, March 21st, 2014**

Needless to say, the first version of this list of goals would have acknowledged the fact that after being bedridden for the 12 previous weeks, I was totally weak physically, couldn't sit up erect and could nowhere near stand, much less think of walking.

Having started from that place, to be where I am now reveals just how powerful this practice is and just how far it has brought me back from the brink of a medical nightmare.

True to the spirit of goal setting that we have already talked about, I used this template to give consideration to all of the aspects that I needed to focus on in my push towards recovery and to solicit everything that I would need to get there from the *Creator*.

I also used this template as a live flowing affirmation, as a script for me to continually speak healing words into my life. Whenever I needed to describe my current state of health and wellness to me or anyone else, these were the words that I would use to do it. And, whenever I needed to keep my mind out of a dark and doubtful place, it was these same pre-planned words that would bring me comfort.

As I reached these goals and/or my physical condition changed I would update and set new goals. I did this on a regular basis and used it to keep me fully engaged and focused on where I wanted to go in regards to a matter that could have easily been mentally debilitating.

For sure, there is no more serious a challenge for any human being than to have your mortality and/or your mobility threatened. When confronted by such a challenge, it would be very easy and almost understandable to become gripped by fear and immobilized in the process.

The last thing that one would think that they have the ability to do is to set goals, much less achieve them. But that is exactly what I did and it worked.

If it can work here, how much easier would it be for this same process to work in your life when the stakes and the challenge that you and I are facing is nowhere near as serious? It would be almost laughable for us to think for even one minute that it wouldn't.

That is why we simply must learn to harness this power of goal setting and drive it to bring us all of the good things that we desire for our lives, both those that we need like in the case of healing for serious diseases and those that we want like financial success or a dream possession.

As I have covered here, we must learn to put it all in the order. We have to stop thinking in terms of our self-imposed limits when we are planning out our goals and start asking the *Creator* for exactly what we need and want.

When the doctors told me that I was confronted with the prospect of life long paralysis, I could have accepted the fate of never walking again. But I didn't. I made it a goal to get out of that bed and to get back on my feet walking and it came to pass. I ask and I received.

The same was true of the cancer that I was diagnosed with. I could have taken my doctors point of view and accepted it as a disease that I have and one from which my recovery was probably not going to take place. But again, I didn't. I saw myself free of this disease and I set my goals accordingly.

Today there are no signs of it in my blood. There are no signs of it growing in my body. And, I have not had any real treatments for it in over a year.

In fact, my doctor is always accusing me of avoiding the maintenance treatments that he wants to put me on. He also has told me on several occasions that he and his colleagues are scratching their heads trying to figure out how and why I recovered.

I have tried to impress upon you here the need for you to set your goals in the form of tasks that when completed would walk you naturally up to your goal. It took me some time to learn over the years that a goal is not a goal until there is a definite plan in place for how to achieve it.

Before learning that fact, I had all types of goals that never came to fruition. No matter how much I wanted them or how much my heart was into them, it didn't matter. They never came true.

Eventually I learned that the simple reason why was because I had no concrete plan for going after them. Because of this fact, no real, sustained action was ever taken to make them come to pass.

Back then, I would put a lot of time into trying to figure out what was wrong with me, the world around me; what was wrong with my philosophy and my thinking, my relationships.

Put simpler, I searched high and low trying to figure out why I was not achieving and never did it dawn on me that my problem was simply that I was setting goals and never giving them the benefit of a properly thought out plan.

Everything turned around for me the day that I learned this powerful truth. I have found over the years that many people suffer from this same affliction. In fact, from what I have seen over the years, many of the people who do plan out their goals often fail to do the needed research to make sure that their plans are sound.

These people choose instead to operate from the seat of emotion and guesswork. Don't you do it. Learn to plan out your goals. As I've discussed and demonstrated here, write out those plans in the form of a list of tasks that once they are completed, walk you naturally and unfailingly to your goal.

Also, I have tried to impress upon you in this point that goal setting works no matter what it is that you are setting the goal for. Thus you really should get in the habit of making everything that you want to come to pass in your life a goal.

We all think about things like starting a business or getting a new job or losing weight. But, what about health goals? What about a financial freedom goal, or a goal to get your financial house in order?

What about goals to rediscover a hobby that brought great joy into your life? If you are now or you ever found yourself confronted with a serious health challenge, what about a recovery and health restoration goal? Or, a goal to come back from that injury?

How about we lose the habit of just accepting the health challenges that can come our way as permanent in our lives? How about we start taking the view that we can restore ourselves to the good health that we once enjoyed? What have we got to lose in taking this view?

No matter what the goal, simply get clear on the steps that you need to take to get to where you want to be then plan out the tasks to get it done and go to work.

On that day way back in 1995, that is what I did and by days end, I found that it worked and I had the prize of that $1,000 bonus firmly in my hands. So go ahead and try it for yourself. I know that you will be shocked at what you can do with this principle.

Lastly, it goes without saying that once you have your goal all planned out and your tasks list in front of you, you need to set a timetable for when you will complete these tasks.

As I have said previously, the circumstance driven goal will usually give you a timetable for which you must achieve success or else face some consequence.

If the goal that you have in front of you is not such an occasion, you must be prepared to set this vital parameter and stick to it if you want to see the real power of goal setting come to life here.

Whichever the case, know that the key point to get is that no matter what the timetable, you have all of the time that you need.

I must remind you that the real power of **FAITH (APPLIED)** is in the fact that it brings to your aid the help of a higher power, another entity that goes to work on your behalf. It literally unleashes the miracle producing power of the universe.

I have used this power with timeframes that were measured in hours, in a day, in days or longer. So don't be afraid to set a timeframe that seems tight if that is indeed the timetable that you have to work with. The key is to set it and go to work on getting the tasks that you have to complete done within the allotted time, period.

With this second principle now under your belt, let's look at the third step in the process of activating the miracle-making power of the universe:

Position yourself for success

Leave your comfort zone and take up an aggressive posture where you can make the most attempts possible at getting your goal. From this position, actively pursue your goal through a focused work effort. If it is a multi-day goal, do something physical each day to get your goal. If it is a one day goal, do something each hour. Do this no matter what the outcome of your last action, or results of the previous day. Don't quit this process until you have the goal.

On July 30th, 1995, I knew that if I were to have any real shot at achieving the seemingly impossible task that was set out before me I would have to go about my affairs in a way that was different from the way I'd normally handle my work day.

I knew that if I did the same old things that I did over the course of every other workday I would get the same result that I had always gotten. I mean literally, for some reason I knew if I thought the same thoughts and had the same attitude, I knew that if I took up the same place that I normally took up in the department; I knew that if I took the same rest breaks that I normally took, I knew that if I took the same time for lunch, or took a lunch at all that I would fail.

In truth, the way I operated on this day was a far cry from how I typically operated back then. Typically, I just tried to get through the hours of my shift and gave no thought to what type of sales results I might get for the day.

At days end, it was whatever it was. If I had a great day of selling that was good, if not, that was good too. And, I paid no special attention to how or where I positioned myself and the impact that this might have on my success or failure. As far as I was concerned, just like many of my colleagues, the factors that controlled my success or failure were outside of my control.

Instead, success and failure were controlled by things like store traffic and customer flow, the particular customers that came my way on a given day, the weather outside, the day of the week or month, or the time of the year, the weekly ad or how management treated me in the moment.

It could also be controlled by any other arbitrary thing that could be thought of, so long as it wasn't me. Out of this frame of mind, the notion that a change in my actions could bring new or different results was totally foreign to me.

It is not all that uncommon for even the best of us to think this way about our ability to be successful or for us to approach a project or a goal without any thought of doing something different than we normally would do to get it.

I would bet that you have heard it said that the definition of insanity is doing the same thing and expecting a different result. Yet that is exactly what most of us tend to do when we are confronted by a challenge or when we are trying to achieve a goal.

We go about it in the same casual manner that we tend to go about our regular, day to day lives. As a result, when all is said and done, because we never bring it, the clock ends and we simply haven't done what it takes to get the outcome that we are seeking. And then we say that it just wasn't meant to be.

On this day, something down inside of me told me not to approach the day in this manner. It told me that if I expected to win the prize that was on the table, I would have to shake things up in every imaginable way.

That meant that I would have to move out into the open space and be seen. From this place I could greet each person that entered my department and offer my assistance. Greeting everyone also meant that I would have to be more aggressive. No time to worry about being rejected or looking like a hungry salesman – something I hated appearing to be.

It also meant that I would have to be persistent and not take the easy *"NO"* for an answer. When the prospective customer tried to brush me off with, *"I'm just looking,"* I had to avoid taking it personally and still stick nearby to let them know that I was there to help them if they needed it. It even meant not being afraid to look at people with dollar signs in my eyes and asking everyone that I spoke with to buy from me.

Normally I would never ever have tried to move a customer to make a decision to buy something from me and to do it on the spot. But on this day, I knew that I needed to break that habit and do my best to be a closer and not just the person content with letting people come and go without buying.

Finally, it meant truly putting the time in. On this day, it wasn't just about doing the hours, it was about getting some real work done with the hours. It was about seeing the people and it was about seeing enough people to hit the target that I sought.

That meant that rest breaks and lunch would have to take a backseat to the goal that I coveted. I knew I could rest once the day was over. I also knew that rest would be much more gratifying if it came with a $1,000 bonus.

In all these ways, I changed who I was and how I handled myself over the course of this workday and because of it, I won the prize. I guess if you had to put all that into a phrase, it could be said that the *Creator* told me that I would have to stand up and be accountable for this goal that I was hoping to achieve.

So often we think of getting what we need by faith as a transaction where the *Creator* does everything to get it to us while we are accountable for nothing. And, many times we want to play it cool when it comes to our goals, but winners don't play that way.

If it is not clear to you by now, when I say to *position yourself for success*, I mean that physically, in the literal sense. As in, on that day, for me to get to my goal I had to abandon everything that I was accustomed to being. I literally had to leave my comfort zone and put myself in the place that allowed me to aggressively go after the goal that I was trying to attain.

Looking back on it even now, I can see how vital this positioning was to the success that I ultimately attained. If I had worked out of the space on the sales floor that I was most accustomed to, if I had not greeted everyone, if I had worried about rejection; if I had not asked everyone to buy or if I had taken time to rest there was just no way that I would have touched enough people. And, for certain, I would not have helped enough people to reach $8,000 in sales on that one day.

Fortunately for me, the spirit led me to take a different approach on that day. At the end of the day, this one seemingly small principle made all of the difference in the world and probably single handedly gave me my goal.

Two ways to position yourself for success

Since becoming fully aware of this formula for **FAITH (APPLIED)**, I have long contemplated the dual aspects of this principle of **Positioning Yourself for Success**.

For sure it is representative of taking an aggressive approach to meeting the challenge that you are confronted with or pursuing your goals.

It should go without saying that there is no way to say that you are serious about winning when you are taking a casual approach to meeting a challenge or goal.

In that way **positioning yourself for success** literally means that you are far from casual in your pursuit of the challenge that you are trying to conquer or the goal that you seek.

Just as I am sure that the story that I related above depicts, I had to get after it, I had to bring it if I truly expected to have a chance to win the prize that I was seeking. I not only had other people that I had to compete with. But I also had the clock that I was racing against.

With both of these elements nipping at my heels the entire day, there had to be a level of urgency, a level of aggression from me or victory was out of the question.

Given the competitiveness of our world, given the callousness of others around us and the limited margin for error that we all live with today, the same is true for you. We simply must have a level of aggressiveness to our pursuit for success.

Of equal weight, I have found that this principle is representative of our need to learn how to shed the comfort zones that keep us from the success that we seek.

It should also go without saying that we all have our comfort zones – we all have a way that we like to go about things. We all have things that we are willing to do and things that we are not willing to do. We all have a pace that we like to work at and a way we like to go about working an assignment.

For that matter, we all have an image that we like to portray. The challenge for many of us is that these comfort zones can often conflict with the actions that we must take to achieve the goals that we are striving to achieve.

In this regard, the ability to *position yourself for success* is about you having the ability to shed the comfort zones that stand to get in the way of you rising to meet the challenge that is confronting you or you getting your goals and dreams. For sure on July 30th, 1995, most of what I did that day was outside of my established comfort zones.

I can also think of many other occasions when I have successfully used these principles in a faith project where I had to move far away from my comfort zone to find victory. In fact, there was usually no way to stay comfortable and achieve the thing that I was after.

I have had to go places that I was uncomfortable going, talk to people that I was uncomfortable talking to. I have had to request things from people that I was uncomfortable asking for those things.

In a professional sense, I have also had to personally make cold sales calls and cold phone calls to secure new business. In these instances I have had to act against my own feelings and emotions in the moment. In pursuit of success, I have had to do all of these things to meet a challenge or achieve a goal.

In trying to activate the miracle-making power of the universe I have especially had to apply both of these elements to *position myself for success*. Because I have had to do it I know that the same tasks are awaiting you if you are serious about achieving success in a faith project.

I changed lanes to position myself for career success

I experienced a perfect example of the power that we have to *position ourselves for success* when I first changed career paths to venture into professional sales. As great as the outcome of this change would go on to be in my life, and with all the great things that it ultimately brought my way, I really can't take credit for making it.

In truth I only made this change in career paths and joined the copier sales industry after some persistent urging from the **Creator**. In fact, the story is typical of how the **Creator** has led me to bigger and better things at various times in my life.

As hard as it is for people who know me now to picture, I was once a low wage worker, working in the retail electronics industry. As I have already alluded to, back then I was a young husband and father struggling to provide for my family.

Despite my best efforts and in spite of the fact that I was getting up and going to work everyday, financially, the ends were just not meeting for me and my family. Accordingly, I was extremely frustrated with what I was doing for a living and I was just itching to find a better way to provide for my family.

Making matters worse, I wasn't blessed with the gift of a developed faith back then. To say that I was totally undeveloped in that area would be an understatement. And, I was completely impatient to top it all off.

As a result, I couldn't see how I could ever go from where I was economically to where I wanted and needed to be. I just had no real clue of how to get myself onto a better career path, one that would give me the ability to provide for my family in the manner that I desired.

Having no answer for the predicament, I would get totally overwhelmed with frustration. It would build until it reached a boiling point and when it reached that point I would quit my job in disgust; usually before I had even found my next job.

As things would work out, by the time I'd quit, I would have a little cushion of cash that would make us ok for at least a few months.

During these times, I would always contemplate doing something entirely different to try and lift my family out of this situation and help us to get on a better financial footing, but I couldn't quite figure out what. All I knew was that I needed to do something different.

Privately, I even thought about trying my hand at going into business for myself. I had tried this before and while it didn't turn out the way that I had hoped it would, it was something that I thought could definitely work.

But selling that idea to my young wife would prove impossible and without her blessing trying to make that the answer to my job plight would be a disaster.

Eventually, while all of this back and forth about what to do was taking place, the little cushion that we had was running dry and with that development I would begin to feel the urge to go out and get the next job fast.

Usually there would be one last ditch effort to try to explain to my young wife the need to do something different. I tried to explain to her that going back to the same old job was like making a lateral move. I tried to get her to see that we were only moving sideways – that we weren't moving up at all by these moves.

I remember making her the folowing diagram in an effort to try and explain all of the peaks and valleys and the overall cycle of employment based financial struggle that we had been stuck in.

Despite all my explaining, she never got it. With that, the pressure would really be on to find something fast, which inevitably meant going back and getting the same job that I had left a few months earlier in frustration and disgust. So that is exactly what I did.

With that as my unwritten strategy, I bounced all around my industry from employer to employer. I went from working at a place called Adray's Electronics, to a mom and pop place called L.A.Tronics Electronic Superstore, and finally, to a place called the Good Guys, all without seeing any improvement in my family's financial condition.

Yet unbeknownst to me, in the backdrop of this moment the spirit of *God* was trying to pull me in a new direction – a direction that would offer me exactly what I needed to not only improve my economic situation in that moment, but to positively alter my financial destiny forever.

Although I couldn't see it at the time, the **Creator** was setting me up for a lane change that would take me from being totally frustrated about my finances, to having more income from a job than I would have ever thought possible for a guy like me.

The process of how I would come to change lanes played out like most of the other moments when the **Creator** has led me by faith to a better place in my life.

To paint you an accurate picture of how this all came to pass, let me first say that back then you searched for jobs in the newspaper. Back then, each time I came to the place where it was time to get a new job, I'd hit the paper with a vengeance.

Each time I did, a particular ad for a field sales job seemed to be waving at me. By this I mean that for some reason not clear to me at that time, my eyes, and perhaps my spirit were always drawn to it. To top it off, every time I saw this ad, the little voice in my head would tell me as clear as day to,

"Go get that job."

Meaning, when I left Adray's and was looking for my next job, I was told to *"go get that field sales job."* And, when I left L.A.Tronics and was looking for my next job, I was told to *"go get that field sales job."* And again, when I left Good Guys and was looking for my next job, I was told to *"go get that field sales job."*

The only problem was that that field sales job went against everything that I stood for and everything that I was looking for in a job. For starters, it was a sales job. Even though I was in retail sales I really didn't like sales back then.

Next, it was an income that was heavily based on commissions. I had been raised to believe that a commission income was a shaky income and would often equal no income at all.

Next, it involved cold calling on strangers, door to door. Not only was I shy back then and hated the thought of going door to door selling anything to anybody, I really hated the notion of having to approach complete strangers and trying to sell them stuff.

Finally, it meant being under pressure to sell and reach a monthly quota. I hated selling in the retail setting and never performed well with a quota in that environment.

In fact, there were times in retail when my bosses would have to threaten to fire me just to get me to make the effort to make sales; and, this was in a low pressure environment where the customers usually came to you looking to buy.

In all these ways the thought of going after that field sales job seriously challenged my ideas about what a good job for me was and was in no way compatible with my established comfort zones.

Therefore it shouldn't shock you to hear that each time that voice told me to, *"Go get that job,"* I just shrugged it off and went out and got the job that I knew that I could get.

That's how I went from Adray's to L.A.Tronics to Good Guys without stopping to realize that each time it was the same job that was not meeting my needs before; the same one that I was frustrated and disgusted with before.

Like anyone could easily imagine however, each time it wasn't long before I once again found myself confronted with the same financial struggles and totally frustrated with my situation.

Because of the fact that by the time I would land this new job I would be in need of a cash infusion, those first few checks would actually feel like they were meeting my needs.

But before too long the honeymoon period brought on by this new money would be over and I would see the truth that my situation had not changed at all.

Finally, the fourth time this cycle played out **God** realized that I was a bit hard headed and decided to change His approach with me. This time instead of saying, *"Go get that job,"* when that same old ad waved at me, the little voice inside simply suggested that I,

"Go hear them out!"

That little change in command made all the difference in the world for a thick headed guy like me. As I quickly said to myself,

"I can do that!"

In fact that little voice then reminded me that I could always go back and get the job that I knew I could get if I didn't like what I heard. And that was certainly true. I could always go on to the next retail electronics joint.

Over the years I had worked at nearly all of them anyway. So there was no doubt that I could do that at any time I chose to.

With that new urging from the **Creator**, I took that ad, called up the company and made an appointment to go in for the interview that would lead to the transformation of my financial situation in the blink of an eye.

Minolta Business Systems: A God sent dream job, come true!

From the very first minute that I arrived for the interview I was glad that I had yielded to the urging of the **Creator**. For starters, I was standing in the office of a multinational corporation – *Minolta Business Systems*, a division of *Minolta Corporation*.

I had always wanted an office job with a big company and now that is exactly where I was standing. Even though the job involved working out in the field, the fact that I would be reporting to an office and the fact that I would be working out of an office was a big deal to me. As far as I saw it, it was a major upgrade to working on a retail sales floor where you don't have your own space.

The office itself was bright and cheery looking. There was a ton of natural sunlight filling the room and you were struck with the feeling that you were still outside when you came in. Unlike the retail stores where I was working, you felt like you were still connected to the outside world when you went in for your shift.

In the background there were people hustling and bustling around. I saw a lot of smiling happy faces moving about. From my vantage point, there were no bosses standing over these workers. It was like everybody here was treated like an adult that could be trusted to perform the duties for which they had been hired to tend to.

I guess I noticed all of this because it was in striking contrast to what I was used to seeing on the sales floors where I had worked most of my adult life to that point.

I was greeted by a nice friendly receptionist upon my arrival. She informed my interviewer that I had arrived and advised me to visit the office kitchen and help myself to some of the goodies that could be found there. If for no other reason than to give myself a chance to walk my nerves off, I decided to take her up on the offer.

What I saw when I went into that kitchen was sign number two that I had made the right decision in yielding to the urging of the *Creator* – a full variety of coffees, teas, juices, fresh fruits, pastries, donuts, bagels and schmears. If you hadn't eaten at home before making it to work, you were sure to be well fed once you got to this office.

I would later learn that some level of these goodies were available on a daily basis. Coming from my working background I came to see that it was just one of the things that people who worked in this type of setting take for granted that all workers receive the same courtesy from their employer. I vowed that if I got hired, I'd never make that mistake.

After grabbing a quick bite I headed back out to the lobby to await my host. It wasn't long before I was approached by two sharply dressed people, a man and a woman.

They turned out to be the branch manager, *Mr. Randy Peck* and the area manager whose team I would be placed on if I got hired, *Mrs. Robin Millard*. They took me into a big Conference & Demonstration room and seated me at this very impressive marble table. And with that, the interview of my young life began.

The interview began like any other job interview with my host telling me all about the job and the company that I was considering going to work for, and of course, me being ask to tell them everything about me and my background that was pertinent to the question of whether or not they should offer me the chance to work there.

With us being in the main demonstration room, they took the opportunity to show me the equipment that I would be selling if I were hired. Of course I knew what a copier machine was, but I never knew all the things that they could do or that they came in so many sizes. I had never seen a full product line of them.

They also took the opportunity to role play me in some selling scenarios. It goes without saying that I was about as nervous as I could get. To be graded in a selling role play when I had never worked with the equipment was a bit of a challenge for me, or so I thought. But in the end both of these people were impressed by my performance.

As sales managers, they were particularly impressed with my smooth and calm demeanor when they tried to throw me curveballs. They told me that they were especially impressed with the choice of words that I had chosen to frame the challenges that they had presented to me.

This led to a whole discussion on the subject of how I had come about my education given that my resume stated that I hadn't completed college. And, it was that line of dialog that led to why I walked out of that office on that day with a job offer that was just too good to pass on.

I didn't have the right credentials but I had read all of the right books

I explained to them that while I didn't finish college in the formal sense, I had been an avid reader and self-improvement junkie for years. I explained that it was never lost on me that the last real attempt that most people make at improving themselves was when they were in grade school.

I had left grade school on that same program. But shortly after leaving school, I had undertook to better myself and to enrich myself through reading and taking courses aimed at teaching me how to become successful and wealthy.

I would have thought that I needed to impress these folks with my credentials and resume or my ability to perform the work. But as it would turn out, these were the magic words that opened the door for me to get the job that I had been urged to go get for nearly a year now.

I couldn't have known it going in but my interviewers loved people who were willing to invest the time to self-improve and because they had done it themselves through their college and professional affiliations, they could tell that I wasn't just blowing smoke. If anything it was amazing to them that I had taken the time to do this on my own initiative, without a scholastic or professional environment that mandated it.

In my case, this too was at the urging of the **Creator** in that it was that same little voice that had told me some years earlier that,

"I was broke, ignorant and headed nowhere!"

Then it told me that, if I would fix my *"Ignorant,"* my *"Broke and Headed Nowhere"* would take care of itself.

My willingness to except that little bit of self-honesty started me on the road to self-improvement and to me becoming a life-long learner. It was out of that moment that I had started reading and educating myself and now that decision was paying its first financial dividend. I guess it could be rightly said that this was truly the first time that I had *positioned myself for success*.

In the end, I did well with my interviewers because of the road that I had travelled to get to that day. I did well with my interviewers because I had read the right books and I had done a great job of educating myself.

Because of that, in spite of the fact that I didn't have the right credentials and in spite of the fact that I had only reluctantly came in for the interview, I was presented with a job offer that was easily too good to believe and too good to pass on for a guy like me.

They made me an offer that I couldn't refuse

For starters, the job was 9 to 5, Monday through Friday. Weekends off, and if it even looked like a holiday, you were off with pay.

By contrast, my old retail jobs involved work hours that could be anywhere from 5 in the morning to 12 midnight. I could draw a work shift on any day, Monday through Sunday, and most holidays involved working without any additional pay.

Next, while you had to arrive at the office by 9 am, you had to be out in the field by 9:30 and remain there until at least 4:30 in the afternoon.

Although it was unspoken, that meant that you had the freedom to do whatever you desired to do between 9:30 and 4:30. As long as you covered your work assignment, no one would bother you with your whereabouts while you were out of the office. If they needed you while you were in the field, they contacted you on the company issued pager or cell phone.

That little bit of flexibility helped me to pick up my son from school every day. At my old retail job, your time was micro-managed down to the minute. You could hardly even get a proper lunch with how they managed you.

Next, was the pay package, I was offered nearly $2,000 just to show up, meaning even before I wrote one sale I would be given $2,000 in salary to live off of. And, this was not drawn against commissions. It was in addition to them. So much for the ignorant notion I had been taught that this commission heavy pay structure would equal a shaky income and ultimately no income at all!

Then there were the commissions. First off, there was a handsome commission paid on every machine that we could sale, just for selling it; anywhere from $100 to as much as $1,000 just for selling a new machine. You got even more for selling a lease return or discontinued machine.

Each machine had a list price and a much higher retail price. The list price was like a rock bottom price that you could use to help you make a sale if you were going up against a competing company and you needed a lower price; while the retail price was the price that the company really wanted to sale a machine for.

The compensation plan offered the sales reps 50% of any dollar that he could get above the list price. Meaning that for the sales representative that knew how to hold margin, if he sold a machine for $10,000 above the list price, he'd get $5,000 on top of his base commission.

This was another of those points of proof that even though it took me some time to get obedient, I had been wise to follow the urging of the *Creator*.

With my background in retail sales, holding margin and selling at full retail value was a skill that I knew I had in abundance. It was the order of the day at all of my old jobs. As such, I expected to make plenty of money from this discipline.

Needless to say, when my host had finished laying all of this out, it was the best job offer that I had ever heard in my life. It was certainly more freedom and money than I had ever thought it was possible to possess and earn. Plus it came with some amazing perks like company paid vacations, monthly achievers dinners and recognition as well.

With such an offer on the table, against all of my hang ups, my raising, my perceived better judgment about being in sales and my emotions in the moment, I quickly said yes and took that job.

I did this in spite of the fact that it was door to door, commissioned sales and in spite of the fact that it meant cold calling on strangers and trying to meet a strict monthly quota.

For that decision, in spite of what I thought would be the case when I looked at that ad in the paper, my life has been forever changed for the better. When all was done, this was the first time that the *Creator* had led me to *position myself for success*.

And, it might sound almost cliché to say this, but of more value to me than the freedom and money that I enjoyed there was the person that I became as a result of yielding to the urging of the *Creator*, going in to hear them out, and ultimately, taking that job.

Just to tell you a bit about how it all turned out. Within 30 days of accepting the offer to join *Minolta Business Systems*, with the help of my sales manager I had closed my first big order and made more money in one month than I would have made in 6 months at my old retail job.

That one sale paid me $7,000!!! I don't think any reasonable person will require any more evidence of the value of following this principle of **Positioning Yourself for Success**.

Consider that along with all of the other things that I would have missed out on had I never yielded to that little voice and just stayed in my comfort zone.

Just like on the day when these 8 principles were first shown to me, there is no way for me to achieve this feat had I not stepped out of myself and did something different, in this case, changing my career path entirely was the change that I had to make to gain a new level of financial well-being. In each case, I had to do the thing that made me the most uncomfortable.

When you consider the fact that even when they accept that something has to change, most people tend to seek to change to something that they are comfortable with, you will see the true value of this principle – as well as the truth that often times we must be willing to do the thing that we fear the most if we expect to activate the miracle-making power of the universe.

After receiving that first humungous check all of my fears about this job went right out of the window. If anything, the drive to find more deals like that one became like a drug to me.

The longer I was in the business, I only got further and further away from my old self. I went from being the guy who was afraid to make cold visits and cold phone calls to the guy who loved popping my head into a new business and who loved working out of the phone book.

I also loved training others how to do the same things. I went from being afraid to ask people for their money to a guy who couldn't wait to get to that part of the sales process and a preferred closer for others in the office.

By the time I left the business I had become a go to guy in the office responsible for bringing rookie reps along. I am not exaggerating to say that the day I walked out of *Minolta Business Systems* for the last time, I was the most profitable sales representative in the entire company during my tenure, a fact that even I couldn't believe when I learned of it. In addition, over 70% of my office was using my cold calling techniques and phone scripts to secure new clients.

I could have never seen all of that coming to pass when I first shrugged off that ad in the newspaper when I was job hunting. I could have never seen that I could become as good at the business as I became.

In fact, most of us never give ourselves credit for the person that we can become by leaving our comfort zones and taking on a new position in our quest to meet a challenge or achieve a goal. Instead we only consider where we are, what we like and what we are comfortable with in the moment.

When it comes to **FAITH (APPLIED)** and learning how to activate the miracle-making power of the universe that is a huge mistake. One of the biggest truths that I ultimately realized from making that shift in my then career path was that,

"You can't get something that isn't even on the table."

When we stay stuck in our comfort zone that is exactly what we are really trying to do – get something, a new result that often times is simply not on the table.

Chances are if what you were doing now was going to give you what you are seeking, you'd have it. At the very least you'd see yourself progressing towards it. Stop and think about it soberly. Don't you see that?

For me the day came when I realized that I was the same person from the day before I yielded to the urging of the *Creator*, went on that interview and accepted this job offer.

From a skills standpoint, I was the same guy that had been accepting those frustrating retail jobs. But now I was making a great income, enjoying great freedom and great perks and all this was simply because I had left my comfort zone and changed lanes.

It was all because I had followed this principle of *Positioning Myself for Success*. That is the biggest reason why you have to change your position if you truly want to succeed.

I had to position myself for healing and restoration to overcome Multiple Myeloma

On July 30th, 1995, *positioning myself for success* meant that I had to abandon many long held comfort zones to aggressively pursue the prize of the $1,000 bonus that management had put on the table.

In July of 2012, *positioning myself for healing* meant that I had to once again abandon many well established comfort zones. Only this time, it was so that the doctors who were charged with the task of restoring me to health could aggressively pursue the healing and restoration from cancer that I had been praying for.

Looking back now, it is easy to see that there were several areas where this was critical to my recovery. From the question of which medicines and treatments to take, to which doctors to work with, there was simply no way to even think about making the right choices if I were operating from a place of comfort. And if I had remained in the comfort shell that I was in prior to this challenge, I likely would not have made it through to where I am now.

You see, prior to this moment, I was like a lot of men in that I didn't have the best relationship with the medical community. I didn't go to the doctor unless something was wrong. And, even when there was something wrong, I still had to get pretty sick and pretty much be dragged in to seek medical attention.

Making matters worse, I had the biggest fear of needles. I would nearly faint at the sight of a needle and taking shots or having my blood drawn were events that I tried to avoid at all cost. I nearly didn't get married for this reason and I had even long refused to get enough life insurance to protect my family because the process involved me submitting to a blood test.

I think that it is safe to say now that if I had not been able to shed this frame of mind, there is no way that I could have ever got into a position that would have brought about my victory over cancer.

Over the years I have certainly heard my share of stories about people battling serious diseases like cancer and having a tough time submitting to the treatment process for similar reasons. In my personal circles, I have seen numerous people shy away from following their doctor's orders or from taking the prescribed medicines or treatments when confronted with this kind of challenge.

I have even been shocked to learn from my doctor how many patients will fight doing the things that might bring them the healing that they so desperately want. What these people fail to realize is that to the degree that they fight their doctor's orders or fight taking the medicines and treatments that they prescribe, they are often taking themselves off the path to healing.

It seems almost unfathomable that anyone would knowingly do such a thing. But sadly, as perhaps we all have witnessed, many people will do exactly that.

For too many people who find themselves confronted with a challenging circumstance like a diagnosis of cancer, it is all too easy to let the spirit of fear and worry rule their decision making. Once ruled by this spirit, they spend more time worrying about the possible harshness of the medicines that they need to take than they do trying to get well.

Will this medicine make me sicker? Will this Chemo treatment make my hair fall out? Will this radiation therapy leave me scarred? I have even heard of men worrying over whether or not they would lose their sex drive and/or their ability to make love. I can certainly understand these thoughts and concerns. I too had my own concerns.

Though I didn't allow myself to dwell on these concerns, this spirit did make an attempt to visit me, as thoughts like these did come to my mind.

And, although I didn't allow myself to fall into a state of worry, I did wonder about what my life would be like in the aftermath of my battle with cancer. Particularly, would I ever get back to the normal state of health and wellness that I once enjoyed.

Fortunately for me, I instinctively knew not to let this spirit take over me and I knew that for me to ***position myself for healing*** I would have to handle these questions with the power of prayer. As far as I was concerned, I would have to go through these things to have any chance at being restored to health. But I never focused on the harshness of the medicines or the treatments that I had to take.

If anything the people around me were the ones who always remarked of how serious all that stuff was. They marveled at the strength that I had for getting through it all. Yet little did they know I made the decision early on to go to the *Creator* in prayer to find the strength that I needed in that moment.

So instead of worrying about the things that I had no choice but to go through, I simply prayed in the place where most others worried. This was the true source of my strength. To be exact, I prayed each time I had to climb into any medical device, or if I had to take a dose of chemo medicine, or if I had to undergo a medical procedure.

And, instead of questioning the soundness or the safety of the medical devices, or the medicines, or the medical procedures, I thanked the *Creator* for these things. Instead of questioning the expertise of the medical professionals that were sincerely working to restore my health, I thanked the *Creator* for these men and women.

And finally, instead of assuming the worst about all of these things, I acknowledged the goodness of them all and that they all flowed from him. In these moments of prayer, I asked the *Creator* to prepare my mind and my body to receive the positive benefits of each of these life-saving resources.

As a result, where others used fear and worry to take them out of the path of healing, I used these techniques to *position myself for the healing* and restoration that I was using the power of *FAITH (APPLIED)* to obtain. As I sit here today I have no doubt in my mind that this seemingly small difference in my approach to healing made a huge difference in why I won my battle against cancer where others unfortunately lost theirs.

So, in a large way, *positioning myself for healing* in the physical sense really did mean stepping out in faith and submitting my body to the doctors, medicines and treatments that stood to give me a real fighting chance. It meant staying out of the spirit of fear and worry and going to the *Creator* in prayer and asking him to prepare and protect me physically for whatever I was about to experience. Then trusting that he would do just that.

I don't know if my case is unique, but I can now say that I didn't suffer with too many adverse effects while I went through the treatment process – if I experienced any negative side effects at all. I can also report that the few negative side effects that I did have to endure have all just about cleared up with time. So it seems that the ***Creator*** did just about what I prayed for him to do.

I dare think of where I would be if I had taken in the negative reports that most people take in regarding how going through these kinds of treatments will bring one harm. I know that I would have likely never ***positioned myself for healing*** if I had.

I had to position myself for healing and restoration by changing the way I was living my inner and outer life

As important as it was for me to position myself for healing in the physical sense, there was one more area that I had to give serious consideration to if I expected to use the power of **FAITH (APPLIED)** to gain a victory over cancer. That area consisted of the way in which I was living my life – both my inner life and my outer life.

It shouldn't come as a surprise to hear that many of the serious maladies that we can find ourselves stricken with find their roots in the condition of our physical health.

Whether it is a question of our physical condition, or how well we are caring for our bodies and working out to keep them fit and healthy. Or, a question of our dietary habits and what we are feeding our bodies in an effort to keep them vibrant and nourished. The plain truth is that the answers that we can give for these questions is often a perfect indicator of whether or not diseases like the one that eventually attacked my body lie ahead in the future.

Speaking for me, prior to July of 2012, I wasn't in the worst shape, but I wasn't anywhere near in the best shape that I could have been in either. While I had no issues with any of my vital organs, or with things like my blood pressure or my blood sugar levels, I was a bit overweight.

At the same time, from a dietary standpoint, while my overall eating habits were pretty good, I did have a love affair with sugar and usually ate something sweet every day. For sure being a sugar addict and overweight could have been contributing factors in why cancer was able to attack my body.

Therefore, *positioning myself for healing* also meant working to clean up these areas of my outer life. As a matter of fact, when I first took on the battle to overcome cancer, I thought that all I had to do was beat the disease itself and my life would automatically return to normal.

But I now know that that's just not true. I now know that I will have to take much better care of my body and work my way back to the health and wellness that I desire to get back to. As such, taking better care of my body, both in terms of what I eat and what I do to condition my body are more important than ever. I can see now that this will play the single biggest role in restoring me to complete wellness.

In fact, from my personal experience I now see the truth is that when a major medical challenge takes away your health or mobility, there is only one way that you get that health or mobility back, you must earn it. And, the two most basic places where you earn it back are at the gym and at the table.

In the spirit of that truth, if you ever find yourself confronted with a challenge like a major illness, for you to *position yourself for healing*, you will likely have to change your diet, your exercise regimen or both. Just like I learned on July 30th, 1995, when these principles were first given to me, what you cannot do is do the same things that got you into your illness and expect a new result – in this case, the result being wellness.

The plain truth is that there are many times when the disease is trying to tell us that there is something wrong with the way that we are living our outer lives. Not getting this truth in the moment of challenge could easily mean the difference between winning your fight over the disease and losing your life to it.

By the same token, neither should it come as a surprise to hear that many of the serious maladies that we can find ourselves stricken with find their roots in the condition of our mental or spiritual health. The fact is that many of the serious maladies that we get confronted with can have their roots there.

One of the things that I heard early on in my battle was the unique definition of disease that broke the word down to spell out, **Dis-ease**. The implication being that the illness or disease that I was now being confronted with was really a sign of some area of *dis-ease* in my life. The thought then became if I expected to get well and stay well, I had better find the source of this *dis-ease* and eliminate it from my life altogether.

To this end, there are those who feel that in almost all instances of major illness, perhaps the disease is showing the stricken that there is a need to change the way that they are living their inner life.

I don't know if I am prepared to say that I agree fully with this view. But speaking for me, to position myself for future wellness I did make a decision to pay closer attention to what's going on with my inner life. I made the decision to be more selective of the matters that I expend my mental and emotional energies on and to let many of the things that used to get me upset role off of my back.

One of the other decisions that I made in my hospital bed was to live by the power of **FAITH (APPLIED)**, and to lean on and trust the **Creator** to help me to be victorious in all the areas of my day to day life. In all of these ways I put every aspect of my life on the table as I sought to *position myself for healing* and recovery.

As far as I can tell, on July 30th, 1995, this single principle perhaps played the greatest role in activating the miracle-making power of the universe and moving the mountain to bring me the $1,000 bonus. Now, in July of 2012, once again this single principle likely played the greatest role in activating the miracle-making power of the universe to bring me the gift of healing from *Multiple Myeloma*.

So there you have the third principle of **FAITH (APPLIED)** that allowed me to overcome impossible odds and claim the $1,000 bonus on July 30th, 1995. Little could I have known that it would ultimately play a role in saving my life on another July day 17 years later. But the fact that it did just that is now a matter of history.

At the end of the day, never ever forget that *positioning yourself for success is about leaving your comfort zone and getting more aggressive to get in the flow of whatever you are standing in faith for.*

On July 30th, 1995, I was standing in faith to earn the $1,000 bonus, but how could I have expected to receive that bonus if I didn't get in the flow of the potential customers that were coming in the door? In July of 2012, I was standing in faith for healing, but how could I expect to receive that healing if I didn't get in the flow of the medicines and treatments that were presented to me?

In both of these instances, there simply would have been no way to receive what I wanted had I not change my position to get in the flow. Therefore as we wind down our discussion of this vital third *FAITH (APPLIED)* principle remember the two questions that you must continually ask yourself to insure that you are in the flow,

"Am I operating in my comfort zone?" If you are, get out of it quickly. Next ask yourself, *"Am I being as aggressive as I can be?"* If you aren't, immediately move to do so.

In a way it might be helpful for you to always remember that what you want already exist, you just don't have it. To get it you simply need to *reposition yourself for success*, most often by *abandoning your comfort zones and getting more aggressive in your approach*.

Also when you think about this principle of *positioning yourself for success*, always remember that if you are trying to rise up to meet a challenge that you have never faced before, you must operate in a way that you have never operated before.

Be sure that as you try to achieve greater results than you have before that you never again make the mistake of doing the same thing that you've done before and expecting a different result. That is so much of what this principle teaches us not to do.

I also feel the need to point out that many of us have been conditioned to believe in general that challenges are our enemy. When we are confronted by trying circumstances often we might even feel that the *Creator* has forsaken us. But I have come to see the exact opposite.

I have come to see that these are really moments where the *Creator* is trying to lead us to higher ground or to show us that we are capable of more than we may believe ourselves to be capable of.

Even though we don't like going through them at the time, being confronted with trying circumstances and rising to the occasion to meet them is the surest way for us to develop our faith and many of the other vital life skills that we need to succeed. It is also the best way for us to see what we are made of.

From my own experience I can tell you that there is no other way to learn many of the faith lessons that we need to learn to master *FAITH (APPLIED)*. I am a living testament to the notion that we really do learn best by our feet being held to the fire and I feel strongly that there is simply no better way to learn faith. And I know that when you learn to embrace your moments of challenge, you will see this truth for yourself.

As it relates to harnessing the power of *FAITH (APPLIED)*, remember that *positioning yourself for success* and getting into the flow of the thing that you are standing in faith for, takes you one step closer to achieving the miraculous and getting what you want.

Now that you have this third principle of the *FAITH (APPLIED)* formula down, let's move on to explore the fourth step in activating the miracle-making power of the universe:

Stay out of the loser clique

Avoid hanging with and socializing with losers who aren't trying to go for the goal anyway. Especially do not talk with them about the goal and take in their negative self-defeating views of, why me; I wouldn't do it, so you can't; fault finding; blame and responsibility shifting.

On July 30th, 1995, I was literally surrounded by a group of people who had all basically taken an internal oath of failure. In fact, from past events it was very obvious these co-workers of mines had decided that for the sake of being friends that they would never try to outdo one another.

This would become yet another occasion when they would exercise that friendly agreement. In deciding that I would accept the challenge and go for the goal of getting this $1,000 bonus that was put on the table before us, this was the *loser clique* that I would have to stay out of.

The funny thing about it was that because of their attitudes I had had similar issues with the various members of this group in the past. It seems that from the first day that I began working at that job, they wanted me to get with their program of self-imposed, group failure.

Like old slaves, they wanted to keep individual productivity and the productivity of the department as a whole down so that management wouldn't have cause to expect high productivity of any one of us.

As they saw it, if one man had success, management would see that we all could have success and demand more as a result. They were always spewing their views that there was no serious success to be had and no real money to be made in this department, or in the store as a whole for that matter.

They were constantly trying to get management to buy their views on this point and to accept it as a sufficient reason for their lack of productivity. When I came along, I quickly became a threat to this point of view. Not only was I not a friend of anyone or beholden to anyone in this store or department, I was not in agreement with this point of view.

Also, many of these guys were bitter old single guys. If they had ever even had wives and/or children, they weren't in their daily lives caring for them. I had both a wife and kids at home that I was intent on feeding and I was here to make all that I could, at all times. As such, this day would come to magnify the rift that existed between us.

From the first minute that management had put this offer on the table, this group of failure minded colleagues did everything they could to cast doubt on whether or not it was achievable. They certainly made it clear that as failure friends they'd never consider entering into a situation where one could succeed while the others failed.

As such, when the doors opened for the day, these guys did anything but engage in trying to hit this goal. In fact, the members of this group spent this day like they had habitually spent every other work day, hanging out in the back of the department socializing with each other – bitching and complaining.

When they weren't doing that, they engaged in busy work; fulfilling duties like cleaning and dusting and playing with the merchandise that we were supposed to be selling. They watched their favorite movies or listened to their favorite CDs. They also took their customary long breaks and lunches.

Any one of these activities was sufficient to prevent any one of us from achieving this goal. But, put all of them together and there was simply no way to even think about succeeding. Yet this was how these guys chose to spend their day.

My approach to the day was the utter opposite of this foolishness. Because I took this stand, by day's end I alone stood victorious in my department and made career long enemies of these self-imposed *losers* in the process. Both of which were ok by me.

From my experience, this is so typical of what you and I can encounter in our surroundings when we are striving to meet a challenge or trying to achieve a goal. Having self-imposed *losers* around us who are trying to turn us into one of their failure friends. We usually know who these people are before we even get going.

This reality is commonplace on our jobs. This reality can be commonplace in our social circles. This reality can even be commonplace in our places of worship. Unfortunately, this reality can also be commonplace in our intimate and family relationships.

I don't know why it is that there are times when the people nearest to us are the main ones trying to discourage us from striving to achieve. But I am pretty sure that each of us has had our fair share of those situations. After all, we are on planet earth, and that seems to be part of the journey.

Perhaps I had an easy time *staying out of this loser clique* because I wasn't beholden to any of these people. But I do know that it is another animal when you find yourself having to rise above the *loser clique* of loved ones.

And yet, I also know that that is exactly the place where many of us are, confronted by the challenge of needing to play above the expectations of the people nearest to us – having this as our backdrop as we attempt to summons the miracle-making power of the universe.

Whether we are trying to rise up to meet a challenge or go for our goals and dreams, the reasons for why the people around us can't support us in our drive to accomplish a given task or succeed in our overall lives are many. Sometimes these people think lowly of us and our abilities; they feel that we are simply not capable of what we are seeking to do.

I have found that in many of these instances, these people are trying to tie us to their own expectations for themselves or to their own beliefs about what they are capable of.

In essence, they are trying to define our capabilities in terms of what they themselves feel they are capable of. Sometimes they are looking from the limited perspective of what they themselves have done or seen others do before.

There are times when these people are of the mindset that they are better than us and if they are not capable, who are we to think that we can accomplish such a feat.

Many times people who are supposed to be close to us can actually have a low opinion of us and try to use that low opinion to define what we are capable of achieving. As they see it, we are simply not the one who is supposed to succeed here, or in life generally, for that matter – perhaps, like most people, we have had some failures in our past and these people are trying to bind us to the record of our past.

Sometimes they are even well meaning in that they are trying to protect us from the hurt of failure or the disappointment that they feel we will inevitably experience for pursuing and failing to achieve what they see as goals that are too lofty for us to attain.

Sometimes these people simply have sinister motives and they are just out to hold us down for some reason that is born out of their own self-centered intentions. Still other times, there is no real rhyme or reason for why these supposed loved ones aren't supporting us.

Maybe for any or all of these reasons, someone nearest to you is the person that you must avoid cliquing up with as you strive to meet the challenge before you or go for that coveted goal. I have certainly found myself in this situation on many occasions in my life.

What I have found through all of these events is that the reason why someone opposes you or your goal doesn't really matter. The fact still remains that as far as this goal is concerned, you must avoid hanging in that *loser clique*. That is the truth whether it is a clique of many or a clique of one.

As I saw back on July 30th, 1995, these people weren't going for the goal anyway. As such, they were not interested in seeing anyone else go for it.

In fact, the last thing that they wanted to see happen was to have someone near them go for it, succeed and prove false all of the excuses that they gave for not going for it themselves. You and I must realize that that dynamic is going on around us all the time.

Some people are always trying to meddle in the lives of others in an effort to bring them to failure so as to justify their own lack of ambition and effort or their own failings and shortcomings – for that matter, their own poor life choices. They try to repackage their issues and try to call their opposition to your striving for success as things like *"common sense"* or *"being realistic."*

They will often try to mask their fears and doubts as strength. It is commonplace for these people to try to guide others around them in a manner that supports their own personal nonsense. If your success defies their beliefs or stands to shatter their excuses or challenge their reality, these people will just about do everything within their power to hold you back.

No matter which of these angles your opposition is coming from, it's a *loser clique* and if you want to see the miracle-making power of this universe bring victory to your life and circumstances, you must avoid hanging around and socializing with these people at all cost.

There is something out here for me. I don't have to know where it is coming from – I just have to be in motion!

To say the least, *staying out of the loser clique* was a key part of what I did on July 30th, 1995. And, I have also had the good sense to do the same thing on many other occasions in my professional sales career when I used the power of the *FAITH (APPLIED)* principles to achieve what was thought to be an unachievable goal.

There came a time in my career when I set out to learn how to work exclusively on the basis of these 8 principles and upon the concept of faith in general. I don't really know how it got started.

In some ways I was not really aware of the full ramifications of my doing this. It certainly wasn't like I became fully conscious about the benefits of using these principles and made a decision from there. Instead it was more like I just fell into the habit of using faith in my work and selling endeavors.

I wouldn't focus so much on how much I did to try to get clients. I didn't focus on how many attempts I had to make to make sales or on how many people I was working with as much as I maintained a belief that success was there for the taking if I just believed that it was.

I basically carried the belief that no matter what appeared to be happening I would end up where I needed to be as long as I kept my mind tuned to this belief.

As an outward expression of this belief, as I went about my work day, as I made prospecting calls, as I cold called businesses in my territory looking for clients, I would repeatedly say this affirmation over and over to myself,

"There is something out here for me. I don't have to know where it is coming from – I just have to be in motion!"

I used this positive confession to permeate all that I did with this powerful spirit and it never failed me. Looking back on it now, this was vitally important, as I ultimately found myself confronted with the challenge of having to *stay out of a loser clique* that presented itself in a whole new form.

It was one thing to *stay out of the loser clique* that was made up of people who were my equals. But the day came in my professional sales career when I realized the need to *stay out of a loser clique* that was made up of people who were my superiors – people who by title had the right and responsibility to check, if not outright set the course of my work efforts.

You see, I had always used this philosophy without regard to what my equals thought. I had used this philosophy without any regard to the deadlines that were screaming at me. I had even managed to use this philosophy without any regard to the fact that it could put my very job on the line.

Because of this I ultimately found myself on the wrong side of my superiors. This was inevitable given the extent of the accountability system that was commonly followed in the professional sales environment.

In the everyday world, back then and now, it seems that almost nobody lives by faith. The notion that I was staking my success on a belief in something that couldn't be touched or seen was just too out there for my bosses to fathom.

The very nature of the accountability that we were all subjected to meant that I would be expected to explain at all times where the results that I was responsible for producing were going to come from. Not only was I suppose to be able to explain myself to my boss, she needed to explain herself and me to her boss. Next, her boss needed to be able to explain himself, and my boss and me to his boss. And, so on up the food chain.

Here I was operating by my ***FAITH (APPLIED)*** principles and believing in a source for success that couldn't be logically explained, and still worse, repeatedly stating the affirmation,

> *"There is something out here for me. I don't have to know where it is coming from – I just have to be in motion!"*

The whole thing could only have looked outrageous from the viewpoint of management.

To my boss and nearly everyone above her in management, it appeared that I was simply a nut case. To them if you weren't out racking your brain trying to make sales in a visible manner, you weren't trying to sale at all.

As such, they simply thought I wasn't working. And, with each boss that I had, once they got wind of this philosophy of mines, the time came when they would try to force me out of the practice of working by these principles.

This new brand of the *loser clique* manifested itself in many different ways and touched several key faith projects that I was trying to accomplish during those years. One of the most notable instances was my wedding in 1996.

Dream weddings do come true, when you avoid the loser clique!

I had always desired to give my wife a dream wedding. Over the years we had wanted to make it happen but our finances were always just too tight.

Neither one of us had families that could afford to throw us a wedding, let alone a dream wedding. So it was up to me to make it happen, if it were to happen at all.

As I started making a little better income in my new career I figured that this would be the best chance I would have of fulfilling this dream. So I decided to ***accept the challenge*** and ***set the goal*** to go out and give her a wedding that she would never forget.

With that decision, I took action. We acted as our own wedding planners. We lined up a venue, the *Ritz Carlton Hotel* in *Marina del Rey, California* (Not cheap). We rented out space at one of the restaurants nearby the hotel to host the reception (again, not cheap).

My wife to be found a place that had the dress she wanted and a seamstress who would make it her own. I found my tuxedo and a tailor to alter it to fit me. We found a florist that would handle the floral work. We found a bakery that would handle the wedding cake. We found a jeweler that would supply the rings. We found a printer to do our invitations and print work. We found a photographer to take the wedding photos. We got our licenses. Our church home supplied the pastor to officiate the wedding.

We found everything that we needed to make this the perfect day and we moved immediately to put our deposits down and lock everything in. There was just one problem, all we had was the deposit money. The money to pay for the event had not been earned yet.

To even my future wife's dismay, I was initiating all of this on the faith that I would find the clients to make this day a reality. By the time everything was set in motion it became clear that I was the only one who possessed the belief that this could be done, let alone the faith needed to actually make it come to pass.

The project was as much a challenge as any of the others that I had faced before. True to the spirit of what I mentioned earlier, in the natural it could have easily appeared like there was nothing going on for most of the time that I was working to make this day come true.

Despite my best efforts and the efforts of my own company paid telemarketer, not a lot of good sales leads were coming in as we headed toward the close of the business month.

To make matters worse, because of how we got paid, to get this money on time, I had to meet a sales deadline that was a full two months in advance.

If I failed to meet this deadline, there was no way to get the money in time and there would have been no way to get my deposits back or change the event date. I would have simply lost the money that I had put out trying to put together a dream wedding.

Everyone else in our social circle at that time had gone to Las Vegas, their local city hall or put on some other form of a *"Shotgun Wedding."*

As you might guess, almost none of these people were pulling for us to succeed in having this dream day. From this crowd I got accused of taking a foolish and unnecessary financial risk. And, we got accused of trying to be too showy.

We had originally planned to go to Hawaii and hold our wedding but chose to keep it at home so that these friends and family members could celebrate with us. But I guess these people were too envious of the fact that we were having a dream wedding to celebrate it.

For reasons that still elude me, some of these people took our wedding as an offense to their wedding. They could not see that I meant no offense to anyone else's wedding choices. I simply didn't want to have my new bride have her wedding day fit into anything that could be categorized as *"Shotgun."*

Of course, this meant that there would be no help and support from this quarter and that I really had to make it happen all by myself.

If anything, this became a ***loser clique*** that I had to definitely avoid. So I turned the...

"There is something out here for me. I don't have to know.
where it is coming from – I just have to be in motion!"

...spirit up to a level 10 or above and I got super focused on this principle as I realized that on this faith project, it was truer than ever. It was certainly true that I had no clue where I would find the sales to make this all come together.

In the backdrop of this project, it was just another month at work and there was a sales quota that I was expected to bring in and I was accountable to my boss for these results. Every Monday morning I had to have a face to face with her and explain what was going on.

As much as it might seem like these goals were one and the same, as in if I hit my quota, I'd make the money to pay for the wedding, that wasn't necessarily true.

Of course, it could work out that way. But as far as management was concerned and the way we were focused to sell, these were two separate situations. To them, closing the sales to hit quota, didn't necessarily mean that I'd make the money needed to pay for my wedding.

Basically, the deals that they wanted me to focus on could bring dollars into the office, but have little profit to pay out commissions. That was commonly what many of the sales people would do to hit their quota – write deals that made the house money and made them nothing.

So these two goals didn't have a natural overlap to them. If they overlapped at all it would be because I did something to pull them both together. So it should be clear to see why as the month shaped up, I was at direct odds with my boss.

Thankfully she was a generally nice person so that when she got wind of what was going on she didn't make a big stink about me shooting for my quota that month. But as she noticed what I was doing to try and solve my dilemma, she did however position herself to become a member of the *loser clique* that I had to avoid if I was going to find success.

As the spirit of *God* revealed to me the three prospective clients that would ultimately get me to where I had to go, I made the mistake of divulging their names in our weekly accountability session.

I really had no choice but to offer up their names. It was bad enough that I wasn't making a serious attempt to go for my quota, the last thing that I could do was to look like I wasn't working at all.

The problem with these prospects was that they had been prospects for some time. They had each been pitched to a few times before, by both past sales reps and me. Each time they had each flat out declined to act on the proposals that had been drawn up for them.

Now here I was telling my boss that this is where I am expecting results to come from, and she in turn, had to go tell her boss the same.

Once my boss realized this, she absolutely hammered me about it. She asked,

> *"How could I let it come down to this?" "You have tried to sale these people previously and they didn't buy, why would now be any different?"*

She even said,

> *"You are planning your wedding around these prospects, there is no way you will make it!"*

From her vantage point, my believing in mind stuff over good old physical labor had finally caught up with me.

To her and the other members of this new **Loser Clique**, that was all this faith stuff was – mind stuff. To them it was something that foolish salespeople try to substitute for good old-fashioned hard work.

She made that clear in no uncertain terms. The only break she cut me was in not sharing this development with the big boss. He not only would have shared her views on the subject, but he would have been far less agreeable to my plan for success and far less willing to give me a pass for the month to focus on my wedding.

I got all of this negative from the very person who trained me in the business. To think that I got all of this negative from someone that I respected and looked to for support and guidance in my career.

After all, I was still relatively new in my selling career at that time – a career that I started on very weak belief and faith, having been told all my life that sales work was something that I should never do for a living.

To have this kind of negativity from a person of my boss's caliber was almost enough to cause me to give up. But like I have tried to drive home to you here, when it comes to activating the miracle-making power of the universe, *you simply must avoid falling into any form of a loser clique*.

It doesn't matter who the *loser clique* consist of. It doesn't matter what their level of expertise. It doesn't even matter whether it is a clique of one or a clique of many.

If someone is trying to discourage you in any way from standing in faith to go for your goal or strive to meet the challenge that is confronting you, you simply have to avoid hanging with and socializing with that person or group of people.

You especially cannot layout your hopes and fears, or your dreams and goals here. For sure, if you can't avoid cliquing up with these people, you will never see the power of the universe come to your aid and do for you, what you could never do for yourself otherwise.

As my boss vented, I just let her talk. I took nothing she said personally and I certainly didn't take it in. I let her words just drop where we sat. Once she was done, I went about my day just as I had planned to.

Specifically, I went to work on getting these prospects to do what they hadn't done before – buy, and buy now. To achieve my aim, I used the 8 principles of the *FAITH (APPLIED)* formula to get each of them to go forward with my proposal and make my dream wedding real.

Namely, **(1)** *I accepted the challenge*. **(2)** *I set the goal* to get each prospect to buy. **(3)** *I positioned myself for success* by visiting each prospect almost daily in some small way. **(4)** *I ignored the loser cliques* that had formed around me both at home and at the office. **(5)** *I ask each prospect to buy again*. **(6)** I was prepared to keep moving and **not waste time on anyone that wouldn't buy**. **(7)** *I delayed judgment* to give my efforts a chance to pan out. And, **(8)** finally, *I worked up to and through the deadline of my faith project.*

In the end, It Worked!!! I ended up closing the first two prospects one day before month end and the last one and the biggest of the three after the close of the business day on the last day. Best of all, I made our dream wedding come true!!!

You should have seen the look on my bosses face when she learned that all three of the people that she said would never buy, had indeed bought. At that moment she was forced to concede that I had not wasted my time at all.

To her credit, at least she was woman enough to admit that she was wrong and that she had been shortsighted. She acknowledge me in front of the entire office staff, the sales staff, service staff, administrative staff and the full management team for doing a great job and doing exactly as she had trained me to do, get results no matter what!

Even though I didn't officially hit my quota that month, I had brought some good profitable deals in. These deals paid both the house and me. It was a true win – win for both sides.

From that day forward, I had no more problems with selling my way with that particular boss. However, over the years there would be others that would take this exact same stance when they learned about my faith selling habits.

With their general lack of faith they were often trying to get me to focus on dealing less in the mind stuff and more in the natural and on staying away from the deals that I could bring to pass through the use of these faith principles.

One of these bosses often accused me of exercising too much faith and patience, as I would never accept the small offers that most sales people took. Instead, I had the habit of trusting in the power of these faith principles to bring the best deal together for me.

Often, I would perfectly use patience to turn a small deal into a bigger, more profitable deal. He would often say that in these moments of patience that I was running the risk of losing the small deal that was offered to me while trying to get the big deal that I wanted.

He would repeatedly say, I was failing to understand that, *"half a loaf, beats no loaf."* And, to him I was always flirting with getting *"No loaf."*

Despite the negative views of this boss, my approach never went unrewarded. In fact, I lost very few of these deals and always made far more income when working my way.

Another boss went so far as to call my wife to try to get her involved with my selling activities. Like my previous boss, he was always itching to have me take small deals from clients while I was usually believing the universe for larger deals, ones that would help me to meet vital needs.

On one such occasion, he called me about a potential lead and as was my custom, I planned to exercise the faith and patience to see how big a lead it could become before I made an effort to take the sale.

Before I knew it, this guy had called my wife to try to get her to talk me into just accepting a small order and being done with it. He had to call her because ***I had been avoiding him and his loser clique views***. I refused to take this negative input, now channeled through my wife and in the end, I was right again.

The little one machine deal that this guy tried to get my wife to encourage me to take, that would have paid me next to nothing, became a big three machine sale that paid me nearly

$5,000. This was one of those times when I had been riding around chanting my affirmation,

> *"There is something out here for me. I don't have to know where it is coming from – I just have to be in motion!"*

Once again, by the power of the **Creator**, something was definitely out there for me. I made a nice amount of money on this deal and I wasn't the one that found the lead. My telemarketer did. I had a ton of sales work out like this when I sold on faith. In fact, I made more money through applying these 8 principles of patient faith in my selling than I ever made through selling any other way.

Again, none of this could have ever happened if I had not learned how *to stay out of the loser clique* and follow my own initiative. Are you starting to see that for yourself? Again, I am telling you stories that are the **God** honest truth.

The *loser clique* can come to you in many forms and from many different angles. As a rule, anytime you are confronted with people who expect you to explain where things are going to come from or who try to explain to you why you will fail if you can't explain where your results will come from, that is a form of the *loser clique* that you must avoid.

While I was going through dealing with these types of bosses, I never liked to explain where my results would come from. Remember, *I don't have to know where my results will come from. I just have to know that they are out there and be in motion trying to find them.*

Neither did I like to explain failure in advance, as in rationalize why I don't know, what I don't know to the point where I am really now predicting the circumstances of my own failure before it actually takes place.

To me, that is what you are doing when you are defending the use of faith in your life and your affairs. And, I hated having to defend my use of faith. Especially when faith was producing great results, results that I could never have achieved otherwise.

Essentially, it was like being asked to explain my belief in **God**. And, that is something that no man has the right to do. I realized then and I still do now that anyone who asks me to do that is a member of the ultimate *loser clique* that I have to stay out of.

To recap, for the most part, *"Staying out of the Loser Clique"* is a simple matter of avoidance, a matter of you just not spending time with people who will discourage you in any way from striving to accomplish the task that either you or circumstances have set out before you.

But as with the story I just related, there are many times when avoidance in the fullest sense may not be possible or may not be enough, particularly when we are talking about the people who are truly nearest to you. People like a boss, a parent, a mate, a close friend or a close colleague or partner all have the power to influence your efforts and generally are not so easily avoidable.

In these instances, you have to learn how to not allow their defeatist attitudes to enter your head space. You have to learn not to allow them to infect you with their general attitude of indifference or indifference for your project or goal.

As a good rule of thumb, if a person is not involved directly in the project, if they are not equally interested in the outcome that you are seeking or if you know that they don't support your efforts, don't try to engage them in your process.

Stop talking to them about the things that go wrong, about the people who don't get it, about the sales that didn't come through. For that matter, don't bad mouth your project, your process or talk about the people that you work with to these people.

It is all too common for people like this to use these things as weapons of discouragement against you. If they really want to be sinister, they will use these things to sow the seeds of doubt within you.

Learn to talk to yourself and to your *God* himself if that is all that you've got. Learn to seek input or guidance from yourself and your *God* if that is truly all that you've got.

But unless you want to see your project die a quick death, don't take your project issues to people who aren't going for it themselves. You can discuss things with these people once all is done and the victory is in your hands, but not before.

Another thing that I have learned is that you can't drag people along who don't want to make it or who are not going for it anyway. They will only slow you down or stop you altogether. I have learned that,

> *"You and I can't give people something they*
> *don't already want for themselves."*

I have literally spent years struggling with this one until finally I got this truth through my head. Finally accepting it freed me to go win in my own life.

It is common of good people to want everyone to do well. I have always had this gene for as long as I can remember. I have always been the type of person who would try to bring the good news that I discovered back to the village under the assumption that everyone wanted to receive good news. If I learned something that could enrich my life and the lives of those around me, I just had to share it with everyone that I knew.

There was even a time when I thought that everyone wanted to be successful and do well financially. But I now know that I was very naïve in that belief. I now realize that everyone wants success and wealth, but the vast majority of people want someone else to get those things for them.

Also, don't make the mistake of believing that the member of the *loser clique* will see things differently if they have a vested interest in the outcome of what you are trying to accomplish. Don't think that because someone stands to sink with you if you fail or swim with you if you succeed that that will make them share in your desire for victory.

Remember, my co-workers would have gotten their own $1,000 had they crossed the finish line victoriously. But those who were negative still chose to be negative. The fact that we could all share in success did not change that. I have seen this truth play out many times in all areas of both my personal and professional life.

Finally, don't feel like you have anything to prove or like you have to give the people around you something to believe in. Yes, you should be winning. But you have to know that you can't make someone believe in you or what you are doing.

I have made this mistake several times as well. But I now understand that operating in faith means that we are required to believe without evidence that we should believe.

In fact, to my way of thinking, if we have prior evidence that what we are doing is going to work, we don't need belief or faith – we have fact.

Thus applying your faith means there will be a time when you not only lack fact, but with a member of the *loser clique*, even fact might not be enough to win them to your side.

So don't you make the mistake of believing that you can show evidence of success to get people around you to be supportive of you. More often than not, it simply does not work.

What I have learned is those who are going to support you are usually willing to do so on your word alone. Those who are not, tend to find some reason to be unsupportive no matter what results you show. They may even become resentful when you start showing clear evidence of the rightfulness of your efforts. Believe me when I say that I have seen this truth play out time and time again.

Also, in this same way, if you have the habit in you of trying to fit in with any person or any group of people, free yourself from that urge. That is another trap that will keep you from seeing the miracle-making power of the universe come to your aid.

In the simplest terms that I could use to explain this to you, realize that every family, every friendship, every group, every church, every business has a culture. If what you are trying to accomplish runs counter to that culture, you are sure to encounter resistance.

If you are beholden to the concept of fitting in, you'll be more apt to succumb to that kind of pressure. Endeavoring in this way will only cause you to stumble and give up when these people fail to get on the bandwagon.

I have seen people go after a task, hoping that people will fall into favor with them when success arrives. In an unspoken way, perhaps these people see these people climbing onto their bandwagon as one of the rewards of success.

They are then sorely disappointed when these people fail to join them in the winner's circle. I have even seen some people give up their goals and dreams altogether when this happens.

You must realize that sometimes success is its own reward. You must understand that striving for your goal is worth it if you got the victory that you sought – so long as you violated no one else in the process. You must also learn that if any so called friend or loved one tries to make you choose between success and your relationship with them, you were not really a friend or loved one to them in the first place.

Also never forget that using **FAITH (APPLIED)** to activate the miracle-making power of the universe calls for raw belief, the kind that is not based upon evidence and that is the exact opposite of what you would be displaying if you were to get engaged in waging a campaign to prove you deserve support.

As you should have gotten through the story about my wedding, it really doesn't matter who the members of the *loser clique* are. They may be supposed experts or people whose advice you often seek, but they could still be wrong. To find victory, you must follow the spirit of **God** and your own initiative. It is the only way for you to see that you are right.

Above all, *never explain failure* in advance of it actually taking place. Don't discuss the negative people around you or their views; especially when they are not around. Just put them out of your mind. Don't let their attitudes become yours or get tainted by their pessimism.

If you simply must say something, remember my affirmation, **"*There is something out here for me. I don't have to know where it is coming from – I just have to be in motion!*"** Use it as I have. I am sure it will serve you well, just as it has worked miracles for me.

Fighting a loser clique while fighting for my very life

It really does bear repeating that a *loser clique* can consist of any group or for that matter, any person that doesn't support you in what you seek. I would have never thought that I would find a *loser clique* in the hospital when I was battling for my very life and mobility, but there was one there. It consisted of some of the nurses and doctors that were charged with the task of dispensing care to me.

You would think that these medical professionals all shared my goal to return to my prior state of physical well-being. You would think that like me, all of these men and women would have stood alongside me in ***accepting the challenge*** to fight to overcome the illness that had been placed upon me.

The truth is that that just was not the case. Don't get me wrong, there were several caring health professionals that worked on me during this time. But sadly, there were far too many that just didn't care about me or the plight that lie ahead of me at all.

These people had no problem bringing their uncaring, pessimistic attitudes into my face and space. These people had no problem putting their own agendas ahead of my agenda as a patient.

These people had no concern for how I actually felt physically and attempted to push me through the healing process and out of the hospital in a manner that was actually making matters worse.

Although I was young and vibrant prior to this challenge, they were ready to cast me off rather quickly and had no problem trying to ship me off to an assisted living home with old and dying people just to accomplish their aims.

Little had they known that I had already made up my mind as to the outcome of this challenge – and in trying to move me in any direction that would not lead to my victory over this illness, they were in for a losing fight.

Very early on in my eight week hospital stay I started realizing that everyone that was assigned to treat me didn't have my best interest at heart. I realized in no time flat that there was a whole cast of characters, a ***loser clique*** that I would have to limit my exposure to if I intended to get well.

As with any workplace, there were those who were just going through the motions of the workday. There were also the insignificant workers who thought they were running the show and didn't need to listen to the orders of me or my doctor.

There were those who were totally unwilling to put themselves out for the patients – these were the people who had lost the concept of basic humanity and had forgotten how to treat the patients the way they themselves would like to be treated.

There were those who felt that if I had any questions about a treatment or procedure that I was questioning their knowledge and expertise. There were those who would attempt to give me advice without first reading my chart to know specifically what was going on with me.

There were those who would try to force procedures upon me without any regard for how the procedure might affect me in the long run. Worst of all, there were those who had no *God*, no spirituality and no faith.

The result of letting these characters run unchecked in my environment was nearly devastating. They gave me terribly wrong advice and information regarding my physical condition and my ability to perform basic everyday duties in that diminished state of being.

There were a few incidents when I was given too much pain medicine, resulting in a state of consciousness that I should hope to never be in again. To this day I don't see how anyone can abuse such medications and use them to get high. For me the feeling was far from enjoyable.

At the worst stages of my illness, I could not move my upper body at all. I had zero control over my ability to lift up or roll over from side to side or anything.

As such, if I needed to be moved, say from my bed to a treatment or exam table, or from a gurney to a treatment or exam table, others had to physically move me.

To make matters worse, because there was a mass pressing up against my spine and my nerves, I would have these seriously painful spasms if I was moved wrong or carelessly.

As you might guess, this caused me some serious problems during my stay. And, for some reason, I ran into the most problems whenever I had to work with male staffers, whether they were doctors, nurses or medical technicians.

The fact is that these people simply weren't listening to me or my body. To them, I guess I was bitching and moaning when I tried to tell them how they needed to handle me.

One in particular made it very clear that he felt as though I was trying to question his abilities to do his job, a job that he had held for more than two decades. And, while he would not listen to my instructions, he caused me numerous painful experiences when I was in his care. Never mind the fact that I had had a team of small women successfully move me on more than one occasion, let him tell it, I had the issue.

The simple fact is that these people were failing to see me as an individual, an individual with my own set of issues. They tried to treat me just as they had treated everyone else when in truth my case was different. Just as I am sure everyone else's case is.

Of course, every male was not the same. There were some that got it and to them I am thankful.

As you might imagine, the issue of these spasms was a matter of great concern for me. Many people are stricken with cancer to be sure. But in my case, the very nature of the disease was such that it seriously attacked my mobility and very few of the people who were charged with treating me were getting that early on.

While they weren't getting it, they were unnecessarily roughing me up in the name of treating the disease. However, this all changed when I got it and started implementing this principle to *keep myself out of their Loser Clique.*

At that point I took over and began to demand the type of care that my unique situation called for, no matter who I offended in the process. I essentially learned to listen to my body and to do what it dictated. I learned to go at the speed that it dictated.

If I needed to be lifted and handled in a certain manner and you were unwilling to handle me in that manner, you didn't touch me. If my body said that today was not a good day to go through with a particular treatment, I did not do it.

If my body said that today was not a good day to work out with the physical therapist, I did not do it. If you didn't deliver the type of care that I needed and expected, you simply had to go. I had no problem telling you to get out of my room and my life.

Ultimately I got everyone straight by taking this stance for my health. But it wasn't without some getting nasty and head banging, even with the doctors.

I must say again that along the way I had no problem putting people out of my environment if they tried to subject me to their unhelpful mentality. I perfectly equated such behavior to be the same as any other *loser clique*.

Don't get me wrong, I am not talking about arbitrarily foregoing lifesaving medical procedures or just blatantly or foolishly disobeying the doctor's orders.

On the whole, all throughout my recovery I have been perfectly willing to submit myself to the treatments and medicines that all of my doctors have told me were necessary for me to get better. But I realized early on that not only did I have rights as a patient, but I had the right to stand on the principles of positivity and faith that I instinctively knew would be a key part of my healing and restoration.

From the moment that I entered the hospital I realized that many of the so-called professionals that I was coming across didn't share that spirit of positivity and faith in any way. As a result, it became critical to my wife and I that we keep these people from influencing the positive healing atmosphere that we had set up in my room.

I would have never dreamt of throwing doctors and nurses alike out of my hospital room, not in a million years. We are all raised to be polite and to respect people like doctors and nurses. In that upbringing I am just like most people; my Mom was even a nurse. But the fact is that there was no way to be polite about it.

I could have let these careless and pessimistic professionals unleash the spirit of sickness, defeat and ultimately death into my hospital room and space and took the risk that this spirit would have eventually invaded my own mind.

I could have continued to give these careless professionals access to my body where they could have continued to rough me up and run my body through treatments and medical procedures that made me worse off for what I was already battling.

I could have become part of this *loser clique* under the guise of being polite, or I could have did exactly as I did and tossed their butts out once they revealed themselves to be members of *the loser clique that I had to stay out of.*

In the end, I know that I made the right call and I would not only do it all over again if I had to, but I would advise anyone going through a similar situation to do the same thing. Again, it doesn't matter who the person is. Either they are in harmony with your desires, or they are part of *the loser clique that you must stay out of.*

As this was playing out, I had no concrete knowledge of the inner thoughts of most of the people that I had to put in check at the hospital. But, I ultimately found out from my doctor that I could not have been more right in my handling of the situation there.

I learned that several of these supposed professionals had made up their minds very early on that I would never regain my mobility and the ability to walk and even thought that I would not overcome the cancer that had invaded my body.

These men and women had quickly given me up for a future that would have had me confined to the bed and even worse, dead. Some gave my doctor grief for doing his best to restore me to health. A couple of these so-called professionals even predicted that I wouldn't live for more than 6 months.

Now what if he had listened to their views? What if I had been more concerned with being polite and not hurting their feelings? What if I had ever thought that I had no right to question their expertise or their credentials?

I probably wouldn't be here writing this to you today. I have no doubt that this disease would have taken me out if I had taken in the pessimistic views that these people had about my ability to recover from this serious illness.

The same would have been true if I had followed the ill-advised and ill-timed treatments and procedures that some of them tried to take me through.

Thankfully, I had no problem listening to my own spirit and my own body. Most of all, thankfully I had no problem listening to my *God*. Because I know that doing so is what saved my life.

Today my doctor marvels at the scope and swiftness of my recovery. He tells me all the time that he can't wrap his mind around how far I have come from the condition that I was in when I was first admitted to the hospital and into his care. He has also told me that his once doubting colleagues are having an even tougher time wrapping their minds around my story of healing.

I have often tried to help him get the true source of my miraculous recovery. Whether or not he will ever get it, I don't know. I do feel that he was sent to me from **God** himself. Without his efforts and actions on the behalf of my health, I have no doubt that it could have been a different story for me. I also have no doubt that he was sent to me because of my stand of FAITH.

I believe that that is the very reason why we connected in the first place. He was part of the response from the universe to my stance that, *"I would beat whatever it is that I was confronted with."* That is why I have always treated him with the utmost respect and trusted him as a professional, in stark contrast to how I have had to treat some of the other doctors, nurses and medical technicians on the same hospital staff.

This little story should finally drive home to you just how serious you have to be about staying out of the *loser clique* and keeping those who don't share your goals out of your presence. You should see again that it really doesn't matter who they are or what their title or expertise is supposed to be.

All that matters is that their thoughts, views, words and actions harmonize with your desired outcome. If it does, roll on. If it doesn't they simply must go, and if you must have the support of another person, you must keep looking until you find someone that will line up with where you are trying to go.

It should even go without saying again that you must be willing to go it alone if you are the only one who has faith for the goal that you seek. If that is the case, except now that you are enough by yourself.

Except now that you are all the earthly support that you need to see your goal through. And, given that by the power of *FAITH (APPLIED)* you have the *Creator* himself backing you, you are not alone by any means. In that you can take full comfort.

I feel the need to make it clear that the point here is not for you yourself to become nasty in the name of trying to meet a challenge or of seeking your goals and dreams without provocation. You should always strive to maintain peace and remain peaceful throughout the process of going after what you seek, even when someone is trying your patience as we've just discussed.

I am saying that when the situation arises that you have to choose between achieving success in your task and getting rid of people who would just as soon bring you to failure, you must rise to the occasion and stand up for what you are going for.

In some cases, while you will have to be firm in your stance, you can still do this peaceably and respectfully. But there are those cases when you will have to meet nasty with nasty and in those times, you must be willing to get down and dirty to defend your interest. So be ready.

Also, I would be kidding myself if I allowed myself to not see that some of you may have a problem with considering your loved ones, your friends and family members as part of a *"Loser Clique."* I know this because I have been there before too. In fact, I struggled with this for a long time – even after I had already received these 8 principles.

For sure it is sometimes tough to see that someone we hold near and dear doesn't support us in our endeavors or in our efforts to succeed in life in general.

But as tough as it may be to see it, no matter how hard we may try to fight it, it is so often true. As tough as that is, it is even tougher to see the people nearest to us as the *losers* that they might really be.

Fortunately for me, I never had a problem calling things as I see them, even in my closest relationships. At the very least, I have always understood that I had to see the behavior of the person for what it is, even while I may continue to love and respect the person.

Being able to see and judge the behavior for what it is has allowed me to stay out of the trap of letting loyalty to loved ones bring me to failure in my life. I have witnessed so many nice people fall prey to this error in judgment. Thus, the ability to cut certain people off is a trait that I believe we all must learn to possess.

With that said, before you take offense to the term *loser clique* as it applies here, it may serve you to know that that is how the principle was first presented to me by the spirit of *God*. It came to me in that exact name when I stepped back and pondered how I had managed to achieve success in *The Great TV Incident*.

My experience over a lot of years has taught me that in spite of our personal discomfort with the label, it usually fits perfectly well.

As much as you or I may wish to kid ourselves, it is our inability to see these loved ones for the members of the *Loser Clique* that they are, that will only keep us vulnerable to their attacks. And, such an error in judgment will ultimately become the source of our failure to successfully activate the miracle-making power of the universe.

I know that we covered a lot of material on this principle. It is the first one of those points where I needed to spend a little time to make things crystal clear for you – to make sure that you know fully why you must now avoid some of your associates if you are serious about using the power of *FAITH (APPLIED)*.

I will trust that you have gotten a clear picture of why *you must stay out of any loser clique* that stands to block the *Creator* of the universe from bringing miracle-making power into your life and your affairs.

So now that we have thoroughly covered this vital fourth principle, let's look at the fifth step in activating the miracle-making power of the universe:

Ask everyone who might help

Try every avenue there is to getting your goal. Don't assume where your results will come from. Just be in motion and try every source until you have your goal. Also, don't be afraid to go high in pursuit of your goal. Often we think that it is easier to achieve small things than big things. We think the doors in lowly places will open for us faster than the doors in high places. Or, we believe it is easier to make it among the unsuccessful or the poor than it is to make it among the rich and successful. Simply put, we think that we are sure to get our goal if we just aim low enough. And, on the contrary, we think there is no way we can get our goal from a higher place. The truth is just the opposite. Often, it can be easier to get what you seek from the higher place than the lower one. It is we who usually struggle to believe that we can go to, and get our goal from the higher places. Realize now that asking everyone who might help means being open to all of your options – the high end ones, as well as the low end ones. You don't know who will help you or where your results will come from, so truly stay open to asking everyone and exploring every avenue – including those in, and of high places.

On July 30th, 1995, I did something that I had never done before in my entire retail sales career to that point and something that I would later learn is vital to achieving success in my faith walk – *I ask for the help that I needed to succeed!* I not only asked, I asked and I asked and I asked everyone that came my way until I had the goal of the $1,000 bonus in my hands.

As I have already mentioned, I had already taken up an aggressive position within my department where everyone who entered would have had to pass me by. In doing this, I had already insured that I would touch a greater number of people over the course of that business day.

Now this was where I made a powerful move to benefit from that positioning by ***asking everyone possible to help me*** in my quest to achieve the sales goal that would give me that extra $1,000.

On that day, no one was off limits, no one was unapproachable. It didn't matter what their career or financial status was. It didn't matter what their age or marital status was. It didn't matter what their race or gender was. It didn't matter whether they were looking for something great or something small.

It didn't matter what the scenario, if they crossed my path, I asked them to buy something from me. I tried to bring each encounter that I had to a place and point where I was helping them with something, and in so doing, they were helping me to achieve my goal of earning the $1,000 bonus.

Not only did I ask, I asked quickly. I didn't allow these encounters to drag out. I tried to bring each customer to a point of decision and to gauge their willingness to help me as fast as possible. And, I asked multiple times before giving up on a potential customer. I didn't take the easy ***"NO."***

I made a real effort to win the customer over to the side of buying something and helping me to reach my goal. I simply took my feelings and emotions out of the equation and just asked everyone to buy something from me.

This was so different from how I would have normally gone about my work on an average day. Normally, I would have never had the courage to take this kind of action. Normally I would have allowed my personal feelings and emotions to dictate my actions regarding whom to approach or whom to ask to do business with me.

Specifically, I would have let the spirit of unbelief control both the quantity and the quality of the actions that I would have taken to get to this goal. In this approach to asking I know that I am not alone.

Many times when human beings don't ask for the things that they need to confront the challenge that is before them or to achieve that goal that they have set out before themselves, it is out of that same spirit of unbelief that I usually allowed to stop me.

For those of us who struggle in this way, therein lies one of the real issues with asking for the help and support that we need to succeed. Operating from this place of unbelief, we can have the tendency to tell ourselves *"NO"* before we even open our mouths.

We don't believe in what we are doing or we think what we seek is impossible. We think we are bothering people or we worry over how we might look to others. We don't want to look like a bum or a derelict or a needy person.

Even in our professional lives we can tend to take the same view and/or believe that people will have the same kinds of views about us. We think that people won't accept our offer or buy what we are selling.

We project our views and limitations onto other people, telling ourselves that our self-imposed limitations reflect their reality. We can even believe that our request is too big to be achieved by us or the *Creator*.

While the excuses that we give for our unbelief are many, the end result of this unbelief is the same – we fail to ask for what we need or want to achieve the success that we are seeking.

No matter what excuse we put on it, our unwillingness to open our mouth and **ASK** is our unbelief displayed perfectly. Maybe you just don't believe in yourself or you don't believe in the person that you are confronted with asking or you don't believe that the *Creator* will deliver for you, or all of the above.

Yet the reality is that before you can harness the power of *FAITH (APPLIED)*, you must be able to believe in your ability to ask for and get those things that you need to achieve success in your faith project.

In fact, you can't step into faith as long as you are struggling with unbelief – no matter what the source or form of that unbelief.

That is why at the very least, you have to learn to suspend the question of what you believe; something that we will talk more about how to do in greater detail later in this work. But for now know that only then can you harness the power of this vital fifth principle of *FAITH (APPLIED)*.

Know that as long as you are dealing with unbelief, you will never undertake the process of providing the physical actions that will allow you to gain those things that you are using your faith to get.

Looking back to July 30th, 1995, the help I needed to get to my goal was people opening up their wallets and making purchases from me, and on that day, I felt an instinctive urge to open my mouth and ask for that help. In the end, I don't know what made me do it. But for some reason, I did.

Looking back on it now there is no way that I could have ever hit my target if I had taken my normal line of action. I simply would not have touched enough people to get the goal that I was seeking.

That's because normally I worked from a base of two habits that were totally destructive to my ability to achieve the goal that I had accepted the challenge of achieving on that day.

The first was the game of guessing who I should approach to offer my assistance to. The second was to try to guess who might have the willingness or the means to allow me to assist them. If I had of engaged in either of these habits, perhaps I wouldn't even have touched the right people to make my goal come true.

Because both of those realities made up my normal mode of operation, I never had the experience of helping as many people as I helped in this single day. And as you probably can imagine, as a result of these two limiting approaches to doing my job, I never had a day of results like I had on that day.

At first glance, you might think that I used these approaches out of laziness or out of some sort of indifferent attitude toward doing my job. Or, you may think that I thought that I was too good to serve the people that came into my job looking to spend their hard earned dollars. However, nothing could have been further from the truth.

While I may have given off that impression or even the appearance of a strong personality, the fact is that both of these approaches were born out of what I believe is the other major reason why most of us never ***ask for the help that we need*** to successfully use the ***God*** given tool of faith – ***FEAR***.

At that time, I had some serious hang ups when it came to working with people. I had some serious hang ups when it came to reaching out for the things that I needed to meet my needs or achieve my goals. I even had some serious hang ups when it came to believing that the ***Creator*** would involve himself in my personal and professional affairs – or the universe would respond to my needs and desires.

As I have already alluded to, *I didn't believe* that I had any right to make demands when it came to any of these areas. As a matter of fact, I believed that if I had success in any of these areas, even momentary success, it was more due to luck than any demands or efforts on my part.

So contrary to how it appeared, at its root, my not approaching people was really about the same spirit of unbelief that we talked about earlier. Out of that unbelief grew the spirit of fear that made me limit the actions that I engaged in while doing my job.

To tell it even more accurately, as a result of this spirit of unbelief, more than anything else, my not approaching people was about me trying to avoid a fear that far too many of us have. It's the fear that we won't get what we want or need – a fear we usually call by the more descriptive name:

The Fear of Rejection

As I hit the work floor on a daily basis, my only goal was to spare myself the pain of being hit with that little big word that we all have been taught to avoid like the plague, the word ***"NO!"***

As little as that word is, it is as powerful as any other when it comes to bringing up negative emotions within us, and back then, like most people my desire was to avoid the pain of having people say that word to me. The trouble is that in my effort to avoid this perceived pain, I was also robbing myself of the ability to pursue this goal, or any other goal that I could ever have, for that matter.

When you come right down to it, it is our fear of the word *"NO"*, or more specifically, our *Fear of Rejection* that is why we don't make a habit of asking for the help that we need to meet the challenges that confront us or to achieve the goals that we set out before ourselves. You could say that in this way the *Fear of Rejection* is keeping us from applying faith and activating the miracle-making power of the universe.

Struggling with a learned fear

For sure, none of us came to the planet afraid that we might get rejected by asking for help. The fact is that our *Fear of Rejection* is entirely learned. It is not something that we were born with as babies.

In fact, they say when we are born we only have two established fears; the fear of falling and the fear of loud noises. They say all other fears that you and I can suffer from are fears that we learn. I don't know how true that is, but I do know we aren't born with a fear of asking for what we want or a fear of hearing the word *"NO!"*

Whenever you watch little children you can clearly see that they have no problems asking for what they want. In fact, more often than not, they have no problem asking and asking and asking until they get their way. All the *"NO's"* in the world don't deter their little egos from asking again and again.

If anything, we adults get tired of saying *"NO"* far faster than they get tired of hearing it said. When all else fails, they will resort to crying until we give in and reward them with what they have been asking us for.

As they get bigger, our kids have no problem scheming and trying to slick their way into getting what they have a desire for. Some will even try to just outright take what they want behind our backs.

Every parent has experienced this moment a time or two. All parents have witnessed a moment where all our kids know is we have what they want, they want it, and they are to only stop asking for it when they have it.

So clearly kids don't come to the planet that way. And, you and I were no different when we first arrived on the scene. It's only as we get older that we become conditioned to fear the word, *"NO"* and to fear asking for what we want or need in general.

For most of us, it was in childhood that we begin receiving this conditioning and learned that we shouldn't be so comfortable with asking others for what we want. Perhaps we get told that it makes us or our families look bad, or we get told that it is impolite to ask people for things that they have, that we want or need. We may have even been told that it was rude to ask grandparents and other relatives for the things that we desire from them.

While some of these views may have been understandable in one context, they are far from true in the blanket way that they are often set before us as youngsters. Nevertheless, they often get internalized and take on a life of their own by the time we are all grown up.

By then, they simply become an edict that we learn to live by that says, *"Ask no one for nothing."* For the most part, most of us stick to this unwritten rule as we go through our adult lives, sadly even when it comes to our dealings with the **Creator** and applying our faith.

But the whole truth is that we know how to get beyond our fear of the word *"NO"* for those things that we have a strong desire for. Take for instance our behavior in our romantic lives. Most of us resemble the little kids that we once were in our willingness to lay it all on the line to get the object of our affection. In that arena we have no problem totally risking rejection.

As a matter of fact, we will do all of the things that children will do to get the person that we want. We will ask over and over if it takes that. Some of us will resort to whining and tears to win over the person of our choosing. While still others will plot, plan and scheme their way into the heart of the person that they are drawn to.

One way or another, we will do everything within our power to get that person. The thing that most of us won't do is let a little thing like *"NO"* get in the way of keeping us from the one we desire. And, for most of us, no amount of rejection is enough to deter us.

Proof of this can be found in the fact that many of us are with a mate today that rejected us when we first asked them to be with us – me included. And, yet we asked again, and again if necessary until we got the *"Yes"* that we were hoping for.

So the ability to overcome the internal *Fear of Rejection* and ask for what we want is in us. The real question is whether or not we are focusing on our deeply held desires or the possibility of being hit by the word *"NO"* and the rejection that we fear.

Whichever one we focus on tends to be the one that wins out. We would be wise to remember this fact when we need to move past our *Fear of Rejection* and ask for what we want or need to meet a challenge or achieve a goal.

Understanding the 10 Truths of Asking brings success

Like all other fears, our *Fear of Rejection* is often born out of ignorance. As in, if only we could put this subject of asking in its proper context or if only we could set some ground rules to govern the process of us asking for what we need to bring about success in our faith projects, we wouldn't have the problem of this *Fear of Rejection* dooming us to failure.

In fact, I believe that part of why we fear asking and being rejected so much is because we don't truly understand all of the dynamics that are involved with successfully asking for and receiving what we seek in pursuit of our goals.

By the time we reach adulthood, we all realize that getting what we want from other human beings is not as simple of a proposition as it might seem. By adulthood, most of us have experienced this truth many times over. But most often we think of it as being a random reality. We may never realize that there are some *Truths of Asking* that apply to the process that we are engaged in.

In fact, I know of 10 specific **Truths of Asking** that your awareness of could mean the difference between success and failure in getting the help and support that you need to achieve your goals. I believe that you knowing and understanding these truths for yourself will help you to put asking in its proper light and perspective. Plus it will help you to not take it personal when you ask someone for their help or support and receive the dreaded *"NO."*

The first of those **Truths of Asking** that we would be wise to learn is this, when it comes to asking for what you need to achieve success through the power of **FAITH (APPLIED)**, you must know that:

Truth #1 – *Success is always in the numbers!*

For starters, the simple truth is that for you or I to achieve success in a faith project and meet the challenge or goal confronting us, we will usually have to gain the help and support of other human beings. If you haven't accepted that fact yet and you are serious about learning how to use the power of **FAITH (APPLIED)**, now is the time to do so.

Now, as scary as that truth is, the full truth is even scarier – that truth is that often we will have to go through SEVERAL people to find the **FEW** that will help and support us. This is one of the hard lessons that I have had to learn in my professional life. I would even say it this way,

> *"When it comes to dealing with people,*
> *success is always in the numbers."*

Simply put, you get what you want by getting to more people, by putting out more effort. There are many areas of life that don't necessarily involve people where this is also true. We could even debate whether or not it is true in all areas of life. I know for certain that the *Creator* has shown me that it is true when it comes to **FAITH (APPLIED)**.

Many times to get what you want, to even get that prayer answered, you must be willing to go through the numbers. You must be willing to knock and knock and knock. You must be willing to seek and seek and seek. It is not a matter of praying harder or believing harder. It is often a matter of going from door to door to door, or from person to person to person until you have your goal in hand.

That is one of **the Truths of Asking** that the **Creator** revealed to me on July 30th, 1995. I have literally witnessed this truth many times over since that day. That is how I know that to find the success that we seek we must be willing to ask everyone that we can ask to help us. To me this act represents the highest level of **FAITH (APPLIED)** and demonstrates a **Leaving No Stones Unturned** mentality that is vital to our success.

Like so many of the other principles that we are talking about here, I first became aware of this truth in my professional life, and not because I had a good working relationship with this truth. For years I thought that if I needed a person to help me, all I had to do was ask a person to help me. If I needed a new client, all I had to do was approach a prospective client and I would get what I asked for.

Operating from this false belief made me an utter failure for a long time and in nearly every business and professional endeavor that I ever undertook.

It wasn't that I didn't have small successes. Of course, I got a few **"Yes's"** here and there. However those **"Yes's"** were fleeting and they never were enough to bring me the larger sustained success that I needed.

Even worse during those years, emotionally, I would go soaring in the clouds with each one of those seemingly small *"Yes's"* and fall down in the dumps with every one of those seemingly big **"NO's."**

As a result, the time came when I thought that there was something wrong with the people that I was approaching. The time came when I thought that there was something wrong with the town that I was endeavoring to build my business or career in.

The time came when I thought that there was something wrong with the business or profession that I was in. And, eventually the time came when I thought that there was something wrong with me and my approach.

I could not figure out for the life of me how I could approach a person for help and not receive what I had asked for. I could not figure out how I could ask a person to become a client or customer and not get the client or customer that I had sought.

The feelings of discouragement that grew out of this reality was usually enough to cause me to become totally reluctant to ask others for help and support or to become a client. After all, it didn't appear that asking would bring me the success that I sought, even when I got *"Yes's"*. It appeared as though I never got the right ones or enough of them to meet my challenge or goal.

It never occurred to me that I didn't get enough of them because I didn't do the numbers or ask enough people. Without this awareness, I would go back to the drawing board time and again to devise new plans of attack, thinking this might be the issue.

Ultimately, I questioned if things would be different in a new place, or a new business, or with different people. Eventually, I questioned if things would be different for someone other than me. All the while, I never suspected that something else could be the real problem. Neither did I suspect that the solution to the real problem that I was having was so simple that it was almost mind blowing.

The Math of Asking

Unfortunately for me and my family, it would take several years and a career change before I found out the truth about what had caused me to fail in those early business and career endeavors. The lesson itself was one of the little gifts or perks that I had received when I joined *Minolta Business Systems*.

One of the things that that company was definitely great for was the degree to which they went to train their staff. They spared no expense in their efforts to bring in the best trainers available to insure that we possessed the best knowledge and information available to help us become effective sales people. They also had many great in-house trainers and leaders.

In *Mr. Randy Peck*, I had the good fortune of working for such a man. From the very first in-house sales training that I had the privilege of sitting in on, I could see clearly why I had failed so miserably in the past. In fact, by the time this training session was over, I literally realized for the first time that,

> *"I couldn't get my businesses off the ground because I simply never did the numbers!!!"*

In this training seminar, I learned what I have come to call the **Math of Asking**, and while the ratios that were expressed in the course related to the business of selling the copier machines that we offered, the greater truth was not lost on me as I have ventured into other fields of business.

What Mr. Peck taught us that day was that to achieve our sales goal and quota of selling **5** new clients in a month, it was necessary for us to talk to **1,200** prospective clients, to find **40** who would agree to sit down with us to have a serious discussion about becoming a buyer, to get **5** to actually go forward and buy.

For sure it would take a ton of **FAITH (APPLIED)** to knock on **1,200** doors and receive that many **"NO's"** and stay the course to get the **5 "Yes's"** that we needed to hit our goals. As Mr. Peck taught us, for a variety of reasons, it took a lot more in terms of effort and in terms of people approached to get a few people to do what you were asking them to do – in this case, buy a new copying system from our firm.

Of course he backed up this success formula with a ton of facts and personal experience; not only his own experience, but the experience of all of the other successful people that he had managed and trained over the years.

As I sit here now, I have seen the truth of these ratios time and time again, making this one of the most vital **Truths of Asking** that I have ever learned in my business walk.

In fact, I now realize that when it comes to dealing with people and seeking people that will support whatever proposition you or I could set out before them, **1 plus 1 doesn't equal 2!** Did you hear that? **1 + 1 = (not) 2!!!**

What that means to you is that you can't ask one person to help you or support you and expect to automatically get what you asked for. You might get what you are seeking! But you also might not!

In fact, the betting odds are that you would not get what you are seeking most of the time. Who knows what equals 2? Perhaps it is not a case of addition as much as it is a case of multiplication and even those numbers don't look appetizing.

For instance, when I sold copiers, I eventually learned that **20 times 1 equaled 2 and 2 equaled 1! (20 x 1 = 2 leads = 1 sale!)** As in, if I made **20 cold phone calls to prospective clients, I'd get 2 new solid leads. Out of that I usually got 1 new sale.**

Man if only I had known this truth in some of my early business endeavors. I am certain that I would have created a lot more success. Without it, I failed miserably for years because I thought something was wrong with me, or my products, or the people that I was working with.

Ultimately, to find success in business and selling I had to just learn to live with the truth of these ratios. In fact, the other part of *Mr. Peck's* message from that day helped me to just accept these ratios and be thankful for them forever.

What he told us was this, if we would just trust him and do the **1,200** to get the **40** and we got the **5**, we would make so much money working with the **5** that we wouldn't care about the **1,195** that said, *"NO."* Guess what? It is true!

If you get the goal, you don't care about what it took to get it. I have done it many times to know it. It is only out of ignorance that we will pay more attention to the effort that we put out to get what we want or need above whether or not that effort is getting us to where we want to go.

As the *Creator* showed me on July 30th, 1995, these same things hold true for successfully using the 8 principles of *FAITH (APPLIED)*. We must learn how to put the numbers on our side by applying the *Math of Asking* to all of our faith projects. We can't concern ourselves with the amount of effort that it takes to achieve our goal.

Simply put, we must care about the end result and not what we went through in terms of action steps or people to get it. When we get this, we have no problem with putting out the effort, doing the numbers or with asking everyone we encounter to help us.

In this same way, when it comes to the *Math of Faith*, success is also in the numbers. In the spirit of this truth, we must learn to do way more in the way of effort to insure that we arouse the miracle-making power of the universe to aid us in our faith endeavors.

What's going through your mind as you contemplate the **Math of Asking?** Are you still interested in learning and mastering the principles of **FAITH (APPLIED)?** Are you discouraged? Or, do you now feel like you have some assurance that **FAITH (APPLIED)** can work to meet your needs or make your goals come true? I hope so.

If you are already engaged in some faith project or pursuing some coveted goal, it might help if you would figure out what your ratios are. How many people do you get out of every **(X)** amount of people that you approach?

Like it did for me in my professional endeavors, just knowing this information will embolden you and give you a sense of certainty that your efforts in asking for help and support will be worthwhile. Buried within this truth is another of the **Truths of Asking** that we would be wise to learn, namely:

Truth #2 – *You won't get everybody!*

This could have nearly been covered in the last point that we dealt with and you can almost think of it as a side "B" to what we just talked about. As the title of this point suggest, for a variety of reasons, *you and I will never get everybody that we approach*.

This is the truth no matter what the challenge that we are confronted with trying to get help with or what the goal is that we are trying to accomplish. And, the truth is that this will play out in many different ways.

In both the personal and the professional arenas, this could range from the people who come right out and tell you *"NO"* from the jump, to people who will give you a *"Yes"* and renege later on; or from the people who don't have the means, to those who sincerely don't have the need.

As a matter of fact, to be real about it, you can experience this at the hands of those who won't help you because they can't, or it can come from those who won't help you because they just don't want to see you succeed.

At the end of the day it doesn't really matter where their motivation to not help and support you is coming from. The fact is that some of the people that you and I approach are never going to be a part of the success of our faith project.

Again, that is why knowing the numbers and doing the numbers is so critical to achieving the success that we seek. It is the only remedy to the truth that *we never get everybody*.

Sometimes it is timing and sometimes it just takes time!

As true as it is that *we never get everybody*, it really could have been said that there are times when, we can get everybody, over time. Sometimes with people it really is a matter of timing. And, still other times, it can just be a matter of time, as in over time, a person that has previously told you *"NO"* might warm up to your request for help.

For instance, in the business arena, a prospective client may have reasons why they cannot or will not buy from you today. But that same prospective client may eventually become your client after multiple attempts at selling them, over time.

I have seen this done several times over the course of my sales and business career. So there is something that can be said for not taking the easy *"NO"* when you are asking people to get involved in helping you or becoming your client.

Perhaps it is one of those cases where you will have to put the time into trying to bring this person on board. We will talk later about knowing when that time is as it relates to using *FAITH (APPLIED)*. But for now just know that sometimes it just may be a timing thing or a case where you need to give your efforts in asking time to pan out.

But the main point to get here is that no matter what the reason, there are some people that you are just not going to get; some not at all and some not in the moment when you need them. So if we are really serious about meeting our challenge or achieving our goal with the aid of the people around us, we must be willing to approach many more people than we are looking to get.

We have to do this because we are not going to get everyone that we approach. No matter what the challenge is or how great our approach and offer, some will say *"NO."* That is a fact that we simply must face before we can even think about reaching success.

Not knowing this can set you up for a mountain of discouragement as you conduct your affairs. While knowing this can give you the peace of mind that comes from knowing that the *"NO's"* that you get most often have nothing to do with you, nor do they have the power to keep you from getting what you seek.

You should also know that it is not uncommon for people to try to make you think that their denial is your fault, something that you have done wrong or a problem with your request or offering. It has been my experience that people never say it is them with the issue.

Let many people tell it, it is always an issue with you or your offering. If you or I don't know better, we can easily be led to believe these lies and give up on our faith projects. This is especially true when we have great respect for the person that is telling us *"NO."*

But by just remembering the truth that *we never get everybody*, you can move on past this debate of why you didn't get someone and continue your search for the people who you can get to help you in your faith project. And, remembering this truth also helps you to not take it personal when someone doesn't want to support you, even if their refusal was personal.

In the end it doesn't matter so long as you keep moving and you find the support that you do need to give you what you are looking for. This leads us to another of the *Truths of Asking* that is vital to our success. That truth is:

Truth #3 – Those who you think will help you won't, those who you think won't help you will!

Call this another one of those side "B" *truths of asking* because it is a point that lines right up to the last one that we discussed. As in, not only do we never get everybody, but *those who we think will help won't and those who we think won't help will!*

Just looking at those two truths side by side, you can see how our ignorance often leads to frustration and frustration leads to giving up and quitting. You can also see why the two habits that I talked about earlier, not approaching everyone and trying to guess who to approach are so deadly to our success.

If you don't get everybody and *the ones who you think will help you won't and the ones who you think won't help will*, trying to base your efforts on guesswork would be a total crapshoot, right? Yet that is exactly what you and I are doing often times when it comes to asking for the support that we need to succeed.

It seems like by design, we are totally blind when it comes to knowing who will respond favorably to our request for help. Many of us may have never even noticed that things seem to work this way.

I first noticed this truth as a kid. But even then I didn't get the fullness of its meaning. I just noticed back then that in my family and social circles, it appeared that when someone was in need, the people who would help, couldn't and those who could, wouldn't. I would later learn that my childhood observation was a greater truth that many grown-ups battled with in their everyday lives.

It goes without saying that I have seen this truth play out time and again in the business arena as well. As you should see from almost every story that I am sharing about my endeavors in my sales career, it seemed that the person that was thought to be the ideal prospect seldom turned out to be the person that did the deal.

As a matter of fact, the truth is that in almost every instance, the person that bought was the person that I, and everyone else thought would never buy. Thankfully I had the habit of keeping my mind open in my dealings with people.

I can't say that I was always this way. As a matter of fact, I can remember an incident early in my retail career when I operated from the exact opposite point of view and it cost me dearly.

Grown ups don't buy $2,000 stereos, kids with loving grandfathers do!

As the story goes, one day I was working in my department and doing those things that I did in not approaching everyone that I could help and trying to guess who I should approach and offer my assistance.

In between guesses, I was watching TV and counting down the minutes until my shift ended when a young teenage boy entered my department and started looking at all of the high-end stereo systems. Before long he began turning them up and messing with the various features of each.

After several minutes of me ignoring him and giving him the evil eye, he approached me and asked if I would help him and show him our top of the line system. I promptly told him that I was busy and went back to watching my TV program and counting down to the end of my shift.

As I saw it, this kid was simply playing with the merchandise and there was obviously no way that he could buy the items that he was playing with. With this attitude, I eventually requested that he stop touching the equipment and leave my department. After all, it wasn't for children and he was clearly a child to me.

Meanwhile, in the time that he was in the department, I approached several adults that I felt had what it took to become a buying customer. As you might guess, in spite of my best efforts, these adults didn't buy a single thing.

Eventually I managed to get the young man to leave my area and I went off to lunch to take a break from what I considered to be a slow selling day. An hour later I returned from lunch to find out just how wrong I was in this choice of actions.

Upon my return I found that the young man had returned and he was being assisted by another one of the sales people in my department that had just came on duty. Only now I could clearly see he wasn't the kid by himself playing with the expensive equipment that no kid his age could buy.

Instead, he was the birthday boy who came into the store with a Grandpa who loved him to bits and was willing to buy him a $2,000 stereo as a gift – a purchase that Grandpa happily put on his Gold American Express card.

It goes without saying that as I watched all of this play out I felt about as dumb as I could have ever felt. I had totally misread the situation. I put my own limiting thoughts into the situation and saw them as the young man's reality. And, as it turned out, I was dead wrong about all of this and dead wrong about what was going on overall.

I guessed that this kid wouldn't, in fact, couldn't become my customer and I guessed wrong. Because of it, I lost out on a great sale and an even greater commission. And, to think that I had this kid all to myself with no one else to help him out but me and I blew it.

The other sales person had just clocked in for the day and made one sale that was big enough to cover his whole day. Contrast that with the fact that I did an 8 hour shift and barely made enough to buy the poor man's lunch that I was so itching to get to.

If that is not prime proof that we must ask everyone for help, nothing can ever be. Also, if that is not a powerful example of the truth that *the ones who we think will do it, won't and the ones who we think won't do it, will,* I don't know what is.

Needless to say I only had to make that mistake once in my career. From that point on I really have made it a habit to give every person whose path I cross the attention that they deserve. Above all, I never try to guess who I should help. Instead I practice the habit of giving each person the best quality of care that I can give and then I let the chips fall where they may.

Now that leads us to the fourth *Truth of Asking.* Understanding this truth will help us distinguish between times when we should fight to get the support that we need and those when we shouldn't waste even a minute of our time. That truth is:

Truth #4 – There is a difference between a Condition and an Objection (Rejection)!

If you are going to ask everyone that you possibly can to help you and run the risk of being hit with the dreaded *"NO"*, it might help you to realize that it is not always that people don't want to help you. Sometimes they may want to help you, but it is that they just cannot.

I feel the need to explain this point as if I am talking to people who don't work in sales and never have. As such, let me start by saying that in sales there are times when a prospective client can say **"Yes"** to your proposal and for some reason, usually unknown to the salesperson they are still saying **"NO."** In those instances, the excuse that they give you is called an **Objection**. I submit to you that the same thing holds true in regular everyday life.

In the professional sense, you are taught that to be considered a good salesperson, you need to learn to overcome objections or the reluctance that people present to going forward with your business propositions. And we could say that the same holds true in regular everyday life.

In fact, didn't we do this growing up? How many times have we asked our parents for the car for the night and they gave us an objection as to why they'd rather not, only to have us work our butts off to overcome their **Objection**? We have all done it. So whether we realize it or not, we have seen the concept even if we have not applied it on a conscious level or knew it by name as we have done it.

There also have been times when we weren't able to overcome the objection before us. No matter how hard we tried, no matter how hard we pleaded, we just couldn't seem to get our way. Or, maybe we got told that the person that we were approaching couldn't give us what we were asking for if they wanted to.

My friend, at that moment what that person may not have had the words to tell you is that the reason why they couldn't give you what you sought is because you weren't being confronted with an **Objection**, you were staring right in the face of a **Condition.**

The difference between an **Objection** and a **Condition** is as broad as the difference between day and night. One is something that is usually smoke and mirrors, while the other is as real as brick and mortar. Once you know how to do it, one is something that you can talk by with relative ease. The other is something that no amount of skill or talking could ever get you around.

In my professional career and my everyday life, I see too many instances where people are trying to treat a *Condition* as if it were a mere *Objection*. I have watched these people drive themselves to the point of sheer frustration because they didn't know that they should just walk away from this unwinnable situation, no matter what the cost.

Can you imagine the challenge that would result from you spending your time asking for help from someone who doesn't have the ability to give you the help that you are seeking? No matter how eloquent you ask, no matter what you promise to give in return, no matter how vital the need or goal is to you, there is no way for you to succeed in this situation. What you seek is simply not on the table or there to be given to you.

Can you see why this is such a critical *Truth of Asking?* Can you see how making this mistake will get in the way of you successfully completing a faith project?

To be sure there are as many *Conditions* as there are *Objections*. And, it would be helpful if you and I learn how to spot them and distinguish them from the plain old rejection that we can encounter when we ask someone to help us on the path to handling our challenges or achieving our goals.

This one skill will save us a ton of time and frustration by insuring that we always ask people who can actually give us what we are seeking.

Next we come to the fifth *Truth of Asking.* Like a couple of the truths before, this point really could almost be considered a side "B" to the last point that we talked about. But it is so vital that you get this truth that it demanded to be dealt with by itself, to insure that its value and importance didn't get lost. The truth that I am talking about is:

Truth #5 – You must ask those who are empowered to help!

I don't know whether or not you realize it, but there are some people on this planet that don't have the power to help you. It is true. There are some people that just cannot give you what you are asking for. They won't tell you that. They may present themselves like they are in charge. However, the truth is far from the image that these people project.

I first became super aware of this in my professional pursuits. But this is a truth that exists in both the professional and personal arenas.

In a professional setting, the implications are obvious. As in, in all professional settings there is a boss and the boss is the only one that is empowered to make decisions about granting the request that people may have for the company.

You come in asking for something and only that boss has the right and power to give you what you are asking for. He or she may deputize others and give them the power to grant request. But the bottom line is that there is a boss that has the final say.

In a personal setting, a home life or family setting, many of us fail to realize that there are bosses as well. Seldom do you have a situation where each person in the family is equally empowered with decision making authority.

In either setting, these key people are called *Decision Makers* and learning how to determine who they are and get to them is a vital key to learning how to get what you want. In fact, a challenge arises in either of these settings when you are asking for support from any person that doesn't have the authority to give you what you are asking for.

Some people can only say "NO"

Talk about the easy way to get a *"NO."* There are none easier than you approaching a person that only has the power to say *"NO"* and asking them to support you. Rather than reveal that they are nobody in the scheme of things, it is often easier for this person to just tell you *"NO"* and save face; at least it is in their minds.

Make no bones about it, there is a real danger in dealing with one of these people. I used to see this all the time in my sales career. I have also seen this play out in many ways in my personal life. Perhaps you want to ask your brother to help you meet a challenging situation that is confronting you; however his wife holds the purse strings and he has zero say in how the finances are handled in his household. Rather than even coming close to admitting that, he just tells you he can't help you. In this case, the only answer that he could have given you was a *"NO."* He doesn't have the authority to say *"YES."*

There are many times in both the professional and personal setting where things work the same way. I have even seen this truth play out when conducting my personal household business.

In fact, it could happen in just about any setting. As an example, I have had customer service issues with companies where I encountered a low level employee who couldn't resolve the matter to my satisfaction.

Usually these employees tried to pass their decisions off as final and binding. Have you ever been in this situation and had the person try to tell you that the higher ups were going to make the same decision? That is what these people would try to make me accept.

The truth is that this person didn't have the power to give me what I wanted and they simply wouldn't admit it. Usually a simple call to the real boss would yield the outcome that I was seeking.

Think about how something like that would impact your ability to succeed in a faith project. If you don't watch out for this, this kind of person can singlehandedly derail your efforts towards gaining the help and support that you need to succeed.

Beware of the Gatekeeper

As deadly as the non-decision maker is to the task of you asking for and getting what you need, there is another person that is even more deadly, the *Gatekeeper*. This is the person whose job it is to keep you from getting to the person that can tell you *"Yes"* to what you are seeking.

In a professional setting, this is usually a secretary or some other low-level worker that has been designated to keep people like you away. It may even be an ambitious or nosey worker who has designated themselves as this person.

In a personal setting, it could be a mate or some other relative who makes it their business to block the path to the people that you need to ask for the support that you need to get to your goal.

Sometimes it could even just be people who are trying to block you from finding the help you seek from any source. No matter what their origins, you must avoid being blocked by the gatekeepers who are trying to prevent your success.

I can remember an instance when I was selling copiers that kind of summed up this whole point of learning to ask people who are empowered to help. The incident had elements of each of the sub points that make up this larger point.

To cut right to the heart of the story, I had been talking to a gentleman for some months about buying a copier from me. The gentleman had held himself out as the key decision maker and he treated me well the whole time that we talked. However, while he never told me *"NO"*, he never made the final buying decision and told me *"Yes."*

Instead he would just put me off and butter me up, as in, he would tell me that I was *"The Man"* or as soon as the company approves the budget, I was the one that they were going to buy from. I heard these put offs for months and I bought them because he made me feel so good as he put me off.

Eventually he went on vacation and the truth finally came to light. As life would have it, I called looking for him and was told that he was on vacation. The person to whom I was speaking then told me that the CFO of the company was handling the pending equipment acquisition and promptly directed me to him.

With a head filled with all of the flattery that this other guy had bestowed on me, my opening line was,

"Hello Mr. So and So, this is Brent! Your guy!!!"

After a long awkward silence, the gentleman said,

"Who is this?"

To which I said, still not getting what was happening in this moment,

> *"This is Brent, your guy – the one that*
> *you are buying the copier from!!!"*

To which he replied,

> *"No we are not."*

He went on to tell me who he was set to buy from and it was nowhere near me. In utter shock, I told him the whole story about my communications with the other guy and found out that I had been talking to a person that never had the power to make a decision to buy from me.

Fortunately for me, after a bit of quick thinking and some even quicker talking I was able to get this gentleman to hold off on completing his purchase with the real guy and submit a bid that ended up winning. In the end, I got the sale because a vacation had got me by my friendly *Gatekeeper* and got me to the real person who was empowered to work with me.

As you go about the process of asking for the help and support that you need to handle that challenge or conquer that goal, be sure that you are dealing with someone who is truly empowered to help you.

Learn to do this whether you are in a professional or a personal setting. Like so many of these points, this one act could mean the difference between success and failure in your faith project.

Now we come to a *Truth of Asking* that is vital to the success of the *FAITH (APPLIED)* system. As a matter of fact, getting this one point improves your chances of success by 1000%! That truth is:

Truth #6 – You have to ask until you have what you seek in hand!

Often times to succeed in a faith project there is a need to fight on, to never give up – to keep pushing until you get what you want or need to succeed.

That means to have success in asking for what you need to confront that challenge or achieve that goal, *you have to keep asking and asking and asking until you have what you seek*

in hand. That is the essence of what this point is all about.

Now to be clear right up front, I am not necessarily talking about asking the same person over and over and over again. Although there can be an element of that at times.

What I am really talking about here is you having an attitude that says that the game is not over until you have what you need in your hands. I am talking about you taking a *"No Quit"* stance that sees you through to the successful completion of your task.

When you are walking by **FAITH (APPLIED)** this is absolutely vital to success. I don't know how many times this one principle has brought me success. I have had a ton of instances where my victory came to me in the 11th or 12th hour of my faith project.

I don't know how many clients were closed at the last possible moment in my faith selling cycle. Neither could I tell you how many challenges were resolved just on the brink of ultimate calamity by way of this one principle.

To me, it seems that success is buried on the other side of this kind of frustration. As in each of the instances would see the clock run late into a project and me get totally frustrated before what I sought came through. I have also seen this many times in working faith projects.

Sometimes it appears that the **Creator** test us or our patience by making us wait for the answer to our prayers until a time that is long past the point where our emotions have been drained. I don't know why that is. But I do know that if we cannot patiently keep pushing beyond this point we often don't see our prayers get answered.

In the same way, if we can't patiently push beyond this frustration we don't often see our faith project succeed. And, as much as it might feel like we are going down to defeat at this moment, when we can pass the **Creator's** test and keep pushing until we have what we seek in our hands, we often get to feel what it feels like to pull victory from the jaws of defeat.

It is those moments that we often regard as miracles. To be sure, they are the result of what happens when you work from an attitude that says,

*"I will continue to ask for what I need
until I have what I seek in hand."*

Learning to keep it moving is the key to asking until you have what you seek in hand

As I mentioned at the start of this point, to be successful in asking for what you need, you have to learn how to keep it moving. To be effective you have to keep asking and asking and asking until you have what you seek in hand.

But this is not about asking the same people for what you need until you wear them down and get them to give in. I have only ever known one person who was good at that, my brother *Todd*.

In our family, we used to say that when it came to asking for and getting whatever he wanted, *Todd* would, *"Beg you down."* When it came to asking for what he wanted, *Todd* had no shame. He wasn't worried about how he looked. And, he wasn't the least bit worried about hearing the word *"NO."*

All he knew was that if you had something that he wanted, he was going to beg you down until you gave in and gave it to him. As comical as that was to watch sometimes, especially if you weren't the one that he was hard begging, that is not what I am talking about here.

In my career, I have been in an environment where that was the philosophy, where you were constantly admonished about the need for you to go back to the same people that had rejected you in the past – waiting for the day when they would come around to your cause.

Many of the people in this environment believe so heavily in this philosophy that they don't move beyond their circle of comfort. They don't go beyond their social sphere to find the support that they need to succeed, and ultimately, many of them simply don't do enough to earn the results that they desire.

These people are good at masking their fears of rejection at the hands of people beyond their comfort zone as strength. They will try to point out notable cases where someone did ultimately come around and victory followed for the asker.

As real as those moments are, the truth is that for the most part this philosophy yields far less fruit than just keeping it moving on to the people beyond their comfort zone.

In too many instances the asker would go through complete hell while they literally sat around waiting for a particular person or group of people to come around to their side.

I have always thought that a better approach was the one espoused by my old boss *Randy Peck*. He taught me while there are times when you double back to the people who previously rejected you, you should also expect to keep it moving and explore other avenues for getting to your goal.

You may even build a strategy for returning to people who previously rejected you into your overall approach to asking for the help and support that you need. But to see the true power of **FAITH (APPLIED)**, you must make it your habit to keep it moving and to ask new people for help and support until you have what you seek in hand. That is what I am really talking about doing here.

At the heart of the matter, I am talking about learning not to give up on yourself or your faith project because a few people or even several people tell you *"NO."* I'm talking about you having a personal policy that says that when confronted with this issue you will ask and ask and ask others until you succeed at getting what you want or need to win. That is what it means to, *"Ask until you have what you seek in hand."*

By following this philosophy, you will insure that your faith is bigger than any person or persons that don't quite see it as you do. And, from my personal experience, this trait is absolutely vital to your ability to get the power of **FAITH (APPLIED)** working in your life.

Remember, when the rubber meets the road the people nearest to you, the ones who you think will help and support you may not see things like you do. Having the courage to move beyond this group could mean the difference between finding all of the help and support that you need to win and watching your faith project die at the hands of people who won't help. Again, that is why learning this point is so important.

Here again, this next **Truth of Asking** is one of those that could have been a side "B" to the one that we just finished. As in, it will be a whole lot easier for you to keep it moving and **ask until you have what you seek in your hand** if like this next truth says, you knew that:

Truth #7 – *You don't have to know where you will get the results that you seek!*

One of the biggest needs that we all can have as human beings is the need to feel a sense of certainty and security in our lives. It is because of this need that I believe most people have a hard time living by the power of faith. They can't deal with feeling insecure – like they are just hanging out there.

I also believe that that is the big challenge with asking for what we need to meet the challenge that is confronting us or in going after the goal that we have set for ourselves. We want to feel like we know where the answers to the concerns that we have are going to come from. We need to know where the things that we are seeking will come from, and yet we all know that it just doesn't work that way. And, thankfully it doesn't.

I have learned that that place of insecurity is one of the greatest blessings that the *Creator* could have ever given us. I believe that he has so made our world that when it comes to applying our faith to confront the challenges or goals that are before us, **we don't have to know where the results that we need will come from.**

If we could just learn how to except this truth and put it to use for the good of all of our wants and needs there is a power and even a freedom that can come from leaving the *"where it will come from"* to the *Creator*.

The fact is that often times we are looking at this blessing in the wrong way. I came to the realization a long time ago that when it comes to asking for what I need to succeed, what we see as certainty and security is really a burden on one hand and a limiting force on the other. This is true both in terms of the people component of asking and the resource being asked for.

Have you ever contemplated the amount of pressure that you take upon yourself by trying to always know who will help you or where the physical things that you need will come from as you work through your faith projects?

And, of equal weight, have you ever considered the limits that you place upon yourself in terms of the people and resources that you can access by having to know where these things will come from based upon your limited resources?

Speaking of the pressure of certainty and security, I used to rack my brain to the point of exhaustion when I still lived by the notion that I had to know where the results would come from to succeed in a faith project. And, still nothing was accomplished.

Often times this pressure had the effect of immobilizing me when I couldn't come up with the answers that I sought. Remember, we already said that *the ones who we think will do it won't and the ones who we think won't will*.

There were also times when this kind of pressure and stress made me ill. The fact that stress and pressure can make us ill is perhaps the greatest proof that the *Creator* never intended for you and I to carry this weight in our minds and bodies.

Eventually I realized that the burden was just too high for me and my limited resources. That fact became real evident in my lean, struggling years. Realizing this fact allowed me to find my way to the greater truth that,

> *"We don't have to know where the results that we seek will come from!"*

It happened as a result of coming up against times and circumstances when failing simply wasn't an option. These were those times when the challenges before me were simply too big, too vital for me to just shrug off and walk away from.

In those moments, the fact that I couldn't see where the people and/or resources needed to meet my needs would come from wasn't a good enough excuse for me to just let these needs go unmet.

These were the times when even the thought of failure was unfathomable, the times when the stakes were so high that I had to push on in the face of that uncertainty that most of us hate to deal with.

In these situations I had to learn how to quiet my mind and not let it run away with the question of where my answers would come from – a question that would ultimately lead to my undoing.

In these moments it just made sense to me to give up the responsibility for finding the people and resources that were needed to a power that was bigger than me. In taking that action I found that this power always delivered the results that I needed, even though I personally could not see any path to those results.

Usually, this power came through in ways that I would have never considered and provided far better than I ever could have. People and resources were led to me that I could have never gotten to on my own.

Doors were open to places and people that would have normally been beyond inaccessible. And, these were not matters of coincidence. They were the result of what happens when the *"where it will come from"* is left to the **Creator**. In fact I feel safe in saying that one of the benefits of leaving the *"where it will come from"* to the **Creator** is,

> *"Things always work out way better than you or I could have ever handled it!"*

The small price that we pay to use this great power is being willing to accept that **we don't have to know where the results that we seek will come from** and step into that place of uncertainty and insecurity while the **Creator** moves on our behalf.

In so doing, we relieve ourselves of the pressure of trying to have answers that we just may not have. We also remove the limits of our small existence and open ourselves up to options that are beyond our normal realm of possibility – options that are as broad as the universe that we are a small part of.

That's why I am so grateful that I came to the realization that I didn't have to know where the things that I needed to succeed in a faith project would come from.

As a matter of fact, as I have seen time and again, the process works best if I never even think about it. Especially since as we have already discussed, the people and resources that we think will come through for us, often don't and the ones that we think won't, do.

Given that we don't know where things will come from, it makes sense that we shouldn't be required to concern ourselves with that question. Does that make sense to you?

For years I had read about similar principles in books and I just couldn't grasp it. It might have been called by different names, but the message was still the same. Yet for some reason it didn't sink in with me until I learned it for myself as a result of my faith walk.

You don't have to know where your results will come from – you just have to be in motion!

Eventually I coined a phrase that helped to keep me perfectly focused on this truth and my real role in this process,

> *"I don't have to know where my results will come from; I just have to be in motion!"*

I don't know if I came up with that myself or if it was something that the *Creator* placed in my heart and mind. But it wasn't long before I saw the power in living by this little phrase. As I would work through my projects, I would repeatedly chant it to myself. Whenever my mind would try to get bogged down with the question of where something would come from, I would chant this phrase to myself instead.

I realize now that the power of this chant is that it moved me to action. I learned a long time ago that it is human nature to become immobilized in times of confusion. I believe that there is no greater path to confusion than a mind trying to figure out where something will come from when you should leave it to the *Creator* through faith.

When confronted by this dilemma, most of us won't be strong enough to march ahead anyway. When confronted by this dilemma, most of us will resort to guesswork. Seldom will we keep an open ear toward the *Creator* or seek his guidance. The net result of this path will always be us getting confused, frustrated, burned out and finally giving up.

By contrast, it is only by knowing that *"you don't have to know where your results will come from"* that you can remain clear minded and in motion towards success. Only this keeps your ears and eyes focused on the guidance from the *Creator*. As it relates to *FAITH (APPLIED)*, it keeps you open to the assistance of the miracle-making power of the universe.

Remember I have said that this system brings to your aid the assistance of another power. Remember I have told you that this system unleashes the miracle-making power of the universe. It's when we use this point properly that our victories are seen as *"miracles."* And, it is when we stop worrying about the *"where your results will come from"* and just stay in motion that the *Creator* can produce the *"miracles"* that are there for each one of us. That is why it is imperative that you adopt this *truth of asking* and make it a part of your own working philosophy.

That leads us to our next *Truth of Asking.* It is another one of those that is critical to our success in asking for the things that we need or want to confront the challenges or achieve the goals that are before us.

As a matter of fact, we would never have a problem asking people for what we need or want if we could get this truth deep inside our heart. That next truth is:

Truth #8 – Asking is never personal, it's just Asking!

There is plenty that I could say about this key *truth of asking.* But simply put, as you go about asking for the things that you want and need to succeed in your faith project you must stay mindful of the truth that *asking for what you want or need to win in your faith project is never personal, it's just asking!*

It is a simple truth to get but most of us have a hard time accepting it. And, it is our failure to get this truth that often leads to us losing all faith that we can find the help and support that we need to meet the challenges that life throws our way or to achieve the goals that we have set out before ourselves.

On the personal side of this point we have to get that we need to leave our emotions out of the process of asking for what we want and need. There are many ways in which we would be wise to consider this vital point.

For example, as much as our natural inclination tells us to, we can't pick and choose who to ask based upon who we like or who we are uncomfortable with. In that moment we are making it personal and trying to tailor the process in a way that we think will preserve our feelings. Yet, the simple fact is, *it's not personal* and our efforts to preserve our feelings can very easily doom our entire project to failure.

Perhaps the person that we are most comfortable with just isn't the one that will give us what we are seeking and the person that we are the least comfortable with is that person. If we have made the process of asking personal, chances are we won't be willing to ask the person that we really need to ask. However we will if we remember that *it's not personal.*

As another example, even though the process of asking might be filled with emotion – either the anticipation of *"Yes"* or the dread of *"NO,"* we have got to stay away from the habit of taking it personal when we don't get the answer that we are looking for.

In too many instances we make the mistake of living and dying with every response that we get throughout our faith project. We are either riding high with each *"Yes"* or sinking into the dumps with every *"NO."* Having made this error early on in my professional career, I can say first hand that there is no greater demoralizer and no quicker path to you giving up on asking for the help and support that you need.

I stopped making this mistake when I finally realized that *it's not personal* – even when I was dealing with someone who was trying to make their response a personal attack or judgment of me or my project or what I am asking them to support. Even in those instances I learned to stop taking it personal.

There were many times when people would try to judge me. But I just didn't let that stuff in. I simply understood that we can't get hung up emotionally on the thoughts or feelings of the people that we have to approach in the process of trying to bring our project to life.

Knowing it's not personal keeps you moving ahead

The problem with getting hung up, whether it is on who to ask, how we might look asking, the answer that we might get or in the sentiments of the person that we are asking, is that in that moment we lose the power that asking everyone brings to our faith projects.

Taking it personal gets us caught up in all the wrong aspects of our process. The biggest thing it does is it keeps us from moving ahead and plowing forward until we reach the goal that we are seeking. It becomes a source of hesitation and blocks us from creating the momentum that will drive us to success in our faith mission.

Remember, the goal is always to keep moving forward, to keep asking for what we need until we have it in hand. That is the key to activating the power of *FAITH (APPLIED)*. Taking it personal and getting our feelings hurt always gets in the way of that.

That is why we must adopt the view that *asking is never personal, it's just asking*. From that vantage point it will be easy to just keep moving ahead while staying mindful of the fact that once we have what we seek in hand, we won't even remember the people who said *"NO"* or tried to give us grief.

When we achieve our goal we will have completely different feelings about everything anyway. As *Mr. Peck* taught me, even though we might go through a lot to get it, when we get what we seek, we don't see the people who didn't work with us the same way anyway.

In other words, you don't take the personal crap that people intended for you in when you win. If anything, you kind of have that, *"I told you I was right!"* swagger.

It is only when we allow ourselves to get stopped short of our goal that the responses or sentiments of our detractors become relevant – and, in allowing ourselves to be stopped, we made them relevant.

Until then it is only by putting our emotions into the equation that these people have their power. That is why it's critical that we learn and apply this crucial *truth of asking*. So from this day forward, always remember that *asking is never personal, it's just asking*.

That leads us to our next ***Truth of Asking.*** It is a truth that really took my understanding of faith to the next level when I first learned it. It is as valuable a truth as any of the others that we have discussed thus far because it has the power to give our efforts to secure the help and support that we need the clear direction that almost always leads to certain success. From my experience, asking for what we need or want becomes a whole lot easier when we understand the truth that:

Truth #9 – There is a market for every message!

One of the best teachings I ever got on the subject of asking was from a senior sales representative that I used to work with at a place called *Copy-R Office Solutions, Mr. Rodney Temple.*

One day this gentleman overheard me working on the phones trying to set up appointments to drum up some sales. What he witnessed was me saying just about anything to get in the door of my prospective customers.

Essentially I was down playing my true intentions to come over and sale them a copier machine in the hope that once in their place of business, I'd be able to turn the corner and make the sale that I was seeking in the first place. You could say that I was trying to use the old, *"bait and switch"* on these unwitting business owners.

This is a technique that I had used many times before with mixed results. It was successful on some occasions, but on most occasions it was a complete failure. Yet I never knew that there was another way.

In fact, I never knew that there was a problem with this approach to asking for the results that I sought. That was until *Mr. Temple* overheard me and decided to share some of his experience and wisdom with me.

What he told me was that if I really wanted to make a sale, I needed to be upfront and tell that to the people that I was calling. As he went on to explain, in being that honest about my intentions when I first called, many of the people would tell me *"NO"* and hang up on me.

At the same time he assured me that there would be others who after hearing my offer would invite me over to talk more about it. Only this time, because I was upfront, the people who invited me over would take me up on that offer and buy from me most of the time.

As uncomfortable as I was with taking this advice and essentially selling over the phone, I did as I was told, and guess what? It was true! In following this advice my call to appointment ratio dropped sharply. I actually made more calls, but I got far fewer appointments from those calls. But while that ratio went south, my sales and income went up significantly.

At first glance, it was hard to believe what I was experiencing. But the more I applied this advice, the greater the results I got. And, despite what I would have thought, these results were consistent.

Before long, this little piece of advice not only changed my finances for the better, but it also led me to the discovery of this powerful ***truth of asking***,

"There is a market for every message."

Before this advice was shared with me, I would have thought that I would have gotten nowhere by telling people in blunt fashion what my intentions were. I would have thought that I would have turned everyone off with this kind of message, and sure some were turned off by my candor.

Some of these were the kind of people who would have granted me an appointment when I used my *"bait and switch"* approach – even though in the end, they wouldn't have bought anything. I thought that everybody operated this way. But to my surprise, there were also others who were nowhere near turned off by my new approach.

These were the people who not only granted me an appointment. These were the people who did just as *Mr. Temple* said they would, they bought from me on the spot without the slightest hesitation – something that never took place when I was using my old *"bait and switch"* tactics.

Ultimately a great truth of asking occurred to me,

"No matter what you are saying there is somebody that will be receptive to that message."

But as true as that main point is, there is an equally important sub point that you must get as well. The person who says yes to message *"A"*, may say no to message *"B."* And, at the same time, the person who says no to message *"A"*, may say yes to message *"B."*

Thus the notion that you or I are going to *"bait and switch"* somebody, the notion that you or I are going to get them in the door with one message, then take them to something else is seldom true.

That's why you have to have the courage to ask for what you're really looking for to begin with. In return for this courage, you can be confident that no matter what you are asking for, there is an audience out there that will be receptive to your message – *there is a market for every message,* even your message.

What you should get from this point is that there is truly no right or wrong message when it comes to asking for what you need or want to succeed. That's even true when operating in **FAITH (APPLIED)**. It is simply about having the courage to truly ask for what you want or need to confront the challenge or achieve the goal that we have in front of us.

Just like you have some people who shop at upscale stores and you have some people who shop at bargain stores. Each person responds to the message that appeals to them.

Simply put, this point teaches us that *everybody is not for everything, and still everything is for someone.* You and I simply have to be careful to ask for what you actually want or need.

It also means that in our asking we must have a specific message and not be all over the place. You are always attracting the people and the resources that correspond to your message. You are always getting what you are asking for.

So there is no need to fear rejection or to shy away from asking for the things that you need to use **FAITH (APPLIED)** because as this **truth of asking** teaches us, *"There is truly a market for every message!"*

We now come to the tenth and final **Truth of Asking.** Even if you perfectly get all of the other nine truths that we have already discussed, this truth is so vital that failure to grasp this single point can literally doom your faith projects to failure.

In fact, this single point can make all of the difference in the world when it comes to you and I unleashing the power of asking in the *FAITH (APPLIED)* system. The final *truth of asking* is:

Truth #10 – Sometimes you must ask high to find what you seek!

No discussion on the subject of the *truths of asking* would be complete without discussing what I have learned is the one thing that most of us struggle with.

Simply said, often times to get what you want or need to succeed in a faith endeavor, you and I must be willing to reach up to the people in higher places – we must be willing to reach out to those that we believe to be above us.

To get the help and support that we need to meet that challenge that is confronting you or to achieve that goal that you are chasing, *sometimes you must ask high to find what you seek!*

That is a fact that is as true as the light of day. And, I must say again that in my travels, I have found that it is the thing that the average person can struggle with the most.

I have seen it a million times in my business walk, highly trained business and sales professionals who are totally uncomfortable with the task of going after what they perceive to be the people in high places. Perhaps our culture is to blame for this condition.

As a society, we do tend to idolize those who are deemed to be successful. All of us learn early on in life to be intimidated by what we perceive to be people of power, people of authority, people of importance and people of wealth.

We often think of these people as being too busy for our petty concerns. We can tend to think of ourselves as not being worthy of being in the company of these people; and it's not at all uncommon for us to think of these people as being unapproachable no matter what the reason for our approach.

For a variety of reasons, we usually think of these as the people who would never be willing to lend us their help and support when we are seeking it. And sadly, I am not talking about celebrities here.

The truth is that we don't just reserve this way of thinking for the wealthy or the successful or for the public figures of our society. For most of us, there are several people in our everyday lives that we bestow this *"superior to us"* treatment on as well.

Think about the people in your neighborhood or the people in your church that you give this status and treatment to. Also think about the people at your job, in your friendship circle or in your family that you classify and treat in this manner.

Think about all of these areas of your life and I am sure that you will find no shortage of people that you extend this level of treatment and respect to. And, the fact that these people can come from places so near to us makes this whole matter even worse.

It would be far better if we were talking about people that we don't have to deal with in our everyday lives. But because we do, we often care too much about what they think about us – the one element that can make this matter all the worse.

There are many times when we are too busy putting on airs to ask for the help and support that we need. People who suffer with this affliction tend to want to look like they are the equals of these people rather than be caught asking for their help and support.

The last thing that they want is to create a situation where they look like they don't have it all together or that they are needy. All of these factors lend themselves to you and I not being willing to **ask high to find the help and support that we seek**.

Conversely, it would seem that all of us are comfortable with those people that we deem to be on or beneath our level. Accordingly, we feel very comfortable approaching this group for help and support.

In spite of the fact that these people fit perfectly within our comfort zone there are many times when they are not willing or able to help or support us in our faith endeavors, there are many instances when they may not even have it to give.

To the extent that we are stuck on only dealing with this group, we can go through our faith project to the very end and yet our needs can go totally unmet. To the extent that we are stuck on only dealing with these lowly people and we refuse to *ask high to find what we need*, at that moment we render the power of *FAITH (APPLIED)* null and void.

The simple truth is that there are many times when there is just no substitute for *asking high to find the help and support that we need to succeed*.

There is simply no way to follow this fifth principle of *Asking Everyone Who Might Help* without you and I having a complete willingness to ask everybody possible, including the people in high places. That is why it's critical that we get the spirit of this final *truth of asking*.

I trust that the point has been driven home here, so I won't belabor it any further. I will simply close it out by saying that in spite of our beliefs to the contrary, all of the reasons why we might be intimidated by the people in high places are the very reasons that make them the ideal people to seek out for the help and support that we need to handle a challenge or conquer a goal that we have.

Just to give you a quick rundown of why asking high can be the best thing that we can do to find what we need, when considering whether or not to *ask high to find what you need*, always remember that more often than not:

– Highly placed people have the power to help!
– Highly placed people have the authority to help!
– Highly placed people have the economic means to help!
– Highly placed people have the influence to move others!
– Highly placed people see the vision or respect your drive! and,
– Highly placed people are often too busy to waste your time!

That is why these are the ideal people for you and I to seek out when we are trying to find the help and support that we need to overcome the challenge that is before us or achieve the goal that we are striving for. All of these points are usually true in both the professional and the personal arena.

The bottom line is that when you develop the habit of asking everyone possible to help you by learning to *ask high to find what you need*, you will almost always walk away with what you need to succeed in your faith projects. There is no way to even think about applying faith or a *"leave no stones unturned"* mentality without you being committed to this key point.

So there you have the 10 *Truths of Asking*. I have found that these truths apply no matter who you are asking for help and support, no matter what you are asking for and no matter how promising your proposition may seem.

To find success, you will have to apply the *Math of Asking* and do the numbers. And, even in your personal life, maybe you will have to seek out the help and support of several friends or family members to find the one or two that will help and support you.

Remember not to hold it personally against those who don't help you; even when they may have meant it personally. The simple fact is that you are in it for a result and you should always strive until you have that outcome in your hand. Like the little child you should have a motto that says,

> *"Someone has it to give, I want or need it and I am to only stop asking for it when I have it."*

Remember, as *Mr. Randy Peck* so rightly taught me, when you have the goal in hand, the reward is so good that you usually couldn't care less about how much effort you had to expend to get it.

In fact, I have heard many successful people say that they'd be willing to expend even more in the way of energy and resources than they originally put out to get the success that they now enjoy. Having now lived with their success for a time, they regarded the price paid as being more than worth it.

I have found the same to be true with regard to pushing past the *fear of rejection* and applying these *10 Truths of Asking* to your faith projects. Try these points for yourself and I am sure you too will be amazed at the results that they produce for you.

In wrapping up our discussion on the *10 Truths of Asking*, we just talked about the importance and power of asking for help and support in high places.

I can remember an incident that took place years ago that served as a graphic example of the power of you and I operating with this point as a personal discipline. It might even be said that the incident pretty much summed up the power of putting all of these *truths of asking* to work in your life. Let me now relate the story of when,

The Power of Asking (High) restored our power

As fitting as it sounds, there was literally an incident when my using the power of asking high restored the power in my family's home. Like all of the other stories that I have shared here about the power of the *FAITH (APPLIED)* principles, this incident took place back in the time when I was really broke and struggling as both a husband and father.

As I have written before, back then it was a big enough struggle just to keep a roof over our head and food on the table. In any given month, after paying these vital bills, there often wasn't much left over to address the other bills that came into the household – like the household utility bills. This was one of those occasions.

Our finances were in a dry space and for a few months in a row there was no money to pay any of these other important bills. It wasn't long before the past due notices began to come in, and with them, the threats to shut off these utilities if the situation wasn't corrected soon. I truly wanted to correct the situation and get everything paid up, but I just couldn't afford to do so.

One of the bills that needed paying was our electricity bill. The *Los Angeles Department of Water and Power (LADWP)* had a reputation for being real aggressive when it came to collecting for their services. We had reached the place where they were starting to unleash their aggressiveness on me.

Remembering how my mother always handled these types of moments when I was a kid living in her home, I tried to negotiate a payment arrangement that would allow me to work the bill down in a manner that was affordable for my family. But unlike in my mom's day, these people were totally unworkable. No matter what I offered, the answer was *"NO."*

Each time I approached them they would turn down my proposal and in its place they'd offer me an all or nothing proposition. Each time I would try to explain that my financial situation wouldn't allow me to meet their terms.

I even tried to explain to them that I had an asthmatic child that required the use of a treatment machine from time to time; a fact that required the electricity to be on at all times since he could have an asthma attack at any unexpected moment.

All of this was to no avail. They simply would not budge and eventually they issued me a final ultimatum. They demanded payment and set a final date for disconnection.

Now that they had escalated the situation, I felt it necessary to escalate my efforts to get someone in this organization to hear my concerns and give me a repayment plan that was workable for my family. I was even beginning to suspect that the treatment that I was receiving had more to do with where I was living at the time and who I was dealing with within this organization than any hard and fast rules that these people had to follow.

Given this new concern, I was starting to think that I'd need to speak with the supervisor of the customer service agents that you commonly reached when you called in. Once again, I recalled that whenever my mother wasn't getting what she wanted from the average customer service agent, reaching out to the supervisor would always yield her the outcome that she was seeking.

Beyond this and the other concerns over having the power shut off that I had already contemplated, it was starting to dawn on me just how much of a challenge this would really bring to our household. In the event that it came to us being disconnected, being without power would also mean cold baths and no heat since both the water and household heaters ran on electricity.

Also, our food would likely spoil since the refrigerator would be out and since the stove was also electric, we wouldn't have the ability to cook, not to mention the darkness that we would have to suffer through once the sun went down. For a young family with two small children to care for all of these conditions would have been tantamount to torture.

With all of this weighing heavy on my mind I demanded to speak to a supervisor. I did so thinking that surely this person would have the compassion to see my dilemma and the power to authorize a more workable solution and that they would be caring enough to do so. However, once I reached this person, I found out very quickly that I could have never been more wrong about how me and my concerns and challenges would be received.

To my shock, the supervisors were even worse than the customer service agents. They really played hard ball. They basically treated me like a guy who was simply trying to avoid paying his bill.

I quickly realized that these people were simply the head of a system that had been set up to be completely adversarial, one where it was next to impossible for the average customer to get a break on paying their bill. It clearly wasn't even designed for me to get to and speak with a supervisor.

In fact, I felt all but certain that the customer service agents were actually just passing the phone to the co-worker in the next cubical when you would ask to speak with a supervisor. That was surely how it felt. It was either that or they truly had the most callous supervisors on the planet.

Needless to say, I found no relief in dealing with this bunch and having reached an impasse, their deadline for payment came and when I couldn't pay, they turned off my family's power.

Once the power was off, all of the more minor inconveniences that I feared quickly came to pass. Not that these challenges were playing out in a minor way. They were definitely major issues. However, they were only minor in contrast to the position that we would have been in if my son had an asthma attack and needed his treatment machine.

Thankfully, he was okay for the first few days of this crisis. But just thinking about the possibility of him needing this equipment created a spirit of desperation within me that made me realize that I had to figure out some way to remove this concern once we were at home.

What I ultimately did to head off this crisis was to run a long extension cord down from my unit to tap into the management's power from the main building. This was not only illegal and unsafe; it would have been a complete embarrassment and grounds for eviction if I had gotten caught.

Making matters worse, I lived in the front of the building facing the boulevard and the buildings that sat directly across the street. As a matter of fact, this illegal hook up was only possible because the front of the building was a bit obscured by a 3 story tall growth of bushes.

Still to avoid being seen plugging in, I had to wait until it was dark to drop my cord down and jump up early enough in the morning to retrieve the cord before either a neighbor or one of the workers from my building was up and about. Obviously, this wasn't a workable, long range solution to my problem.

When I finally became fed up with this state of existence, I made up my mind to get back in the fight and take that fight to the tip top person in the *LADWP* chain of command. As far as these low and mid-level customer service agents and managers were concerned, they had me boxed in and it would be their way or no way at all. They often treated the customers from my neighborhood this way. But they didn't realize who they were dealing with in me.

To begin with, I came from the stock of a grandmother that didn't tolerate low and mid-level workers giving her a hard time and not giving her what she wanted, and perhaps, rightfully deserved. She was famous in our family for having once literally called President Ronald Reagan himself when a local government worker had failed to help her in the way she felt he should have.

She didn't manage to get President Reagan on the phone. But as a result of the call, staff members from his office did reach down to those workers in our small town who thought they weren't going to help her and made them give her what she wanted.

In the end she got her way. And, as a result, everyone in our family learned a valuable lesson about being willing to take your fight all the way to the top to get the support that you need to meet the challenge that is confronting you.

Second of all, they didn't know that because of my profession, I had developed the ability to get to any person that I needed to talk to, especially over the phone – and their efforts to block me from speaking with a real manager had only fired up my competitive spirit and my willingness to take the bold action of using these skills.

"How did you get me on the phone?"

By this point in my career, even though I wasn't yet stable financially, my sales training had taught me exactly what to say and what not to say to get by the gatekeepers who try to screen the calls of important people. Now I used those skills to take my case directly to *Mr. S. David Freeman*, the general manager and head of one of the largest public utilities in the United States and the world for that matter.

In his shock, the first thing that *Mr. Freeman* said once he realized that I was an average customer who had managed to get him on the phone was,

> *"How did you get me on the phone?*
> *Who transferred you to me?"*

To which I replied,

> *"It's my job! I get people on the phone for a living! And, there aren't too many people that I can't get on the phone."*

After his shock wore off, we got down to business and I let him know why it was that I had to call all the way to the top of the command chain to ask him for the fairness and assistance that I needed to get a payment arrangement in place that would allow for my power to be restored.

I made him aware of the behavior of his subordinates, both the regular customer service workers and the supervisors. I made clear my position that this was fairness and assistance that I really should have been able to find in the low-level workers that had tried to bully me into coming up with money that I just didn't have to give – a point that he perfectly agreed with me on.

He definitely had a problem with the fact that he had to talk to a regular customer about a billing and payment issue. This obviously put him in a position that no chief executive wants to find themselves in.

What an embarrassment it would have been if he gave me the same hard time that these other supposed supervisors were giving me. Think of the ramifications if my son had gotten sick and couldn't get his medicine and the top executive was part of why the power was off?

Needless to say, when the call was over, *Mr. Freeman* issued a directive downstairs and just like in my grandmother's case, I got the results that I needed to get my family out of the dark. In so doing I brought remedy to all of the challenges that we were dealing with as a result of being without power and insured that my son had access to the life-saving medicine that he could have needed at any moment.

I also learned in this one moment that sometimes there is just no substitute for **asking in high places**. I had spun my wheels for days, perhaps even weeks with those lower level workers and supervisors and each one made no effort to help in any reasonable manner. And ultimately, one phone call to the top got me exactly what I had been asking for, literally – as *Mr. Freeman* basically just took my order and gave me the exact terms that I was looking for.

When I had been dealing with the customer service agents and managers that weren't trying to help me, I had begun to bend my terms in an effort to get some solution. If one of them had agreed I was risking not being able to keep my end up because I was still being stretched beyond what I could really handle. But now I was getting exactly what I needed to make this all work.

It should not surprise you to know that this totally pissed off the people who had tried to bully me into taking those terms that didn't work for my family. I ultimately learned that they had put all kinds of comments in the system to insure that I would always have a hard time if I had to work with them in the future.

A couple of these people even tried to undue portions of the agreement that I had won with *Mr. Freeman*, prompting me to have to get him back on the phone two additional times before the entire matter of this past due bill was finally resolved.

Each time, once he realized that I was a regular customer calling about a billing and payment matter, he opened up with the same question, *"How did you get me on the phone?"* And, each time I would give him the same reply, *"It's my job! I get people on the phone for a living! And, there aren't too many people that I can't get on the phone."* And, once again by the time the call would end, I would have gotten exactly what I was looking for.

I would later learn that this same *LADWP* and all of the other utility companies in that area had a totally different way of dealing with people from the supposed right side of town that couldn't pay their bills. That proved to me beyond all doubt that I had been right in my assertion that I wasn't being treated fairly during this incident.

Once I had become more successful and moved over to one of the more affluent parts of the same city, there were several times when I failed to pay my bill with *LADWP*. Despite the fact that the past due balance was higher and the time past due was longer I didn't get nearly the same treatment.

If anything it took them a substantial amount of time longer to even step forward to make a demand for the missed payments. And, when they did finally step forward, I got all of the fairness and assistance that I had been seeking in the past – a fact that made me all the more glad that I had had the guts to **ask high the get what I needed** back in the day.

To be sure asking high in this way is a practice and skill that I have used several times since this incident. In fact, beyond even this discussion, this is a principle that I live by.

I am pleased to see that it is even rubbing off on my sons. Even my youngest son, then a high school age kid had an incident where a low-level employee in a store where he shops tried to unfairly deny him the right to return a defective item that he had bought.

He took his fight all the way to the top of this pretty large company and not only got his money from the return of the defective item back, but he also got some extra cash, in the form of gift cards to buy something better from the company for his trouble.

He did all of this on his own initiative, without any help from me or his mother. Without a doubt we were both extremely proud of him for standing up for his rights by taking his fight up high. Believe me, it truly works.

Hopefully you too can see why this little *LADWP* story is a perfect example of why this and all of the *10 Truths of Asking* are so powerful. More than just seeing how *asking high got me the help and support that I needed*, you can also see all of the other *truths of asking* at work in my success here. Just to recap them for you:

Truth #1 – Success is always in the numbers!
Truth #2 – You won't get everybody!
Truth #3 – Those who you think will help you won't, those who you think won't help you will!
Truth #4 – There is a difference between a Condition and an Objection (Rejection)!
Truth #5 – You must ask those who are empowered to help!
Truth #6 – You have to ask until you have what you seek in hand!
Truth #7 – You don't have to know where you will get the results that you seek!
Truth #8 – Asking is never personal, it's just asking!
Truth #9 – There is a market for every message!
Truth #10 – Sometimes you must ask high to find what you seek!

This story is also a great example of the power of *leaving no stones unturned* in asking for the help that you need and of standing in faith and *asking until you receive what you need in your hand.*

Remember, to have the greatest chance at finding success through the use of *FAITH (APPLIED)*, you must make it a habit to try every avenue there is to getting your goal. Don't ever assume where your results will come from. Just be in motion and try every source available to you until you have your goal in your hands.

Also it really can't be overemphasized, never be afraid to *ask high in pursuit of your goal*. Often we think that it is easier for us to achieve smaller goals than for us to achieve bigger goals. We often think that the doors in lowly places will open for us faster than the doors in high places. And, we believe it is easier to make it among the unsuccessful or the needy than it is to make it among the successful and the rich.

Basically we think that we are sure to get our goal if we just aim low enough. And, on the contrary, we think that there is no way that we can get our goal by aiming high. Yet the truth is just the opposite.

Often, it is easier to get what you seek from the higher place than the lower place. It is we who struggle to believe that we can go to, and get what we need or want from the higher places.

To truly experience the magic of **FAITH (APPLIED)** through **the power of asking**, you must first realize that **asking everyone who might help** means being open to all of your options – the high-end ones, as well as the low-end ones.

More often than not, you don't know who will help you or where your results will come from. Therefore you must truly stay open to asking everyone and exploring every avenue – including those in, and of high places.

I ask for help and support to regain my mobility and overcome Multiple Myeloma

Prior to the moment that *Multiple Myeloma* interrupted my life, I was a young, healthy and vibrant man. I lived a very physical existence, both in the sense of working out, jogging and hitting the gym and in the sense of how I lived my everyday life.

In addition to living my life in this physical manner, mentally I was fiercely independent and a bit of the classic macho man. I was anything but a person who would have ever thought I would soon need help and support with the most basic task of everyday life.

I lived my life by a philosophy that I called *"Man World."* It was a way of thinking and acting that was all about being strong and self-reliant. It was a way of life that was all about taking complete responsibility for providing everything that me or my family needed to make it in life.

Because I lacked the support of the family that I grew up with, it was about making all things happen myself when something needed to get done. It was about being the source of power and strength for my family. It was a way of thinking and acting that I was committed to and one that I was actively trying to drum into my two young sons.

This is how I was raised and how I had lived my life for the 46 years that I had lived prior to this moment. In all this time there wasn't much that I was used to asking others to help me with.

Even as a family man I had been perfectly self-reliant for years. To show how far I took this ethic of self-reliance, when my family was faced with having to move over the years, I was usually my own one man moving crew. No matter what needed to be moved, I moved it.

Even on occasions when my family was faced with serious challenges, things like needing major car repairs, I became my own mechanic. No matter what needed to be repaired on our car, I repaired it.

Over the years, I have tackled major repair jobs that would challenge even the best trained mechanics – and this despite the fact that I didn't grow up working on cars, didn't grow up with a male influence in my life to teach me such things and had no training as a mechanic. All I had was the spirit of my *"Man World"* philosophy.

With this spirit I had been the man and the physical force in my life and my family's life for more than two decades. With this spirit, I had managed to live a perfectly self-reliant way of life and avoided the need to ask anyone for anything for years.

So imagine what it was like for me when it begin to settle in on me that all of that was taken away from me in an instant on July 14th, 2012. Imagine what it felt like when I realized for the first time in my life, that I needed help and support to do even the most basic things in life.

I had to humble myself to ask for the help and support I needed to defeat Multiple Myeloma

As my doctor has shared with me, many people will have the unfortunate experience of having their life interrupted by cancer. And yet in most of these cases, the victim will never have their mobility challenged by that cancer. In this way my case was totally unique.

In my case, the cancer known as *Multiple Myeloma* that attacked my body took me completely off of my feet when it first landed on July 14, 2012. Because it took me off of my feet, I went from being the totally self-reliant macho man living by my *"Man World"* philosophy, to a man who needed help in ways that I never would have thought I would need another human being to help me, especially at such a young age in my life.

As this moment unfolded upon me, I quickly had no choice but to realize that I needed to ask for the help and support to get through the average day. All at once I needed help with literally everything in my life. It was like I was a newborn baby again and couldn't do a single thing for myself.

When I was in the hospital I had to rely on the nurses for my care and keeping. And once I came home I had to rely on my wife and sons in the same way. Just mentally managing this new reality took great help and support.

To be sure there was no way that I could have even thought about making it through the physical aspects of this reality without the help and support of those around me. And, that was to say nothing of what I would need to successfully battle the cancer that had attacked me.

This moment that I would later learn to call, **"My New Normal"** was a humbling experience to say the least. Making the moment even more challenging was the fact that I had no guarantee that my situation would ever get better.

In fact, most of the doctors that were treating me were betting that it wouldn't – a fact that all but meant that I couldn't look to this medical corner to support my stand of faith against the illness that had attacked me.

Just being confronted with the doubts of these supposed medical experts could have made me turn inward and fall back on my pride. It could have easily made me try to run my old self-reliance program. That is what so many others would do in a similar situation.

But fortunately I instinctively knew that to get through this moment and overcome *Multiple Myeloma* I would have to totally humble myself, check my pride and ask beyond this group to find the help and support that I needed.

It goes without saying that a diagnosis like cancer can and often does turn your life upside down. At least in the short term, it can change everything about your approach to living.

For sure overcoming a serious illness like this requires that you have a ton of help and support. Yet even in a moment as trying as this, many people are too proud to ask for the help that they rightfully need. But this is clearly not a time for pride.

To the contrary, this is a time when you may truly need to lean on those around you in every conceivable way. This is especially true when you are serious about fighting and beating the disease. In my case, I even had to reach out for the help and support of a brother who lived in another state altogether.

It really doesn't matter what type of faith project you are engaged in, just like in my case, you might need to reach out and request help and support from places far from where you are. Doing so will likely mean that you must humble yourself and speak your request for help.

The simple fact is that you must be there for the success of your faith project. No matter whether that project is about finding healing and restoration like I was seeking or any other goal, 100% of your being and focus must be on this goal if you expect to find success.

Yet the truth is that in many cases we aren't aware of the role that help and support will play in our achieving and maintaining that 100% commitment and focus on our goal. And not seeing this truth can often keep us from seeing that we need to humble ourselves and seek the help and support of those around us.

Thankfully the *Creator* helped me to see this truth in my battle with cancer from the outset of the fight. Because of it, I went beyond those doctors or anyone else that wasn't there to help me and ask (*and ask, and ask*) until I found those people who would help me and support me. I also found those people who would offer me the resources that I needed to come away with a victory over cancer.

So from a personal standpoint, one aspect of using this principle to overcome cancer meant asking for the help and support that I would first need to get through everyday life, and second to find healing. While at the same time, from a medical standpoint, successfully using this principle to find victory meant being open to doing everything possible to find that healing.

It took a "Leave No Stones Unturned" mentality to find my healing and restoration

When it comes to battling a serious illness like cancer, being open to doing everything possible to find healing can only ever mean one thing – having that same *"Leave No Stones Unturned"* mentality that we've already talked about in this principle. From my experience, there is simply no way to truly find healing without having this mentality.

In nearly every case where I have watched someone lose a battle to a serious illness, I learned after the fact that the person had a laundry list of things that he/she was unwilling to do, stones that he/she was unwilling to turn in pursuit of healing.

In each one of these cases this unwillingness grew out of either the spirit of fear or a state of ignorance, and many times both. It goes without saying that it really doesn't matter what the source of this unwillingness to explore all options and *"Leave No Stone Unturned,"* the fact is that there is generally no way to successfully employ the power of *FAITH (APPLIED)* without this mentality. For starters, fear is the opposite of faith and the ignorance often leads to fear.

Being ruled by such forces as fear and ignorance can only lead you to fail to recognize the true number of resources that are available to you for the success of your faith project. Many people who are confronted by a challenging circumstance only see a narrow slice of the resources and options that the *Creator* has placed in the universe for us to use as the tools of our faith.

With what I know now, I can't help but think that if those people that I have watched lose their battle to illness had explored their full range of options and turned every stone in their search for healing and restoration, they would have found the victory that they were seeking.

Instead of limiting themselves to a narrow portion of the medicine and treatment options at their disposal, maybe if they had truly educated themselves about and explored every viable option available to fight their illness, they would still be here today.

Let me clearly state here that I am not trying to pass judgment on or make light out of the tragedy of anyone's untimely passing. Nor am I trying to second guess any of these folks when obviously they knew their situation better than I did.

What I am attempting to do is contrast my own case with facts that I know about the cases of some of the people that I know who lost their battle with illness, at the same time that I was receiving my victory over a very serious illness – an illness that made matters worse by totally stripping me of my mobility when it first entered my life.

None of the people that I could speak of here ever had that to worry about. Many of them had greater resources than I had at my disposal, especially in terms of their finances and access to medical professionals and resources. And, despite all of these advantages, perhaps because of fear and ignorance and because *they left stones unturned*, they lost their fight.

While despite the fact that I had none of these advantages and resources going for me, I was able to find victory through the greatest resource of all, *FAITH (APPLIED)*, and largely because I knew the importance of operating from a *"Leaving No Stones Unturned"* mentality.

That's why I am trying to share with you this vital truth of my recovery and to give you a glimpse into what my mindset was. I am trying to show you what the actions were that I took that I know made the difference in my case.

Above all, I am trying to show you how possessing this *"Leave No Stones Unturned"* mentality gave the *Creator* a pathway to bless me with healing through the power of *FAITH (APPLIED)*.

You must "Leave No Stones Unturned" to find healing, even when it means facing pain

It may be helpful for me to point out that in my experience I had to go through some treatments and take some medicines that I didn't particularly like on my road to healing.

From the very first medical procedure that I was confronted with in my battle with *Multiple Myeloma*, the bone marrow biopsy that was used to diagnose the cancer, I found myself dealing with an experience so painful that it could have easily motivated me to shut down all of the efforts that had gotten underway to regain my health and mobility.

My doctor had talked me into allowing this vital procedure to be performed on me, in the process using a bunch of fancy terms to disguise the truth about what I was signing up for. By the time he was done selling me on the ease of this procedure, he had managed to make hammering a big needle into the center of my skeleton to suck out some of my bone marrow sound like a non-event.

By the time his staff was done with the procedure and I lay there feeling like someone had just ran a billion volts of electricity through my body, I knew that the path to the healing that I was standing in faith for was going to be anything but a comfortable journey.

If I hadn't possessed a *"Leave No Stones Unturned"* mentality from the outset of this battle there is no way that I would have been willing to leave the memory of that procedure behind and go forward with the long list of medical procedures and treatments that lie waiting for me on my route to recovery. Just remembering the pain of that procedure today is still a haunting experience.

If it were not for my *"Leave No Stones Unturned"* mentality, maybe I would have looked more at the immediate effects and the side effects that moments like that were having on my body and my way of life. Then perhaps I would have opted to remain in my comfort zone and I wouldn't have went through all of the needed procedures and treatments that were used to heal me. And, perhaps then I would have ended up being one of those people that lost the battle against disease.

Choosing to "Leave No Stones Unturned" wasn't always easy, but it was always worth it

I can certainly understand how easy it is to be unwilling to let the doctors do everything that they can to help restore you to health. Remember that in the first hours after I had been stricken with *Multiple Myeloma* I too seemed almost unwilling to cooperate with the doctors and nurses that were trying to simply get to the bottom of what was going on. Remember, I am the same guy who thought that I would go home from the emergency room and deal with the whole matter later.

I can say however that this reaction was born out of the general denial that I was suffering from in regards to the whole situation. I had no clue that I couldn't even sit up and get out of the bed. I had no clue that I had no control over my upper body or that I couldn't walk.

I didn't at all accept that something was truly going on within my body. And I didn't even realize that the great pain that I was in when I came into the hospital had only subsided because of all of the pain medication that they were pumping into me.

But as soon as I got a grip on the moment and on everything that was happening I settled down and changed my attitude. So much so that by the time I got to *Long Beach Memorial Hospital* I was ready to go through any and everything that I would have to endure to find the healing and restoration that I was standing in faith for. In fact, once I tuned into the reality of what was going on, I made my mind up at *Marina del Rey Hospital* that I would beat whatever diagnosis came my way.

For sure I understood that there is no way to successfully apply faith to this decision as long as I was willing to leave even a single stone unturned. It has long been my view that the forces that would stand to see you defeated in your quest for a faith victory will and often do perfectly hide behind the stone that we are unwilling to turn. From my observation, this is true in all the areas of your life and in any type of faith project that you can undertake.

In a moment as serious as that of battling a deadly illness, if you are fortunate you and your doctor will be blessed with a variety of options for treating the disease that you are fighting. It is in your best interest to know and explore the full range of those options that are available to you until you have the victory that you seek in hand. For if you fail to do so, who is to say that the medicine or the procedure that you won't take is the very one that could save your life? You will only know if you go through with it.

It might also be worthwhile for me to advise you to pursue these options in a spirit of complete faith and open mindedness. That is what I have done throughout this process and perhaps that is why, by the grace of **God**, I got the results that I did. Perhaps that is why the principles of **FAITH (APPLIED)** worked for me.

It might also be necessary for me to point out that it has not always been comfortable to live up to this **"Leaving No Stones Unturned"** mentality. As I have been confronted with the unpleasant medicines, treatments, circumstances, people or task that I have had to endure on this road, I have often felt the urge to push back or to back away from going through with those things that seemed like they would be unpleasant.

There have been many moments that have been initially met with a spirit of disapproval from me. At the very beginning of this illness, there have been times when my wife has had to settle me down and get me to make the proper decision or even make that decision and speak for me when I just wouldn't.

But here again, once I got into the reality of this moment I have always been able to get a hold of myself and make the right call in spite of any personal fears or hang ups that I may have had.

From the moment that my health had greatly improved, my main doctor has often accused me of not being the perfect patient. I haven't followed the perfect treatment schedule and I have always been mindful to only take a medicine regimen when it is absolutely necessary.

Given that these medicines can also carry negative effects, I am careful to only take any medicine if there is still a need for it. As my health has improved to the place where test have consistently shown the cancer to be in remission, I have opted to cut back on the use of any of the harsher medicines that I have taken to get to that place.

But when it was necessary to turn these stones, I willingly allowed them to be turned. And, if there is any point in the future when turning these or similar stones becomes necessary, I will do it all over again.

Given the results that I received from this philosophy, I can say that if you find yourself struggling with an unwillingness to move past you and adopt a *"Leave No Stones Unturned"* mentality, maybe it will be helpful if you elect someone to move you to that place when you can't or won't do it for yourself.

The important thing to get here is that you need to possess the *"Leave No Stones Unturned"* mentality to secure a faith victory or find the healing that you seek and you can't even let you stand in the way of that.

To that end, in this or any other faith project, you have to know and explore all legitimate options in seeking victory, both those in the faith realm and the physical realm. That is what I had to do to find the victory that I won over *Multiple Myeloma*.

By contrast, I cannot stress enough that it is one of the things that I have noticed a lot of the people who I personally know who have lost their battle against illness didn't do. These people had a host of unwarranted restrictions on what they were willing to do and not do, and in the end, perhaps that is why victory eluded them.

It is my hope that if you are battling a serious illness now, or you ever find yourself doing so in the future that this will never be you. I know from personal experience that possessing the *"Leave No Stones Unturned"* mentality is the surest way to make sure that this will never be you.

I know that I have given you a lot to think about in relationship to this principle. But the main theme should still be simple and clear. To successfully use *FAITH (APPLIED)* and activate the miracle-making power of the universe, you must be willing to ask for the help and support that you need and you must be willing to *ask everyone who might help*.

You must also adopt a *"Leave No Stones Unturned"* mentality. That almost always means you must push past the spirit of unbelief and the fear of that big little word *"NO"* and any *Fear of Rejection* that might reside within you.

I should also say here that there is one other enemy of asking that you must be sure that you don't possess. *It is the inability to handle disappointment.* You simply can't make it a big deal when things don't appear to be going your way. We will talk later about a specific way to do this. But for now just know that you have got to avoid being one of those people who get bummed out when things don't appear to be going your way.

As I related from my own past experience, this all works best if you could learn to develop the habit of not getting too high with the things that go right for you or too down in the dumps with the things that would appear to be going wrong for you. If you could truly learn to be okay either way, if you could learn to be the same upbeat person in all instances, you will truly have taken a powerful step in the direction of being a master at asking.

You should also know that I have given you so much info here because this is essentially the heart of this work. This principle, more than any of the others represents the seat of action in this *FAITH (APPLIED)* philosophy. As they say, this is where the rubber meets the road. While each of these principles is vital, this is the one that will make or break your success in using the power of *FAITH (APPLIED)*.

You can get all of the rest of these principles perfectly, but if you don't learn how to *ask for what you want and/or need to succeed*, if you don't learn all of the dynamics involved; or how to put the process of asking in the right context and if you don't learn how to ask *(and ask, and ask)* until you get what you seek, you will likely never see the real power of *FAITH (APPLIED)*.

For that reason, I had to put the necessary time into giving you a thorough understanding of this principle and I had to cover it from all possible angles. Hopefully in so doing, you now have a perfect understanding of the role that successfully *asking everyone who might help* you for those things that you need plays in your ability to achieve victory in whatever faith project you may ever choose to pursue.

Finally, although it may not be written out correctly by being in quotation marks, bold, italic and in all caps, throughout this work, I have purposely played up the word *"NO."* I did so because I want you to see the true size of a word that many of us allow to rule our lives – spiritually, economically, occupationally, romantically and so on.

On July 30th, 1995, at the end of the day, earning the $1,000 bonus was a matter of me helping enough people to reach the sales goal that made it possible. And, there was no way for me to get there without me *asking everyone who might help* if they would do so by buying something.

In asking everyone possible, I found success through the volume of people that I approached and helped. In that way, success on that day was in the numbers. And, since that time there have been numerous other projects that I worked that played out in the same exact manner.

If at any point in these projects, I had worried about that little big word *"NO"* or tried to engage in my old habits of not approaching everyone or trying to guess who may have had the willingness or means to buy from me in the first place, I would have certainly been doomed to failure.

Thankfully the spirit of *God* led me in a new direction on that day. In this way, the *Creator* not only helped me to achieve the task of earning that $1,000 bonus, but he opened the door to a whole new world of possibilities for me. For that gift, I am forever grateful.

Again, I know that we have covered a lot of material on this principle and I will trust that you have gotten a clear picture of why learning to *ask everyone who might help* is such a vital part of unleashing the power of *FAITH (APPLIED)* into your life and your affairs. So now, let's look at the sixth step in activating the miracle-making power of the universe:

Don't waste time on people and situations that don't help you get your goal.

Move on once you see that you will not get what you need from a person or situation, no matter who it is or how promising it looks. It's better to pursue the lowly that will help you than to waste time chasing or waiting around for the mighty or the promising who will not help you. Often times, in the time that it takes to get one waste of time person to come around or give you their final "NO" you could have gotten five other people to go your way.

On July 30[th,] 1995, I perfected my practice of a principle that I had already witnessed the value of in my career. Fortunately for me, I had learned years prior that to achieve success in any faith project it's important that I stay in motion until I have the victory that I am seeking in hand.

Now in your quest for victory over the challenge that confronts you or in the goal that you are working towards you need to know that the same fact holds true for you.

The only way to stay in motion is if you *don't waste time on people and situations that don't help you get your goal!* One of the single biggest enemies of *FAITH (APPLIED)* is time wasted on people who will either never be part of the success that you are seeking or those who will keep you from other people who will.

On that day back in July of 1995, I instinctively knew that for me to reach my goal I had to be about my business and waste no time on people who were not willing to help me with that goal. Several years before this day, this was something that I had learned the hard way.

You see, in my professional life, I used to operate in the exact opposite manner. I was one of those sales people that would perfectly allow people to waste my time.

It didn't matter if they were there to do business or just kill time. It didn't matter if they were the kind of person who couldn't make a decision about what to buy or if they were the kind of person who had decided not to buy and couldn't bring themselves to just tell me so. For whatever reason they were before me wasting my time, I would perfectly allow them to do so.

Looking back on it now, I guess I tolerated this because I thought that it was part of my job to do so. I thought that it was part of being polite and nice to the prospective customers that flowed through our store.

I also feel that part of why I put up with this behavior is because I lacked the skill and courage to quickly and firmly move people to make a buying decision or move on from them if they wouldn't or couldn't.

No matter what the reasons were, this bad habit changed the day one of the top salespeople at one of my old jobs took notice of me and the fact that I was struggling with this issue.

That salesman, ***Mr. Willie Thomas*** pulled me aside and gave me the advice that would forever set me straight on this issue. After observing me for some time, this gentleman approached me and asked me if I'd be willing to hear a little unsolicited advice on how I might improve my sales.

Since I didn't have a problem with taking advice and I desperately wanted to improve my effectiveness in dealing with customers, not to mention my income, I very quickly and enthusiastically said, please do share!

Mr. Thomas opened up by saying,

"Young man, I have been watching you for a good amount of time now and I can't help but notice that you are not doing so well at selling here. I also noticed you seem to be clueless as to why that is, do I have it right?

I said,

"Yes" and confirmed his observations.

Then he said,

"To tell you what I see, I noticed that you basically allow these people to jerk you around in any way that they want to." He went on to explain, *"It's like you allow these people to basically drag you around by your tie and make you jump through all sorts of hoops with no intention of buying anything. And, when you do finally ask them to buy something, they ultimately tell you 'NO' and leave, having perfectly wasted your time. You will never reach your goals; much less earn a living as long as you keep allowing people to waste your time in this way."*

And then he hit me with a nugget of advice that forever set me straight on this subject, in closing his talk with me, he told me this,

"Young man, while you tolerate the foolishness of these would be customers, while you allow them to waste your valuable time, you don't notice that in the time it is taking you to get one 'NO' you could have gotten five other people to say 'YES' to you."

This was advice that I desperately needed to hear at that moment. As I have already mentioned, up to that point in my career I had been struggling to make sales and to generate income for myself and my family. In fact, each month I had been making very few sales and very little money for years up to that point.

However, while working in the exact same environment, *Mr. Thomas* was making a ton of sales and he was earning a great income, month in and month out. He was most often the top salesperson in our store, and often times, in the entire company.

While I was generally working for and surviving off of the meager monthly draw that we each were paid, *Mr. Thomas* earned huge commission checks every month. So coming from him, this was advice that could change the course of my career for sure and I got it from the first moment that it was bestowed upon me.

For every one of these reasons, I took this advice to heart and worked my best to apply it to my efforts on the sales floor. And, guess what? It worked like a charm! Before I knew it, my sales and income skyrocketed.

I quickly got to see with my own eyes that what *Mr. Thomas* had said was true. When I stopped wasting time with people, I started hitting my goals and making money immediately.

Not wasting time was key to achieving a $1,000 bonus

On July 30th, 1995, with this lesson well under my belt I knew instinctively that I had to be direct in my dealings with each person that I approached and find the ones that were there to buy and help me reach my goal of earning that $1,000 bonus.

At the end of the day, I know that this principle was a vital key to me achieving success. For a variety of reasons, there is no way that I could have hit this goal if I had wasted time on non-buying customers.

First of all, from a time standpoint, there is just no way for me to waste time with people who wouldn't help me to achieve this goal and get to the goal. Remember, this was not only a one day challenge – it was set before us on a Sunday, the shortest selling day of the week.

As such there was literally zero time granted to any of us who were going for the goal for waste. Results had to be the order of the day if we were to have any real chance at hitting the target that was being aimed for. I certainly know that this was true for me.

Next, from a practical standpoint, wasting time with people who weren't there to help me hit my goal would have prevented me from finding and working with the people who would be willing to help.

I don't have to tell you that it is physically impossible to be in two places at the same time. To have any chance of reaching my goal I needed to physically be in front of the people who would help me and not hung up with those who wouldn't.

I could not afford to spend major time on someone only to get a *"NO"* when it was all said and done. Like *Mr. Thomas* had taught me, I had to remember that,

"In the time it took to get that one person to say 'NO' to me, I could have gotten five others to say 'YES' to me."

And, pursuing that course of action would be far more conducive to my success than wasting time only to get a *"NO"* in the end.

Lastly, from a morale standpoint, when you waste time with people who won't help you to achieve your goal, it takes something out of you. That is the truth no matter what the arena. This would have certainly been true for me had I made that mistake on July 30th, 1995.

It took everything in me to even believe that I could rise up to meet this challenge. Had I wasted even a few of the precious moments that I had with people who weren't there to help me achieve my goal I know that it would have been all too easy for me to get down on myself and give up.

Because time was of the essence on this day, watching the clock tick down without seeing real results come in would have easily opened the door to doubt.

When you waste time with people who don't help you, who don't buy from you or who don't accept your proposal it is easy to believe that their attitude about you and/or your offering represents the attitude of the masses. It is easy to believe that everyone thinks the way that they do.

Even worse, these people will usually do their part to perpetuate this notion when in reality they are most often speaking for only themselves.

If we aren't careful these waste of time people will awaken that spirit of doubt that lies within each of us. And, there is no bigger morale killing force than doubt.

For each of these reasons and probably many others that weren't clear to me on that day, thank goodness that I had already been taught the importance of this principle. And, thankfully I perfectly employed it on this day. As a result not one minute was wasted. I literally took the necessary actions to get to the buying decision as quickly as possible.

No matter if the answer was going to be a *"YES"* or a *"NO,"* I made sure that I got that answer early in the process of working with each prospective client.

When the person couldn't make up their mind, I simply moved on and left that indecisive person to be assisted by one of the other sales people in the department, most of whom weren't going for the bonus anyway. And, if the person did manage to buy something, be it big or small, I in no way took it as a loss to me.

In nearly all of those instances, it was like *Mr. Willie Thomas* had told me, in the time that it took the other sales person to get that one *"Yes"* I had sold far more than just that one person.

In the end, I met the challenge and achieved my goal of getting the $1,000 bonus and the sales people who spent their time on the time draining and potentially time wasting clients, even when they bought something, fell way short.

Not wasting time is a key element of FAITH (APPLIED)

In the aftermath of July 30th, 1995, the *Creator* showed me how following this same advice when it came to *FAITH (APPLIED)* was a key element to the success that I could ultimately achieve.

To be specific, he showed me how not allowing people to waste my time positioned me in a manner that allowed the universe to unfold its miracle-making power before me.

While on the contrary, he showed me how allowing people to waste our time tainted our attitudes and robbed us of the momentum that we all need to achieve success in a faith project.

And, just like it used to be for me before *Mr. Thomas* set my thinking straight on the subject, the *Creator* showed me how we tolerate all of this bad behavior from people who never have any intention of helping or supporting us in our faith projects.

Just like in my old professional endeavors, the reasons why we tolerate this behavior are many. But no matter how rightful these excuses that we tell ourselves may seem to be in the moment, they really don't matter.

The fact is this time waste still robs us of the power of *FAITH (APPLIED)*, and in turn, it still keeps us from experiencing the miracle-making power of this universe.

There have been few gifts greater than the wisdom that the **Creator** brought to me through the lesson *Mr. Thomas* shared with me.

In the aftermath of getting this timely advice, I not only went on to become one of the top salespeople in the company that we worked at, but I also carried that distinction to every other company within that industry that I worked at after that time.

On the one hand, my newfound success meant increased earnings, recognition and increased opportunities for career advancement – all things that most of us enjoy and strive for. Yet, on the other hand, this newfound success came with one big problem.

Once on this more successful side of life, I had to endure people who began to consider me rude and pushy because of my insistence that they either give me the help and support that I was seeking in a reasonable amount of time or allow me to move on to someone who would.

One of the things that I learned from *Mr. Thomas* was that our endeavoring to not waste time means that you and I must always be closing. Said differently, you and I must get in the habit of always asking for what we want or need from the people that we approach for help quickly.

How else would you know who is wasting your time and who is not if you don't make it a habit to bring every request for help to a close as rapidly and straight forwardly as possible?

We have just spent a great deal of time on the subject of **Asking**, but let us consider the matter from still another angle. I know that a problem that many of us can have with not getting the help and support that we need is that we are uncomfortable with the notion of asking for that help or support in plain language.

We can beat around the bush forever and ever without just asking for what we came to get. I have found this to be especially true in our faith endeavors.

Most of how and why we waste time with people who have no intention of helping us is because we never move to bring the process of asking to a swift close, thereby giving us a frame from which to judge whether or not we are moving towards our desired ends or just wasting our time.

Thus, developing the habit of being a *"Closer"* and always looking to get to the point of your *Asking* is a big key to limiting time waste.

From that position, you will be able to better appreciate one of the biggest truths that *Mr Thomas'* advice ultimately taught me,

> *"What one person won't do, another person will. What one person won't buy, another person will. Where one person won't help and support you, another person will. Where one person won't give, another person will."*

You have to have the awareness that *"what you seek is out there,"* and you must have the absolute determination to *"keep moving until you get it."*

I believe that when you get this truth down inside of you, you will never allow people to waste your time because knowing that there are plenty of people who will help and support you will literally keep you moving and seeking until you find them.

The DNA of Time Wasters

It is almost funny what I began to see once I put this advice into practice. In the retail environment where I worked back then, I began to notice a pattern or a standard mode of operation that all of the *Time Wasters* that visited our store possessed. This pattern also exist in the realm of *FAITH*.

As I learned to call it, there was a *DNA of Time Wasters* – a set of basic traits that these people tended to have in common. Just recognizing their **DNA** made all of the difference in the world when it came to guarding against these individuals wasting my time. While not recognizing these traits often left you vulnerable to the failure inducing tactics of these goal stoppers.

In the old retail setting and a *FAITH* project, there is one group that is known as,

170

The Videophiles and Audiophiles (The Enthusiast)

These were people who loved everything about the Video and Audio equipment that we sold. They knew everything about it. They loved to play with it, read about it and talk about it. They loved everything but buying it.

It is safe to say that there are these types of people in almost every aspect of life, even in a faith project. They are often easily identified as, *"the people who love to talk the talk, but who never do anything to walk the walk."*

In that old retail world, if you even came close to getting these folks to help you or support your cause it would only come after you had spent countless hours talking the talk with them. In the realm of *FAITH*, they talk the talk of *FAITH*, but never lend any real support.

There is a way to deal with them respectfully without wasting your time. But if you failed to identify that technique, it would be very easy for this type of *Time Waster* to doom you to failure and keep you from achieving the success that you seek. And, surely the same would hold true if you fell victim to one of these people while you were in pursuit of success in a faith project.

There was another group of *time wasters* that I called,

The Nice People

These were the people who were too *"Nice"* to use the word *"NO"* when they were dealing with you. There were many reasons why these people couldn't bring themselves to just say *"NO."* At times those reasons were about not being mean or hurting your feelings. At other times, those reasons could have been more about them not dealing in the reality of their situation and the real world conditions that kept them from helping you.

Perhaps they didn't have the money or the means to answer the request that you put before them and they couldn't bring themselves to admit that fact to themselves, much less to you.

So instead of saying *"NO"*, they just strung you along and jerked you around without end – they never said *"NO"* and yet they never said *"Yes"* either. They may have even interacted with you multiple times, each time taking up your valuable time, but still at the end of each visit they didn't move forward with your pleas for support.

Again, I have seen these same people over the years in my faith endeavors as well. In fact, it goes without saying that each of us will encounter people like this in our faith projects, i.e., people who won't say *"NO"* to our request for help and support, but who won't give us the help and support that we are seeking either.

In trying to get what we need from these people we can be left spinning our wheels and never get what we need to see the power of *FAITH (APPLIED)* deliver for us.

The next group of *time wasters* that I encountered back then was the group that I called the,

The Procrastinators

These were the people who were experts at putting off the decision of whether or not to grant your request for help, and for that matter, putting you off forever if they could. They would say things like,

"I would like to help you. But let me think about it for a few days before I give you an answer." Or, "I think I can help you, but I don't like to make quick decisions. Let me sleep on it and get back to you in a few days."

The only problem is that that day seems to never come no matter how much time you give them or put into trying to convince them to support you.

Because we buy into the lip service that these people pay for wanting to help and support us, we often waste more than a little bit of time trying to get the phantom results that they waive in front of us. As these would be supporters drag you into their cycle of *Procrastination*, your goal gets further and further out of sight.

Again, this can be especially true in your faith projects if you find yourself relying upon these types of folks to help you overcome a challenge that is before you or to achieve a goal that you have set out before yourself. I can even remember a time when I was working in a certain community where this problem was all too real for me.

The day eventually came when I realized that the people that I was dealing with were so flaky in their dealings with me, that in turn, they made me look flaky in my dealings with the people in my life.

As they drug their feet and dropped the ball on the things that I was trying to do with them, I was often forced to put off and cancel the things that I was trying to do with the people in my own life. It ultimately made me look like I too was a huge foot dragger. In the end, I watched their broken promises to me, become my broken promises to others.

Needless to say, when this truth became clear to me, I stopped wasting my time with this bunch and put an end to this madness by moving my business to a whole new community and working with a new set of people – ones who would keep their word with me, so I could keep my word with others.

Finally, in that old retail world, there was one more type of *Time Waster* that I found to be all too common. Those people were the ones that I called,

The Non-Qualified People

On one side of the coin, these were the people who didn't qualify to help me but couldn't bring themselves to just tell me so. In so much as they couldn't bring themselves to admit to me that they just didn't qualify to help me, these folks became major *Time Wasters* for me.

On the flipside of those people who didn't qualify to help and would waste my time were the people who don't have the ability or the authority to help me, for whatever the reason may have been.

Just as in the previous case, the problem arose when these people couldn't or wouldn't bring themselves to just be honest and tell me that I would be wasting my time to expect help from them.

In my experience, I have seen a ton of precious time go down the drain as a result of getting stuck working with a person who has one or both of these issues. And, without a doubt this can be a major problem in any faith endeavor just as much as it can give you a challenge in your everyday personal and professional life.

Learning to determine quickly whether or not someone is qualified to actually help or support you is a critical skill to have if you are serious about achieving success through the power of *FAITH (APPLIED)*.

Again, if you have had any experience in an environment like my old retail or even my old professional sales environments, you could probably add some other members to the cast of characters listed here.

The bottom-line is that I knew that I couldn't get stuck dealing with these people if it meant that I was being hindered from achieving my goal. And, that is what this principle is really all about.

It also might be worthwhile for me to point out that there likely is a unique cast of characters that go along with every faith project or situation. I would imagine that there is probably a unique cast for your church group and another unique cast that exist within your friendship and family circles.

But ultimately, the dynamics are always the same and dealing with a *Time Waster* will have the same effect on you and your quest to achieve your goal no matter what the specific reason is for why or how they are wasting your time. Ultimately, they will prevent you from finding the true help and support, and ultimately, the success that you seek.

I also feel the need to point out that there are times when some of the tactics of these people are understandable and when they might even mean well, at least for themselves, or at least they don't really mean you any harm. But still as it relates to you achieving your own goals, you simply don't have the time to waste. So don't allow this to happen.

As I have already alluded to, part of the problem with dealing with these types of people is that they can warp your perspective on dealing with people in general.

As I said earlier, we each have to be conscious of how we are being affected when dealing with people who are not interested in being part of the solution that we seek.

It's also worth noting here again that some of the people who can't or won't help or support you can often have a tendency of trying to make you think that no one else will help and support you.

If left unchecked, these people will try to persuade you to believe that no one will work with you. And, they will totally burn you out and make your head bad for other people.

In the end, they will sour you on working with other people who may be more than willing to work with you or help you. In this way they are worse than simple **Time Wasters**.

All this and they are not giving you what you need or want to win. Obviously the same can be true in your faith projects. For all of these reasons, accept now that no true professional would ever go for people wasting their time. That is what *Mr. Thomas* got me to see.

He made me see that I was being less than a professional by standing for this behavior. It bears repeating here that you have to face the fact that you don't get everybody.

Out of that truth, you must learn to move on graciously whenever you began to notice that your time is being wasted. You don't have to burn bridges as you step off, as you never know when or if someone that is wasting your time today will come around tomorrow.

But the fact is that sometimes you just need to keep at it with new and fresh people. Doing this will help you to stay fresh not only in your person and spirit, but it will also keep you fresh in and for your offering – as talking to the same hard-headed people can tend to put a sour or stale tone, even a pleading tone in your communications.

Before long, without you realizing it, you will find yourself approaching everyone in this tone, including people who you are approaching for help or who are hearing you for the first time.

In this tone, you run the risk of turning these new people off or being short with them or misjudging their interest in helping you.

Knowing the difference between a Suspect and a Prospect protects against time waste

When I was first being trained as a sales professional, I learned that part of the challenge that we can have with discerning where to place our time in pursuit of gaining the things that we need to succeed in our faith projects is in our not knowing the difference between a suspect and a prospect.

This is another one of those lessons that took my career to a whole other level because it taught me how to properly grade the would-be clients that I worked with.

To say it simply, before learning this lesson, I thought that everyone that I approached was a prospective client or customer. I thought that if a person had a need or a use for what I was offering that that automatically meant that they would work with me.

In fact, I thought that they should work with me, I felt that they were all but compelled by their need to do whatever I was asking them to do.

That is a lot like you or I can see our family and friends when we are asking for their help with our faith projects. We can tend to think that there is some bond that compels them to help us.

But the reality is that my thoughts and views were nowhere near true. These people were not at all required to work with me. Much like your loved ones are nowhere near obligated to help you.

From the very outset of the matter, these people were only suspects, i.e., people who were possibly willing to work with me based upon the need that I had observed.

I eventually learned from a seasoned sales manager that a suspect (a person) only becomes a genuine prospect when that person acknowledges the need and willingness to work with you for themselves. Until then, they are only a suspect.

On the professional front, learning this lesson cleared up a lot of confusion for me and got me out of the business of wasting my time trying to cram things down people's throats that they didn't want.

In my personal life, it stopped me from wasting my time trying to get the help of people who weren't interested in giving me that help.

Once I got this lesson, I got out of the habit of expecting to gain help and support from the **suspects** that **should** help or support me. I instead learned to invest my time in pursuit of the true **prospects** that **would** help, even if they had no mandate to do so.

It was in these moments that I learned that there are many instances where your friends, or even a perfect stranger can sometimes be better allies than your family. I can tell you that a ton of time is wasted in faith projects by people who don't know the difference between a suspect and a prospect.

For sure, having the wisdom to discern the difference between people that we suspect might be willing to help us achieve our goal and the true prospects that will be willing to help is an invaluable skill to possess. This one skill in itself will spare you from the major headache of putting time into people that you never should have even talked to.

In much the same way, learning to truly differentiate the resources that we suspect might help us from the true prospective resources that are available to us will make all of the difference in the world in terms of helping us to achieve the success that we seek in our faith projects.

You simply have to learn the importance of working with the resources that are in your hand at all times – as opposed to being one of those people who are always wishing for the things or people that you don't have that you suspect might help.

While in the narrow sense this principle is about learning to move on and not waste your time with people who won't physically support your project, there is a much broader way that we'd be wise to also weigh this wisdom.

In a philosophical sense, it would also be wise for us to learn to apply this wisdom to the subject of you and I making a habit of putting people in their place or of trying to win people over to our side.

In much the same sense of what *Mr. Thomas* told me,

"In the same time that you could successfully
win one person over to your side, you could
have won five others over."

Sure there are times when we may want to put forth the extra effort to win key people over to our cause, but even then, be careful not to sink too much into this task – as even in those cases you could win over multiple people in the same time that it took you to get that one key person to come around.

I do understand the notion that the key person might bring more to the table than the five people combined. But just the same the key person might do nothing with all that they bring to the table while the five lessor people wind up producing actual measureable results. This is where it is great to remember that,

> *"It is better to pursue the lowly that will help*
> *and support you than it is to pursue the*
> *mighty and promising who will not."*

In this way the lowly 5 are better than the key 1 everyday of the week. And, don't be one of those people who will forget about the lowly five the day that the key 1 appears to come around. I have seen many people make this fatal mistake and wind up with no one supporting them in the end.

In their effort to connect with the key 1, these people make the mistake of disrespecting the contributions of the lowly 5, ultimately chasing them off. Only to find out that the key 1 was never sincere and certainly wasn't willing to help and support in the way that the lowly 5 once did.

To avoid this fatal mistake, remember these words of wisdom from our own *Dr. Phil McGraw,*

> *"Remember to dance with the person who brought you."*

As a general rule, always go with the people who got you to where you are. Never put anyone above that crew – especially those who haven't delivered the way they have. You can never go wrong with this discipline.

Wasting your time can be a matter of life or death

In this principle we have been talking about the importance of learning to *never waste time on people who don't help you* in your quest to meet a challenge that may be confronting you or those who don't support you in your push to achieve a highly coveted goal that you may have.

In the broader sense, I have been talking throughout this work about how these principles have played a big role in my healing and restoration from cancer. And, I can tell you with absolute certainty that I never would have been able to receive this miracle from the *Creator* had I not known the value of *not wasting my time on the people who didn't get behind my goal of beating this very serious disease.*

Given that I just went through this very real situation, I can tell you firsthand that *wasting your time can be a matter of life and death,* literally.

As much as my story turned out positive, I just had a longtime friend of mines, *Mr. Earnest Peacock III* go through the exact same situation, only tragically, his story played out in stark contrast to my own. In this gentleman's case, his life was unfortunately cut short, as he lost his battle with cancer.

I believe he lost his battle in large part because he didn't understand the principles of *FAITH (APPLIED),* chief among them, the importance of *not wasting his time with anyone who wasn't giving him what he needed to confront the challenge that was before him.*

From the time that I got dispatched into his situation to try and aid him in his push to find healing, I noticed that my friend was literally surrounded by people who were not there to play a role in his recovery and restoration from a very serious cancer. And, I mean he was surrounded by these people.

From the medical professionals who were treating him, to his girlfriend/caregiver, to his family, it seemed that all of these people were preoccupied with everything other than him getting well. And as the battle for his life progressed, this reality only became more and more evident.

For starters, there were the doctors and nurses treating him. These so-called professionals took a very unaggressive approach to healing my friend. They wouldn't see him for months at a time and when they finally did see him, they made no effort to explain the protocols that they were using to treat the cancer that had attacked his body.

As a matter of fact, it could almost be said that they kept him in the dark about the disease that he was battling altogether and did little to give him the confidence that they were fighting to save his life.

From the very first time that I was made aware of these facts, I knew that he needed to seek other doctors, and not just for the customary second opinion, but to find some professionals that would do everything within their power to restore him to health.

At the least, he needed to find some true professionals to give him the sense of comfort that comes from knowing that some capable person is on the case and has your back.

Sadly, he tolerated this behavior as if he believed he had no right to speak up and request doctors that would do their job and put both his physical and emotional well-being ahead of all other concerns.

Contrast that with my case. I have a medical team that has been a true *God* send. Unlike my friend's situation, this group of doctors and their support staff are totally consumed with the healing and restoration of all of their patients. These folks are so committed that they leave their practice open 7 days a week, all year around.

By contrast, I have had to beat my doctor off at times, as he's been extremely thorough and proactive about providing me with both the procedures and medicines that were needed to save my life.

These folks have even gone so far as to make me consider the areas of my private and professional life that stood to impact the lifesaving work that they were trying to do.

They counseled and assisted me in finding the help and support that I needed in these areas to prevent a mistake that could have ultimately cost me my life.

However, this treatment is a far cry from the way things were shaping up when I first got to the hospital. There my main doctor tried to treat me in the same manner that my friend's doctor treated him.

This behavior was easily noticeable and once I became aware of it, I firmly cut this so-called doctor off. I know now that I couldn't have been more right in this action.

I recently learned that this doctor had quickly given me up for dead and even tried to ship me to a hospice prematurely to do my dying. This was tried in spite of the fact that I had just came into his care and nothing had yet been done to even try to fight the disease that I had.

Instead of giving it some time to see how I would respond to a treatment plan, this so-called doctor just made a judgment call, and this he did without even giving me a chance to weigh in or to fight for my life.

Thank *God* I had the good sense to know not to waste time with this joker. Thank *God* that I knew that when you are using the power of *FAITH (APPLIED)* to fight for a cause or a goal you are not running a popularity contest. Neither are you there to get along with anyone who is not fighting for the same thing that you are fighting for.

Thank *God* that unlike my friend I knew that when it comes to using the power of *FAITH (APPLIED)* you aren't supposed to be a respecter of people's titles or credentials. No matter who the person is, if they aren't there to support you in what you are seeking, you have to *avoid wasting your time with them*, period.

It might also be worth noting that I dealt the same blow to every other medical professional who entered my environment in a similar or wrong spirit.

We even did the same thing for my wife. She was having some minor but potentially serious health concerns and she was being confronted with doctors who were bouncing her around without getting to the bottom of the matter. Once I grew tired of this farce I guided her on how to correct the situation by getting access to the same doctor that had been so wonderfully assisting me.

In her case, that meant literally changing her health insurance designations. But the end result was that she now has the same great doctor and her health matter has been resolved favorably. It is because of experiences like this one that I know,

> *"You don't have to waste time with any would-be*
> *medical professional that isn't helping you to*
> *achieve your health and wellness goals."*

If only my friend had known that he had the right and perhaps the responsibility to do the same thing that I did to get rid of these uncaring doctors as he fought his health battle.

Next there was his lady friend and caregiver. From the first time that I met this lady, I knew that she wasn't in the right spirit – I knew her focus was in all the wrong places.

Call it a spiritual read perhaps, but even though this was the first time I'd ever met her, something told me that she was more interested in what she might gain upon my friend's passing than what kind of life they could enjoy together if he lived.

Granted, I didn't have any form of a relationship with this lady prior to this moment with which I could contrast the behavior that I was seeing. But in dealing with her for the small amount of time that we had prior to my friend's passing, the story of how she handled his will preparation was an incident that perfectly fueled my suspicions.

By the time that I learned that he was ill and arrived on the scene, my friend was already in the process of trying to prepare his will. From what I would come to understand, he had been trying to get the paperwork completed and in the mail to his attorneys for some months.

This was a task that required him to not only complete a lengthy questionnaire, but to also pull the records on all his most valuable possessions to get accurate information on their worth.

Given the symptoms of his disease and the side effects of the treatments that he had to endure and the pain medication that he was on, it was clear for all to see that he was in desperate need of someone to help him pull everything together.

It stood to reason that a person who was supposed to be his caregiver, someone who would be charged with caring for his daily needs should be the most logical person to assist him in this task.

Given that this lady was not only his caregiver, but was also supposedly the lady in his life, I thought it a bit strange to find out that she wasn't providing him with the help that he needed. It wasn't long before I found out that he found it a bit discomforting that she wouldn't assist him with this important task as well.

Despite the appearance of impropriety and being cunning, she never did make any effort to help get the will completed. It is like she was oblivious to how this looked to others. I had the strong sense that she was stalling or simply trying to let the clock run out on my friend's life without the will being prepared.

After a few more months of this task going unattended to, my own wife/caregiver took on the added task of helping our friend handle the matter. Once this woman became aware of this development, a whole new person appeared. All of the sudden, the uninterested caregiver and lady friend became more than interested in the matter of the will.

All of the sudden, she had professionals that were capable of working on the will that she wanted to bring into the fold. All of the sudden, she wanted to dig out the needed paperwork and keep track of the will paperwork.

All of the sudden, she became the sweet voiced, caring person that wanted to be involved in all aspects of getting the will completed. And, all of the sudden, the person who was almost never there when we were there was there to screen both his visits and his calls.

As much as she tried to say that this was just about *not wasting his time on the people who were not helping him in his healing*, this was clearly more about her trying to gain insight, input and ultimately control over the process of the will being created.

In spite of her best efforts, once we got involved she never did gain what she was seeking with respect to the preparation of the will, and the day came when she realized that she wasn't going to get anywhere with us now at the helm of the will project.

In her desperation, she made a move that all of my professional training told me was as wrong and deceitful as the ocean is deep.

To make that long story short, once the required documents were rounded up and it was time for my friend to sign the will questionnaire, at just that physical moment, this lady stepped in to give him a high dose of pain medication that was neither requested by him, nor needed at that moment.

The obvious purpose of which was to render him legally incapable of giving his consent at that moment – as by law, one must be in their right state of mind, not impaired by drugs or alcohol at the time of any signing of a legal document.

I am sure that if the time would have arisen where she wanted to object to what was in this will she would have used his drug induced impairment as a means to object to the validity of this will. Of course, she would have left out the fact that she created this impairment by way of the timing that she used to administer these drugs.

In the aftermath of his untimely death, the full and true colors of this shady woman finally came to light and more than confirmed all the things that I had speculated to be perfectly true.

When all was said and done, although all of the effort that she put into trying to hold up the will being prepared was ultimately unsuccessful, she did manage to block the mailing from his attorney and his final approval of the will.

In this action, she was able to make the will that we had worked so hard to get done, invalid. And, once she accomplished this feat, she then moved to try and validate another will that gave her far more from his estate than he had wished to leave to her.

In addition, this new will made her the executor of his estate and allowed her to begin playing all sorts of games and to make serious attempts to withhold his property from its rightful heirs – all of this totally against what she and I knew to be his strongly expressed wishes.

Lastly there was the behavior of his family, behavior which was scarcely any better. It appeared that these people too were more concerned about what was in the will and what was being left for them than whether or not my friend was headed towards recovery.

To my amazement, whenever these people would arrive in town, I would get a phone call. But these calls were not about the state of my friend's health. Instead these calls were regarding the state and whereabouts of the will.

In fact, in all of the months that I was engaged in trying to help my friend find his path to healing and recovery, I have never had a conversation with any of his family members about this subject. But I did get several inquiries about his will.

These calls even became more frequent as he got sicker and moved nearer to his passing. It seemed that whenever one of his family members arrived in town, the first thing that they did was reach out to me or my wife to try to ascertain what we knew about the will.

I had many occasions where I was so offended by this unbelievable preoccupation with the will that I had to get these people off of my phone before I lost it totally. I was blown away by the fact that if they had their way, these people would have seen this will before my friend even passed.

I worried that if they realized that the will wasn't favorable to them they might in turn dispense care to their own loved one accordingly. I questioned that if they knew they weren't getting anything in the will, would they even give him care at all?

If they did, would that care be substandard? After all, it is not very common for heirs and potential heirs to know what they would inherit before the death of the person that they would be receiving their inheritance from.

Once my friend had reached his final days and was moved to a hospice, I was told that as he lay in what was ultimately to become his death bed, these uncaring people were still perfectly preoccupied with getting their hands on the will to determine what they were in line to receive upon his passing.

From all observation, at no time did any of these individuals give any indication that they were hoping that their blood relative would recover from his affliction. At no time did any of them show any sadness or anguish at the thought of their brother or uncle or cousin passing from this earth after only 54 years living.

To a person, all that they seemed to be concerned with was what they'd receive at the moment that this tragic event took place. With these kinds of attitudes and spirits surrounding you in the form of your own family, I would imagine that it is pretty hard to even believe that your healing and restoration from a serious disease is possible.

Again, by contrast, I was blessed with some real angels who stepped up and did whatever they could to keep me free of the cares of life and focused on the one thing that mattered most in that moment, my healing and restoration from cancer.

Not only did I have a caring wife, I had two great sons who stepped up and totally made my environment all about my healing. My sons alone stepped up in ways that I would have never expected nor asked them to.

They literally became the true men of the house in every imaginable way. The older one stepped up to give his mom both financial and moral support. The younger one stepped up to run the house, literally cooking and cleaning, in turn freeing my wife to be there fully for me to bring a sense of normalcy to my eight (8) week hospital stay.

Once I came home, each one of them continued to do whatever they could to make my life easy and give me the freedom of mind to focus on my recovery.

They were joined by my younger brother who traveled from another state to help me around the house with cleaning and meal preparation – and to keep me company and bring a link to the old world that would keep me in high spirits at this potentially dark time.

And, I have not begun to mention all of the friends, colleagues and clients of mines who showed genuine caring and concern for me during this trying time.

I will forever be indebted to each of these people and will more than return the same favor should they ever find themselves in a similar time of need.

I am not sure if my friend's own views about his illness and the prospects of his recovery, in addition to his willingness to tolerate this kind of behavior played a role in why he was surrounded by this cast of characters.

I do know that my own views were the exact opposite of his and I was totally unwilling to put up with anyone that wasn't there to play a part in my beating cancer.

It bears restating that every one of the medical professionals that I encountered was not in the right spirit or supportive of my healing. And, I also might as well state for the record that everyone in my personal life wasn't perfectly supportive of my healing.

I had family members who didn't seem at all concerned with my health situation. These were the people who didn't call or come visit me. Or, perhaps they came by once and never visited again.

I even noticed that there were some people who seemed to almost be disappointed as I recovered and got better – as if they were pulling for me to lose my battle with the disease that had attacked me. At the end of the day, these were the people that I chose not to *waste my time on because they were not there to help me get to my goal.*

These were the people that I paid no attention to and ultimately dismissed from my life, choosing rather to engross myself in the love, help and support of those who were clearly pulling for my success.

In the end, my friend is unfortunately gone and I am still here. I believe that the starting point of why can be found in the two very different attitudes that we had about battling illness and the views that we each held about the prospects of our recovery. I am also convinced that a large part of why is because I didn't tolerate any of the behavior and the attitudes that he had to endure in my environment.

In the end, he was surrounded by medical professionals, as well as people in his private life whose behavior ranged from callousness to outright on the take. While by contrast, I only allowed caring doctors and nurses to be in my midst at this critical time.

In my private life I only allowed loving friends, family members, colleagues and clients who were all pulling for me to overcome the challenge that was before me to be in my midst while I was engaged in this fight for life.

It's hard for me not to believe that it was these two very different healing environments that made the difference between life in my case and death in the case of my friend.

In the end, my not wasting time on the people who weren't willing to help and support me and my friend's wasting time on the people who weren't there to help and support him were literally the difference between my life and his death. I know those may seem like bold or harsh words. But nonetheless, they are words that I believe to be true.

I know that our *Creator* can't do anything for us that we don't first choose for ourselves. Refusing to waste time on people who don't help and support us and keeping it moving is a critical part of choosing a path where the *Creator* can deliver a miracle like healing us from serious disease – just as sure as it is a vital part of the successful use of *FAITH (APPLIED)*.

Don't waste time trying to win with haters, doubters or detractors

To take it from another angle, it is of equal importance that you don't waste your time trying to correct people or win them over to your side.

Realize that you have nothing to prove to anyone that doesn't help you or support you along your faith journey. With that spirit in mind, know that you should never ever waste your time trying to show up your haters, doubters or detractors.

Additionally, don't allow yourself to become mentally or emotionally engaged in any childish back and forth with those people near to you who fall into this category, especially with those who tend to be competitive with you.

Getting caught up in trying to show up people from any one of these groups of non-supporters is usually a no win proposition for you and, more often than not, a big source of time waste. So just don't do it.

I might also warn you to keep an eye out for the people in or near to your inner circle who can easily fall into this role if you are not watching. Even I have had several instances where I was urged by my foolish mate to get along with people that I should not have been wasting my time with.

There were incidents where I was even urged to be like people who were headed the wrong way – people who were not living by faith and who were trying to get me off of the path that the ***Creator*** placed me on.

Time would ultimately go on to reveal that I was right to not waste my time with these people. Time also revealed that following them would have even had a negative impact on the same mate that was foolishly urging me to deal with them.

Thankfully for me, I had already learned not to waste time on this foolishness or with waste of time people in general. Again I must say that thankfully, I knew that striving to overcome a challenge or to achieve my goals through the might of ***FAITH (APPLIED)*** is not a popularity contest.

In the same way, you must now and forever realize these truths. It's not about getting along with, or blending in with, being like or being liked by anyone that is not willing to help and support you in your quest to see your faith project through.

If I didn't know this it could have cost me my life, like it did my friend *Earnest Peacock III*. Don't waste your time trying to link up with anyone who doesn't help or support you and your goal.

Always remember that time waste is time waste and all of it is detrimental to the successful use of ***FAITH (APPLIED)***. This is really something that you have to get down in your heart and soul. Getting this inside of you means getting the truth that it's not about worrying about what you look like as you step away from a time waster.

One of the things that *Mr. Willie Thomas* demonstrated to me from the first day that he taught me the truth that I should ***stop letting people waste my time*** was that some people will be offended when you stop allowing them to control your time and attention.

While you should always strive to step away in a good natured manner, there may be times when someone will just take offense to the fact that you have stepped off. It's in these kinds of situations that you can't worry about how you are viewed.

Instead of allowing yourself to worry about what impact your stepping away is having on the time waster that you just left, you must allow the urgency and/or the importance of your faith project to dictate that you keep it moving so that you can find the person or people who will help and support you.

The fact is that time is of the essence and the more time you spend on time wasters, the less time you have to seek out and work with those who will help and support you.

Stay mindful of this truth and use it to remind yourself to work from the habit of staying in motion until you find the help and support and get the results that you need or want to achieve success in your faith endeavors.

As a rule of thumb, don't stop between people or as you move from person to person, or pitch to pitch. Instead just keep moving from help request to help request, and from result to result and only allow yourself to recognize when you are receiving the results that you are looking for.

Use this strategy to build a base of options and to build momentum in seeking the help and resources that are the byproducts of *FAITH (APPLIED)*.

Don't waste any more time on a "MAYBE" than you would on a "NO"

Lastly, realize that as much as we love the *"YES's"* and hate the *"NO's"*, these aren't the only responses that we have to keep an eye on, nor are they the ones that we have to watch out for the most.

The fact is that there is one response that most of us never think twice about receiving, that most of us actually record as a positive and all the while it's killing any chance that we might have of seeing the real power of *FAITH (APPLIED)*.

In truth, it is not the *"NO's"* that are our biggest enemy. Instead it is the *"MAYBE'S"* that we get to our request for help and support that we should be the most worried about. These are the responses that often do us the most harm.

Perhaps this is an angle of this principle that I should have spent more time covering, but let me just say here that learning how to deal with *"MAYBE"* can easily be more important than learning how to deal with *"NO."*

I've seen it a thousand times in both my faith walk and in my professional journey, people who lose their way because they don't know how to properly address the *"MAYBE"* that they encounter as they ask someone to help and support them; or as they ask a prospective client to do business with them.

No matter how polite, friendly and promising a *"MAYBE"* sounds, it does nothing to move you closer to securing the help and support that you need to succeed. Therefore, you must learn to either convert a *"MAYBE"* into a fast and firm *"YES"* or treat it just like you would a *"NO."*

In the spirit of this principle, you must not waste time with this person no more than you should waste time with a person who has told you *"NO."*

You must realize that you could likely get the same five people to tell you *"YES"* in the time that you are waiting for this person to move from *"MAYBE"* as you could trying to convert a person that is telling you *"NO."*

No matter how sharp the person is that is telling you *"MAYBE,"* they are as much a waste of time and a hindrance to *FAITH (APPLIED)* as the person that flat out tells you that they won't help you.

In my business, I see this all the time – people who fail in their business goals while they sit around waiting for some sharp person to come around to their proposition. They do this while never seeing the truth that there are a ton of other people that they could approach who would say *"YES"* to that same proposition right now. Don't you do it.

Don't you allow yourself to lose to that challenge or fail to achieve your goal behind the *"MAYBE's."* Treat them just like you would a *"NO"* and always remember that in the same time that it takes you to convert one of them, you could have gotten five others to say *"YES."*

To get this principle flowing in your life and your faith projects right now, declare out loud to the universe,

> *"I don't waste time on people and situations*
> *that don't help me get my goal!"*

Make a commitment to yourself that while you may have made this mistake in the past, you never will again. This entire principle really could have been a side "B" to the fifth principle. But just like with a few of the *Truths of Asking*, it is so important that it deserved a thorough explanation.

It has long been clear to me that you have to make a commitment to yourself to *never waste time on people and situations that don't help you get your goal.*

To not make this commitment, to not make it part of your guiding principles when you find yourself confronted by a challenging circumstance, or in the pursuit of a coveted goal is to leave yourself at the mercy of the people who you ask for the help you need to meet that challenge or achieve your goal.

Ultimately meaning that to not get this principle would be to limit yourself to the whims of the *haters, doubters and detractors* – people who would just as soon see you fall short of achieving the goal that you have been fighting so hard to make come true. That's why getting this principle is so vital to the success of *FAITH (APPLIED).* I believe that it's why the *Creator* gave it to me as a separate principle.

I will trust that you now can clearly see why you must *never waste time on people and situations that don't help you get your goal* and the role that having this discipline plays in unleashing the power of *FAITH (APPLIED)* into your life and faith projects. Therefore, let us now look at the seventh step in activating the miracle-making power of the universe:

Delay Judgment

While keeping your mind fixed on your challenge and goal intensely throughout the day or the days that are allotted for it's achievement, don't let the clock, the calendar, your own doubtful thoughts or the doubts and/or words of others discourage you and/or make you judge or doubt whether you will get to your goal. Don't let the judgment of others become your own judgment. Also, don't let the fact that things don't seem to be moving in your favor, i.e., prospective helpers canceling meetings, deals not closing, money not coming in when you thought it would, a slow answer to a request for help or an application you have submitted cause you to doubt that you will get your goal. Exercise patience here. At this moment, just take a deep breath, relax, clear your mind of any negative, doubtful thoughts and restate what is done and what needs to be done. Put off thinking and/or judging beyond that and just keep moving as if things are going your way.

As the clock ticked down on July 30th, 1995, my mind was bombarded with all manner of negative and doubtful thoughts about whether I would successfully come through this challenge that I had accepted and achieve the goal that was now set out before me.

One of the strange things about life is the fact that we can be so negative on ourselves. I don't know whether this is a condition of mind that we arrive on this planet with or like the fear of hearing the word *"NO"* and being rejected, it is something that is conditioned into us. But I think that most people would agree with me when I say that the greatest form of doubt for most of us is self-doubt.

Once I had set my plan into motion on this day, once I had *accepted the challenge, set the goal, positioned myself for success, avoided the loser clique,* made it a point to *ask everyone I could to help me, avoided wasting my time with those who could not or would not help me* – once I had done all of these things, the real battle began and I found myself engaged in a struggle with the only being that had sufficient power to stop me from achieving my challenge and goal – **ME**.

On this day more than any other, it seems that with each minute that passed my mind was hit with a quit message that I had the choice of either listening to or ignoring.

Perhaps because I had never stretched myself to go for a challenge of this nature before, I can't recall a day when I was bombarded with so many negative and doubtful thoughts. It seemed like the volume of that little negative inner voice had been cranked up to full blast because for what felt like the first time I heard every thought that passed through my mind loud and clear.

The voice was trying to tell me that I should quit and forget about getting the $1,000 that management had put on the table. Maybe the voice and these messages had always been there and I just didn't hear them. Maybe because management had never given me anything to reach for there was no need for that little voice to try to discourage me.

In my everyday personal life, maybe because I normally stayed in my place of financial struggle, there was no need for that little voice to crank it up to be heard. It is almost like my pastor says,

"The negative force of this world doesn't need to come against people who aren't striving for anything positive."

Whatever it was, there was no mistaking the fact that something speaking from within me was trying to get me to just give up before I had even given myself a chance to succeed. There is also no mistaking the fact that we all can face this same negative inner voice as we strive to confront a challenge or endeavor to reach a goal that is set out before us.

It is bad enough that we can get a ton of grief from the people around us who don't have faith or who are just negative, or even from those who aren't going for their own goals or standing up to the challenges in their own lives.

As bad as that is, at least we can do something physically to put distance between ourselves and those people. It is a whole other issue, when you are the person who is doubtful or negative. It is a whole other thing when you are the one who is trying to talk you out of going for it.

Yet that is often just what we do when confronted by a challenging situation. And, the fact is that that is exactly what most of us do with the goals and dreams that we have for our lives. We talk ourselves out of stepping up and going for it.

Sure in the end we blame others around us for being the source of our frustration and doubt. And at times we may seriously be dealing with the reality of negative and doubtful people in or near to our inner circle.

Perhaps it is a mate, or a best friend, or a close relative. I have even had incidents over the years where business colleagues, bosses or leaders that I had to report to failed to see my vision or have faith in what I was trying to accomplish.

But I know from many of these incidents that it just doesn't matter what the people around us think, say or do so long as we stand where we need to stand on the matter. These moments have taught me clearly that if we can master our own negative inner voice – if we can master our own self-doubt, it really won't matter what anyone else thinks about our ability to overcome our challenges or achieve our goals.

These moments have also taught me that there is a rock solid principle that will allow you and I to master that self-doubt. Understanding the truth of this principle and putting it into practical application will give you a powerful tool to use in your battle with the real person who stands to keep you from meeting your challenge or achieving your goal –**YOU**.

Maybe you can't believe, but you can delay judgment

For some reason on that day back in July of 1995 when these principles were handed to me, I got wind of a truth that has served me well ever since.

Simply put, maybe you and I just are not capable of convincing ourselves that we can do what we have set out to do. Maybe you and I just can't get ourselves to believe that things will turn out the way that we would like them to. But I will tell you what I realized I could do on that day; I realized that I could simply *delay judgment!*

I mean that in the literal sense of the statement. I realized that I could simply delay rendering an opinion on the process that I was engaged in. I realized that I could simply put off deciding whether or not what I was doing was working.

I don't know where I found the wisdom or the stomach to do this all important step in the process of going after my challenge and goal. But I do know that it could have easily been considered one of the single most important principles of the 8 involved.

From the very start of the day, my mind was hit with the thought,

"Are you out of your mind? There is 'NO'
way that you can reach this goal!"

And as I said earlier, I was bombarded all day with this manner of negative and doubtful thoughts from within myself.

As the day went on, this negative self-talk took the form of statements like, *"Really, you think you can do in one day, what took you 29 other days to do?" There is no way to sale that amount of money at this store." "There is never enough traffic at this place to support such a challenge." "The floor is stacked with too many sales people for any of you to achieve this goal."*

Statements like these and many others that were just as deadly were continually bubbling up to the surface of my mind as I worked through the day. I don't know if they were really my thoughts or the thoughts cast off by the negative people around me, the members of the *loser clique* in my department. After all, they had been throwing out these types of thoughts and opinions from the first moment that management made the announcement that they were offering this special prize.

At the end of the day, it really didn't matter whether they were their opinions or my own thoughts. The fact was that any one of them easily packed the power within itself to cause me to give up and thus derail my efforts to claim the prize of that $1,000 bonus on that day. And, the impact of their cumulative weight as the day progressed made the matter of dealing with this negative force of thought even worse.

As the day stretched out the thoughts that filled my head took on many different forms. Just when I got the thought of going for the challenge handled, I found myself confronted with thoughts like, *"You tried your best, but now there just isn't enough going on to get you to success." "If 4 hours barely got you moving, how can you expect the 4 hours that you have left in this day to be any different?" "Why don't you just give up, there are only 2 hours left and you aren't even half way to your goal."*

And, as if these thoughts weren't enough to deal with, in the closing moments of the day, as I made a final push to hit my goal, that negative little voice also made a final push to get me to throw in the towel and accept my defeat. When the clock ticked down to the final 20 minutes of the work day, as if I was being quizzed by a higher power, two pointed questions rocked my mind:

> *"Are you ready to give up? You only have 20 minutes and you are still more than half way away from your target, do you still believe you can hit it?"*

These questions shot into my mind like a bolt of lightning and could have easily been seen as valid and justifiable. With 20 minutes left to go, I had only managed to get about half way to the goal for the day.

Meaning that in the broader context, at that moment 29 days, 7 hours and 40 minutes had gone by and I had only managed to produce three fourths of the special quota that I needed to hit to receive the $1,000 bonus.

Now with just 20 minutes left in the workday, I still needed to produce a full one fourth of the results, I still needed $4,000 in sales to suddenly materialize to succeed at this challenge.

Looking at things from that point of view, could I still believe that this goal was possible? And, if I could, what in reality could that belief be based upon? To be sure there was nothing that I could point to logically to justify believing that I could still succeed.

At a moment like this, faith is the only thing that you or I can apply to give us the power to still believe. Just as faith is the only thing that you or I can apply to give us the power to believe that we can overcome a serious challenge or conquer a potentially fatal disease. And, just like on this day, finding the power to assert that belief and apply that faith will likely come down to your ability to withstand thoughts like the ones that dogged me on July 30th, 1995.

Again, any of these thoughts, in and of themselves, packs sufficient power to end your quest to achieve success in a faith project. When grouped together, the force and weight of these thoughts would be all but unbearable for most of us.

Without the power to withstand all of that pressure, finding victory by way of faith is simply not possible. As the *Creator* showed me on that day, there is only one way to withstand the power of thoughts like these – that is to *delay judgment* on them altogether.

Breathe, relax, clear your mind, state what's done and restate what needs to be done – A God-given formula for delaying judgment

In the literal sense, this was the formula for how I managed to *delay judgment*. I don't know where the wisdom to do this came from. This was not something that I had done previous to this day. It wasn't anything that I had witnessed being done before. Instead, it just seemed to flow from within me as a natural response to all of the negative messages that were firing off in my head.

When I say that this was literally the formula, I mean it was literally what I did on this day. Whenever these kinds of thoughts occurred I would *take a deep breath, relax, clear my mind of any and all negative or doubtful thoughts and remind myself of what is done and what needed to be done.*

In this way, I put off thinking about the matter or judging it beyond this narrow view. In this state of mind I was able to just keep moving and working toward the goal as if things were working in my favor. In this way I managed to exercise a level of patience that I had never known before this day. Once I was able to look back on it, I could clearly see how this was the catalyst to my staying active long enough to successfully grab the $1,000 bonus that I so desperately needed.

Obviously I have long since realized that this was *God* given wisdom. I ultimately came to realize that my being led to use this wisdom on July 30th, 1995 was no accident. In fact, having and using it was critical to applying the power of faith and summoning the miracle-making power that I activated on that day.

Since that day I have followed this formula too many times to list and each time the end result has always been the same – success! In any of these instances, had I ever stopped to judge the matter, I would have been left no other logical choice but to see the improbability of it all.

And, had I stopped to consider the improbability of reaching this goal, I would have never taken the physical and spiritual steps necessary to awaken the aid of the supernatural force that the *Creator* puts to work on our behalf when we tap the power of *FAITH (APPLIED)*.

Luckily for me on this day, I didn't stop to think that far, and in turn, the *Creator* revealed to me a power that went on to save my life.

By learning to *breathe, relax, clear my mind of any and all negative or doubtful thoughts and remind myself of what is done and what needs to be done* in moments of doubt, I have been able to call upon that power to help me solve problems and achieve goals that could have easily been considered impossible.

Applying this powerful formula has also helped me lay to rest a true enemy of *FAITH (APPLIED)*, not to mention our peace of mind and overall health – the habit of Worry.

One of the greatest enemies of *FAITH (APPLIED)* is worry. Worry is the epitome of self-doubt. This is especially true in a challenging situation.

There is no way to successfully apply faith with a mind filled with worry. It is most often the spirit of worry that makes you and I give up before faith has had a chance to work a miracle on our behalf. For this single reason alone the state of mind that you must assume is one of certainty that faith will prevail.

While *you may not know where your results will come from* or what the answer will look like when it shows up, you still have to operate with certainty that you will receive what you are seeking if you want to see the power of *FAITH (APPLIED)* work on your behalf.

You can't operate from a spirit of worry and activate the miracle-making power of the universe at the same time. Learning to *delay judgment* will give you the antidote to worry. This is one of the most important action steps for the mind in the *FAITH (APPLIED)* philosophy.

Instead of being consumed with your challenge or with thoughts of all the things that could go wrong, you have to learn to use the power of *Delayed Judgment* to fill your mind with thoughts of the success of your project and with taking the actions that could get you there.

Instead of allowing your mind to be filled with the images of you not getting what you want, you must learn to use your mental energy to fill your mind with images of the actions that you could take to handle the challenge that is confronting you or to achieve the goal that you covet. That is the power of *Delayed Judgment*.

Strategic Silence: The power of Delayed Judgment in action

So how did I do it? First of all, I did it literally. Whenever I had a negative or doubtful thought the first thing that I did was *took a deep breath and just relaxed.* I didn't get all bent out of shape and give the thought a life.

Instead, I simply *put off answering the thought or question in the moment*. Many times, I would *cut the thought off in my mind, not allowing it to run to the end*. As in, if a thought were trying to come through that said, *"This is not going to work."* I would cut it off at, *"This is not...."*

In this way I would simply choose not to let the rest of the words fire off in my mind. In this way, I cleared my mind of any negative or doubtful thought that tried to enter my mind. Of course I knew where the thought was going. However, just not allowing it to fully materialize had a powerful effect upon keeping me positive and keeping me moving forward.

Another thing that I did was to *never dwell on a negative thought. Whether it was a partial thought or a full thought that got through, I just let it fall to the ground of my mind. I didn't pick it up and run with it. I didn't further analyze it. I didn't have an internal debate about its rightfulness or truthfulness. I just let it drop. As in, it was thought once and was not thought again.*

Another technique that I used to *delay judgment* and probably one of the most important ones was to *never verbalize any negative or doubtful thought* on that day.

One of the most powerful things that you and I can do is to give voice to the words that go through our minds – be it good or bad words. Thus while you are engaged in the process of trying to meet a challenge or go after your goal, *the worst thing that you can do is give voice to a negative or doubtful thought.*

Your project will absolutely die the minute you speak its doom. It really doesn't matter what you said or why you took the action of saying it. All bets are off the minute you say in any form or fashion,

"This is not going to work!"

On this day, I just instinctively knew not to do it. In the place of all of these negative thoughts and questions, I did something that seemed to energize me and literally draw the help, support and resources that I needed from the universe to me. That powerful action was to simply *use my words to state where I was in terms of results attained, and then, I restated aloud what results I still needed to produce.*

This too I mean in the literal sense of the statement. As in, on that day, my progress could be tracked moment to moment by way of the same computer terminals that we used to ring up the customer sales.

These terminals were in every department of the store. So at any moment that I wanted to update myself with where I was at in the process of achieving my goal, no matter where I was at in the store, there was a computer that I could log into and get a progress report on where I was at in relationship to my goal.

On this day, I instinctively knew to take full advantage of this resource. *Throughout the day, whenever I had one of those doubtful moments, instead of letting that feeling run amuck, I would go to the computer, log in and refocus my attention on where I was at, and the task still at hand. I would then verbalize this information aloud and move on to find the next potential customer for me to help. In so doing, I kept my mind and my statements focused on where I wanted to go and off of the thoughts and doubts about where I wasn't at or how the process didn't appear to be playing out, or how difficult things may have looked at a given moment, or any other form of what I didn't want.*

This is so different from how I would have normally operated at the time. Normally I would have been more inclined to take my cues from the physical data that was pouring in to me. What I was experiencing in the physical world around me would have had the greatest influence over me and my thoughts, and ultimately my words.

I would have had no inclination to, nor made any effort to control my thoughts. And, my words would have flowed with all manner of the negative thoughts that entered into my mind. The thought of not verbalizing the thoughts and feelings that I was experiencing would have never occurred to me. And, the thought to stand in faith to achieve the goal that I sought would have seemed foreign.

On the contrary, it would have felt more natural to speak all of my self-doubt and to talk myself right out of going for this goal just like the rest of my co-workers. While I didn't share their views or subscribe to a lot of their tactics, I would have followed a path of my own making that would have easily carried me to their same ends. And obviously I am not alone in these tendencies.

In fact, how much stuff do we all talk ourselves out of when we allow ourselves to get carried away with the negative thoughts that flow to our minds as we pursue our faith projects? How would things be different if we could just get ourselves to let things play out to their rightful conclusion? How different would our results be if we would learn to stay positive and give ourselves the benefit of using all of the time that we have at our disposal?

Only time will tell how things will turn out – If only we will let time take its course

When you think about it logically, it really makes sense that we should at least *delay judgment* and let time take its course as we go through the process of trying to meet a challenge or achieve a goal. After all, how can we really know how the process will work out short of seeing it through to the end?

From there even if we failed to achieve what we set out to achieve, if in seeing our project through to the end we wind up having advanced our cause, wouldn't that be a victory in itself?

Back before I was aware of these principles I tried to tell myself as much when I was engaged in some project where I seemed in over my head or where it seemed like I wouldn't be able to successfully meet the goal that I was chasing. But for some reason that truth was always hard to grasp.

Back then I had an *"All or nothing"* mindset so that *progress without success still equated to failure to me.* Even though in the vast majority of cases that was and still is far from true.

I should have realized that progress on any goal, even without full out success is a level of success. I should have realized that in spite of the fact that I may have been running a little behind, more often than not, I needed only to sustain my focus in the late going to cross the finish line to the final victory.

In this truth I should have known that when it comes to success in most areas of life,

"It is always better late than never."

If only I could have gotten myself to view things in this manner, if we could get ourselves to view things in this manner, perhaps we could get ourselves to just relax and go through the process trusting that whatever we achieve will be good for us and help us to achieve the results that we seek in the long run.

As a result of the events of that day back in July of 1995, I learned that it's that letting go, that *delaying of judgment* that will give us the power to succeed. I learned then that there is power in just going through the process with a non-judgmental mindset. I now know that this is one of the key factors in the formula that will allow you and me to activate the miracle-making power of the universe. I saw it on that day and on many other occasions since then.

Delayed judgment delivered me from a decade of financial bondage

There was a single incident in my life that will forever illustrate the power and importance of *delaying judgment* to me. This incident began when the *Los Angeles County District Attorney* erroneously labeled me a deadbeat father and placed me in their *Child Support Enforcement* program.

What started out as a simple misunderstanding turned into a full out assault on my professional and financial life that wreaked havoc on nearly every area of my personal life – from employment and finance, to housing and transportation.

When all was said and done, just surviving all of the issues brought on by this unforeseen crisis would challenge me to my core and took everything in me to overcome – faith, abilities, strengths and skills that I didn't even know I had in me.

The events that led up to this great faith challenge began innocently enough. At the time of the birth of my first child, I was a blue collar worker who had no health benefits. As such, I had to pay out of my pocket for all of the prenatal care that my wife was to receive.

While I was able to squeeze these small payments out of our tight budget, I was not aware that the time would come when the cost of bringing our child into the world would be more than my wallet could handle.

Ultimately my wife's doctor became aware of my financial situation and sat us down to offer some advice on exactly what lay ahead of us financially in having our child. He explained to us that as great as it was that I had been able to muster up the financial resources to pay for the office visits and prenatal care that my wife was going to receive throughout the pregnancy, the delivery of the child would be a whole other reality.

He made it clear that in our then financial position, we would not be able to afford the cost associated with bringing a baby into the world in the private hospital where he worked. Finally he advised my wife and me to put aside any pride that we might have been suffering with and take ourselves down to our local county office to apply for government health benefits.

I guess he knew exactly what I needed to hear because at that time in my life, I was not one to look to the government to support me in any way. Perhaps it was simply pride, but I wasn't in anyway interested in having the government be the source of my growing family's financial well-being.

As an able bodied man, I didn't want the handouts or the hassle that I perceived went along with receiving government assistance. Not to mention the fact that I had been raised to believe that this kind of aid was for those who didn't want to work for their own care and keeping.

Given these views, to say that I was reluctant to take the advice of our doctor would have been an understatement. But this was the same doctor who had delivered me 25 years earlier, as well as all my siblings and some of their kids. As such he had a lot of credibility and trust with my family and thus his advice was given serious weight and consideration.

In the end, my wife and I both took it up with the people within our families that we felt we could trust to give us proper guidance. And after receiving their input, we made the only decision that we could have made and followed the advice of our doctor. Unbeknownst to us at the time, this seemingly helpful advice set in motion a set of circumstances and consequences that would come back to harm us greatly.

Outdated knowledge turned good advice into bad advice

Once the decision was made to seek aid for the birth of our child, the task of going down and signing up for the aid was given to my wife. Following the advice of our trusted family advisors, she went out one day and came back with a package of benefits and aid that seemed to resolve the problem. And for the next few months we received all of the things that our doctor said we needed for my wife to have a healthy pregnancy and delivery.

Everyone from the doctor to our families was relieved to know that everything was in place to bring our first child into the world. And, I would even have to admit that the medical insurance was a welcomed relief to my pockets, as I no longer had to shell out the money for the monthly doctor's visits and prenatal medicines and supplements that she needed while pregnant.

But it eventually became clear that in weighing in on the advice that our doctor gave to us, much of the input that these trusted family advisors offered to us was rooted in seriously outdated information. In listening to them we were not only led to seek the aid that we needed under the wrong pretense, we were also led to accept benefits and aid that we had no real desire or need for.

In the end, as a result of acting on this bad advice, we committed what time would ultimately reveal to be our first fatal error, one that would ultimately cause me to be listed as a single, non-custodial parent who wasn't paying for the care and keep of his child. And, while we didn't see or feel the effects of this error right away, the fact was that a silent time bomb was placed in the background of our lives, one that would ultimately blow up in our finances when we least expected it.

As much as this aid served an important purpose, my feelings about receiving it were still the same and no sooner than our son was born healthy, I was all too eager to have us walk away from these benefits without looking back.

In leaving these benefits behind and once again relying on the income that I brought in as the sole means of taking care of our little family, we thought the matter was closed. But time would ultimately reveal that in dropping these benefits in the way that we did, we had actually committed a final fatal error, the one that actually started the time bomb ticking.

Just when things were getting good, it all turned bad

Fast forward to 1995. Nearly five years had passed since the time when our doctor advised us to seek the health benefits needed to bring our son in the world, and with the passing of this time, our finances and lifestyle had experienced a dramatic improvement. At the urging of the spirit of **God**, I had sought out and landed a dream job in professional sales that finally allowed me to provide for my family in the style that I desired.

After years of working for local companies in dead-end, low paying jobs, I had finally landed in a career type position with a big multinational corporation. As a result, I was finally making the type of money that would enable me to push past the financial struggles that I had been confronted with in my early years as a husband and father.

By now, with the birth of our second son, our little family had grown to four and for the first time we were no longer living paycheck to paycheck. I was making so much money at this time that I almost never even had to pick up my checks on payday. In fact, we no longer had to concern ourselves with the basic money worries that used to rule our lives.

By this time we were used to living off of my commission checks and I usually picked up my salary checks whenever I got around to it. We were doing so well that on any given day there were a couple of these checks in my desk at work and a few thousand dollars in cash on top of the refrigerator at home. All of this newfound extra money just lay there until we had a need for it, which we never did.

In addition to the success that I was having in my new career, I was also able to use the training and contacts that I was receiving in this position to successfully start up a side business selling insurance and investments. All of this income was finally making for a nice lifestyle for my family and they were perfectly enjoying the feeling of peace and security that this new financial abundance brought.

My wife and my kids were getting just about anything that they wanted. Given the struggles and lack that they were once forced to endure, when they asked for something the word *"NO"* seldom came out of my mouth.

In terms of our residence, I had chosen to settle my family down in *Marina Del Rey*, a great beach community in *Southern California*. My wife and sons loved the neighborhood and quickly developed a ton of great friendships there.

This neighborhood offered everything that we could have ever wanted in a community – from shopping and entertainment, to great schools and great neighbors. It was peaceful and quiet, safe and clean. It was truly a great place to live – the kind of place that I had always dreamed of living.

As a teenager I even used to drive 40 or 50 miles roundtrip from where I lived to hang out in this area. It was a place that I used to take my wife on dates to impress her. Now we lived there with our family.

Considering where we had come from and all that we had been through as a family, things were definitely starting to get good. However, just as we were starting to settle into this new way of life, *L.A. County Child Support Enforcement* had begun to construct an image and profile of me that was in very sharp contrast to everything that I was beginning to represent.

By the time this nightmare managed to work its way to the surface, I was a hard working husband and father who could finally support his family and I had no clue that there was even anyone out there who begged to differ. Yet, this agency was building a file on me that painted a totally different picture of what I thought was reality.

In their version of reality, I was a single, non-custodial parent all along and I wasn't ever paying for the care and keep of my wife and children. And, because of this profile, at the same time that things were starting to get good, punitive measures were being taken that would soon make things real bad.

We never knew it at the time, but this contradictory picture of who I was had begun running in the background of our lives shortly after we had gone to the government for help paying for the birth of our first child. Now, it was coming to the surface and it was threatening to undo all of the economic and lifestyle gains that we had made, and doing it just as we were starting to get a taste of financial well-being.

What was worse, because of the way we had collected the assistance in the past, these people were not able to see that I was living with, and supporting both the woman and child that they claimed to be collecting for. This could happen so easily without our knowing it because a core piece of the bad advice that we were given was to not involve me in the process of securing the aid that would help us to bring our child into the world.

As such, I had no contact with the agency that gave us the aid and never even thought that I needed to. As a result, this agency had no way of letting me know that given how our aid case was started, they had a legal obligation to open a child support case and hold me responsible for every dollar of aid that we would ultimately be given. Meaning that for every dollar of positive aid that was supposedly given for the benefit of my family with me as the husband and father, a dollar plus interest was charged negatively against me as a single man. My wife likewise was listed as a single woman.

Given the nature of how this case had begun and was playing out, I never even knew that the same agency that was supposedly coming to my family's aid, listed us bothas single and expected me to make a monthly effort to repay the money as if I wasn't with my family and providing for them. Yet the fact is that they had gone to court and gotten a judge to sign an order that said just that and bound me to make just such a payment.

Having no knowledge that such an order was issued, meant that I was doomed to fail to make these payments right from the start. It also meant that it wouldn't be long before the missed payments reached the point where the case would be in serious default.

From there, it definitely meant that it wouldn't be long before the arrears would grow to the level where I looked just like the average deadbeat dad who was willfully refusing to provide for his children.

Once I fell into this category, a barrage of punitive sanctions would be unleashed on me and my finances that would eventually kill all aspects of the good life that we were just beginning to enjoy. And, still with no knowledge that any of this was taking place, I would have no way to corral this bad and no way to protect me and my family from the great financial storm that would result from it.

By this faulty plan, this aid was not really aid at all. At best it was a *"momentary fix"* to a short-term problem. At its worst, it created a big misunderstanding that stood to do permanent harm to every aspect of my life and ruin me both professionally and financially for years to come.

They must have the wrong Brent Mandolph!

Fast forward to 1999. When this case and the effects of the financial sanctions that had been leveled upon me finally came to the surface, it could not have come at a more inopportune time.

Having found success in the sales job that I was once reluctant to take, I was in the process of moving on to a big prestigious company and an even better employment offer.

The position not only came with all of the great pay and perks that my family and I had grown used to, but it also offered a guaranteed opportunity to be promoted into a management position with the company.

Of course, that position would have meant even greater pay and perks than I was already receiving in my current position. Plus, now as a veteran of the industry, I would also be getting a hiring bonus of a few thousand dollars just for taking the job.

Needless to say, I was extremely excited about all of this, and my family and I both were looking forward to these great improvements to our financial situation.

I had gone through a round of pre-employment interviews and passed each with flying colors. Now the only thing left to pass was the customary background check and this job was all mines.

Given my squeaky clean past, I was absolutely certain that I was fine and had nothing to worry about. I was so sure that there was nothing that could get in the way of me getting this job that I resigned from my current position ahead of time – I even told my soon to be ex-boss that I was leaving for greener pastures.

By the way that I had planned this move, I would be out of work for two weeks before I started in my new position. I planned to use this time to take a bit of a break, a mini-vacation before my official start date with the new company.

To my soon to be new boss's point of view, since I was coming over from a competing company, this background check was just a formality and all of us were certain that in no time flat we would get the call giving me the *"all clear"* to come in and get to work.

But instead of receiving the *"all clear"* that we all had expected to get and a date to start work, I got a message on my answering machine in a tone of voice that told me that something was very wrong. Just hearing that message gave me a queasy feeling in my stomach and totally killed the mood of my mini-vacation.

Needless to say, as soon as I awoke the next day, I was on the phone trying to find someone who could explain the message on my machine. In a twist that I would have never seen coming, I ultimately found out there was a problem with the very background check that I was so sure I would pass.

When the manager called me to say that I had not passed, my first reaction was to ask,

> *"Are you sure that your people entered the*
> *correct information? There's no way I could*
> *have failed your background check!"*

I could say this with all confidence because up to that point in my life, I had lived a clean life. I had worked for many years and had never been fired from a previous job or brought harm to any company that I had ever worked at. I had told the truth on my resume and provided accurate references on my application. I didn't smoke or do drugs and only occasionally drank, and even that was never to the point of excess or drunkenness.

Probably of more importance, I had never in my life committed a crime or been in trouble with the law. I owned a squeaky clean background. So if I had failed the background check, there had to have been a mistake.

Maybe someone had entered the wrong input information. Or, if they had entered the right information, whoever performed their background checks *must have given them the results for the wrong Brent Mandolph!*

I was so in disbelief about this development and so convinced that they had the wrong guy that it prompted the manager who was trying to hire me to get further involved to get to the bottom of what was going on.

It wasn't long before he got an answer; one that I would have never guessed I would have heard in a million years. The reason that I had failed the background check was both simple and sinister at the same time – and it came totally out of left field.

As it turned out, the reason that I didn't get this dream job is because the background check revealed that I had a revoked Driver's License. Now I really knew that someone had the wrong man. Now, I couldn't help but ask,

> *"Are you sure that your people entered the correct information? There's no way I could have failed a DMV check!"*

I had never had an accident. I owed no outstanding fees related to my car or license. I never even so much as had an unpaid ticket, not for parking or any traffic matter. For all of these reasons I just knew that *the DMV must have had the wrong Brent Mandolph!*

Once again I was so convinced that I wasn't the guy being portrayed in this failed background report that the manager felt prompted to get involved. He used a contact that he had at the DMV to find out why, without my knowledge, my driving privileges had been taken away.

When the answer came back that my license had been taken by order of the county where I lived for non-payment of child support, I was thrown into a total state of disbelief and I just knew that someone had the wrong man.

I knew that I was not a person that was failing to support his kids. My wife and both of my children were living with me and I was their sole source of support. I also knew that I didn't have any children previous to or outside of my marriage. Thus, I questioned how anyone could have me listed as a person who was failing to pay his child support.

At the time I didn't have the answer to this, or any of the other questions that were swirling around in my own head, but something inside of me told me to just *delay judgment* on the matter until I talked to the proper authorities. So that is exactly what I did.

Los Angeles County (& Gala/Brandon Mandolph) vs. Brent Mandolph (& Gala/Brandon Mandolph)

As I stepped forward to get to the bottom of how anyone could have me listed as a deadbeat dad, I had no clue where this could be coming from. And, I had no clue that getting this situation turned around would soon become the biggest faith project that I had experienced to that point in my life.

To my way of thinking, I wasn't a deadbeat dad. I wasn't the guy that they had portrayed in the file that they had on me, so clearing my name should be a simple matter of coming forward and proclaiming as much.

In reality I had no clue just how naïve I was in thinking that overcoming this label would be easy. Likewise, I had no clue of what was really at stake or just how much being given this erroneous label and subsequently being enrolled in the child support enforcement program would ultimately cost me. Nor did I realize just how important the principle of *delayed judgment* would be to overcoming the many challenges that this label would bring my way.

With the information that I now had in hand and with everything that was on the line, I moved immediately to get in touch with the proper authorities to proclaim my innocence. I was hoping to bring a quick resolution to the matter and to that end, I tried to provide all of the information and cooperation that would help them to see that they had the wrong man.

But as much as I did to plead my case that I was a stand up father and prove that they had the wrong guy, the agents that were handling the case seem to do all that they could do to both jerk me around and insure that there would be no quick fix to the situation.

In terms of the dollars and cents of the matter, by the time I had come forward the amount of money that I stood accused of owing had grown to more than $5,000. Plus, there was an ongoing obligation of nearly $200 that I was expected to pay each month. And, with each month that I failed to make this payment, the $5,000 balance grew by the missed amount, plus interest and penalty.

To not know that I had this case, then to find out that I not only had it, but I was being held legally liable for paying thousands of dollars was crazy to me. Just hearing that I was being held responsible for paying so much money totally floored me. It was even crazier that I was to pay this money to a governmental agency that claimed to be representing the same wife and child that I was actively supporting.

As I spoke up to proclaimed my innocence, I am sure that the child support enforcement agents saw me as just another deadbeat father trying to skip out on the high cost of supporting a child. In fact, I would imagine that to these people, the same people who were responsible for branding me a deadbeat father in the first place, I was just another guy trying to play the innocent victim.

When judging me through the lens of the supposed unpaid balance and the ever-growing debt, it was easy to see why these agents were resistant to my claims of innocence. This would have been especially true if they could look at my innocence claims without looking at the individual facts of the case against me.

With the record of missed payments and these numbers going against me, I certainly looked like one of those guys that got paraded in front of the news media as examples of fathers that were failing to meet their parental obligations. It quickly became clear to me that whenever I talked with representatives of this agency these two factors dictated each and every aspect of the conversation.

It seemed that by their protocol, they were instructed to look at the number of payments made or missed and the amount of money owed to determine if they should extend any measure of relieve to the crippling sanctions that they used for enforcement.

Based upon my record, it seems like they dug their heels in right from the start and refused to extend me and my family any relief to the sanctions that were beginning to ruin us financially. Based upon my record, it was hard to even find an open and sympathetic ear.

Without finding someone to listen to me, it would be impossible to bring a quick remedy to this case. And, as long as these people couldn't hear that my case wasn't the typical case, as long as they couldn't hear my truth, this nightmare would rage on with no end in sight and engulf all of my newfound career and financial success in the process.

My finances were unraveling fast and the stakes were rising

In what seemed like the blink of an eye, time started to fly by. It had been a few years since this case was opened against me and the efforts to enforce the court order that had been acquired behind my back were really starting to pick up. As these actions picked up, my pleadings of innocence fell more and more on deaf ears.

As all this played out, the success and abundance that we had come to experience as our daily reality started to evaporate fast – leaving us feeling almost as if this success and abundance had never even been there.

All of the sudden I found my bank account was levied. My earnings were subject to being garnished. I couldn't pass a background check for new employment. Having already left my previous copier company for the promise of a better opportunity and sure job with a competing firm, I now found myself unemployed.

I was literally stuck between jobs – as none of the companies in my new industry could hire me without a valid driver's license and many wouldn't hire me with my background check issues and the prospect of me being subject to a wage garnishment order.

And, in a final blow to my fleeting economic success, the professional licenses that allowed me to make money from the sale of insurance and investments were all taken away. Without these licenses, I was quickly put out of my side business. I was effectively without a single source of income and it was starting to become clear just what was at stake for me.

Now that I was a victim of this program I started to take notice of all of the ways beyond the basic punitive sanctions that people who didn't meet their child support obligations were punished into compliance. In an instant these too became a part of my living nightmare.

All of the sudden I was faced with the threat of arrest. I was faced with the threat of having my taxes confiscated, and, just filing was an act that made the threat of arrest all the more real.

All of the sudden I was faced with the threat of being publicly shamed as many child support enforcement agencies had a tradition of dragging the men who had these cases out before the news media to let the world know that they were either looking for them or that they had found them. Either their personal photo or their mugshot would be placed on full display for all the world to see.

Normally I would have never taken the time to pay attention to this type of stuff. But, now I was one of the fathers that was subject to all of these things, a new reality that forced me to change my routine to try to avoid having this nightmare become true.

Even though I knew I was innocent, I was forced to take on the thinking of those deadbeat dads who didn't want to find themselves the victim of these harsher enforcement measures.

On the economic front, within a matter of a few months of being hit with the opening round of sanctions, I found myself near penniless. Gone were the big commission checks that used to take weeks to spend through. Gone were the paychecks that used to sit in my desk drawer until I got around to cashing them. And, gone was the stack of cash that used to sit on top of the refrigerator. Not to mention the fact that having a delinquent child support case instantaneously ruined my credit score, a factor that meant that my finances were being assaulted from all angles.

On the home front, as the stability in my financial life began to decline, the instability in our living situation returned. When this crisis began, we were living in a home and a community that we absolutely loved.

Now as the sanctions started to take their toll, we found ourselves confronted with some of the same old housing issues that we used to face when I was a young, struggling husband and father. In fact, it wasn't too long after these sanctions were leveled against me that we found ourselves struggling to just pay the rent.

When this crisis had come upon us I was working less hard than I ever had before, making more money than I had ever thought possible and I was easily able to provide my family with a great place to live.

Now those times were gone and we were getting back to the place where my family and I were being confronted with the kind of circumstances that could easily have put us out in the streets. If this were a game of chess, we had just reached the place where our opponent could have called *checkmate*.

To say that the stakes were extremely high would have been an understatement. Especially when you consider that from our point of view we were headed towards losing the best place that we had lived and the best lifestyle that we had lived in all of our years as a family.

With all of these matters hanging over my head, it had become crystal clear that I would need to fight harder than ever before and that this fight would require me to use all the power that I could garner from these **FAITH (APPLIED)** principles.

For their part, it seemed that the government had a full bag of tricks to fight with and from the very outset of the battle it was made abundantly clear that they were willing to use them all. Adding to the challenge that I was facing was the fact that this was a legal case and the real battle was made up of events that had to play out in the courts.

Participating in these events meant submitting and answering to legal filings that had to be formally written in legalese – a language that I obviously didn't speak or write, much less understand. It also meant attending court hearings that were also conducted in this same insider's only language.

I really could have used good legal representation to fight on my behalf. But the fact was that my diminishing finances didn't afford me such a luxury. So I was forced to try to fight this battle on my own.

All my efforts to get free only made the matter worse

Fast forward to 2003. As much as we all like to see a miracle in times like this, the truth is that most of our faith victories don't happen overnight. My fight to clear my name was no different. The battle had now been raging for four years and more than feeling like it had become a long drawn out affair.

Over the years I had tried everything that I could think of and everything that had been recommended for me to do to try and clear my name. I had sought fee-based legal assistance. I had sought out pro-bono legal assistance. I had acted as my own lawyer and tried to represent myself.

All of these actions and a few others that I choose not to recount were undertaken in an effort to clear my name. But all of these things were of no avail, and as the case blew through the fourth year in existence, none of them had had any success at budging the growing debt. Even worse, by 2005, I had been forced to watch the balance grow to over $12,000.

As the battle continued on, people had begun to tell me that, rightly or wrongly, I would have to buy my way out of this program. My normal response to these suggestions was to flat out reject the very idea of paying what I saw as the equivalent of a ransom request to put this case behind me.

Even when a close family friend that I discovered worked for the agency told me the very same thing, I strongly took this same stance. I had reached out to him to try and gain some insider tips on how I might go about defeating the case when it became clear that all of my efforts had failed to free me.

Disappointingly, he had nothing to offer in the way of information that would help me to put this nightmare behind me. While he held the credibility of an insider, when he voiced his opinion that I must and I should just pay the bill requested and move on with my life if I wanted my freedom, something inside of me told me not to accept this point of view.

In principle, I could have never brought myself to accept the responsibility of paying money that I knew I didn't owe. To me, it didn't matter who was suggesting that I should. The idea of simply surrendering to this demand for payment of a debt that I knew didn't belong to me was especially troubling because the amount of money involved could have did so much good for my family.

This kind of money could have educated my kids, or served as a down payment for a family home. It could even have been put into a savings or investment program to serve as the foundation of the economic stability that we desperately needed. It could have done much to make our lives better and more stable and because of this fact, giving it away to a debt that I didn't believe I owed was totally unconscionable to me.

My audit request brought $16,000 plus in new debt and raised the stakes even higher

Fast forward to 2007. By the time the case had wound into its eighth year in existence, as much as I hated the thought of buying my freedom, with the passage of time, my attitude began to soften.

Over this period of time I had put out a ton of effort to clear my name without success. I had watched myself fall further into an ever deepening financial hole. I had watched the great lifestyle that I had worked hard to build for my family evaporate into thin air.

Much worse, I had lived in fear of being publicly humiliated or even jailed for years now. With no end to this case or these serious threats in sight, the time had come where I was forced to give serious consideration to what people had been telling me for years – that I needed to take a serious look at the notion of paying up if I really wanted my freedom.

As this thought set in on me, I started toying with an idea of how to approach the whole matter that would make paying this unjustified debt as tolerable as it could be made for me. I had begun to reason that the only way for me to stomach it was if I could somehow be allowed to go back to the beginning of the case and pay the original amount that was requested, just about $5,000.

At that moment, *L.A. County Child Support Enforcement* was requesting that I pay more than $12,000. Of that amount, $7,000 was not only made up of interest dollars, but those dollars had accumulated right in front of my face. To me, even though I didn't owe the $5,000, at least I didn't watch it build up out of nothing.

I wouldn't doubt that the original $5,000 had built up in much that same manner. But I didn't see it happen. That wasn't the case with this $7,000, and for that reason alone, it would be tough for me to pay – especially when it clearly never even went to my family.

On these grounds and for this reason I was compelled to ask for an audit of the case. In this letter I made it clear that I was hoping to get the debt amount back down to the original $5,000 tab and then settle the case.

I submitted a letter that read in part,

"Dear Sir or Madam,

I am now willing to pay to settle this case. But as I don't believe that I owe the $12,000 that is currently being requested of me, I am requesting that an audit of the case be conducted so that we may arrive at an accurate accounting of the amount owing. Once this audit is complete, I believe that you will see that the real amount owing is closer to the $5,000 that was originally requested.

Given that the original aid case was only open for a short period of time, more than half of the amount now requested was never paid out as a benefit. Once this audit is completed, I believe that the facts will show this clearly and the balance will be reduced to reflect as much. Once this happens, it is my intention to pay the full amount owing and settle the matter."

I submitted this letter in good faith that these people would be able to see this truth and play fair. I further thought that even if they saw it differently, just seeing that the majority of the dollars that they were requesting were interest dollars would have caused somebody in this office to do the right thing and cut me some slack.

Once again I couldn't have been more naïve in this thinking. Instead of seeing things my way, when *L.A. County Child Support Enforcement* got back in touch with me, this is what they literally had to say:

"Dear Mr. Mandolph,

Thank you for your offer to settle. In reviewing your case, we have determined that you were right in your claim that $12,000 is not the correct amount that you owe. After completing a thorough audit of your case, we are revising the numbers upward to reflect our findings.

Please see the results of our audit and the amount of arrears that you currently owe below...

Initial Amount was $4,893.00
Recent Amount was $12,670.00
New Audited Amount is $29,191.90

Please contact our office to discuss settlement options at: 866–901–XXXX"

As you read those results, did it hit you, like it did me when I first read it? My family and I had eagerly awaited an answer to my audit request, hoping that it would return with some news that might spell the beginning of the end of this nightmare. And, when it finally arrived, it said that I was right. But unfortunately for me and my family, their idea of me being right, could have never been more wrong.

As their audit now revealed, by their count, I didn't owe $12,000. If it had stopped there and headed south, it would have been a great moment. But instead, by their new count, they said I didn't owe $12,000, I actually owed over $29,000!!! To say that these findings came as a total shock to me would again be to understate what my feelings were at that moment.

I don't know what kind of math they were using. I could have believed that they would have said that after the audit, they found no cause to reduce the amount I owed and that they were standing by the $12,000 number. But in an audit that took less than 30 days to complete, they had come back and said that they now found me responsible for owing an additional $16,000, plus. That's a turn of events that I never even came close to expecting.

And, right on cue, they folded these new dollars into my ledger and once they put it there, they immediately went about the task of trying to collect on this new debt with even more fervor than they had tried to collect the previous amount. Even worse for me, this new amount not only made me look like more of a deadbeat father in the eyes of the agents that I communicated with, it also made the likelihood of me experiencing the more harsh sanctions more real.

With this new balance, I now found myself in the company of the deadbeat parents that they would drag out before the media to make an example out of. I was made to feel as much when I did try to approach the agency about the case.

After the results of this audit were revealed to me, I was starting to feel like I would never get out from under this burden. I had now truly exhausted all of my options for finding a reasonable resolution to the matter. I had done everything that I could think to do to present my case and free myself, yet nothing had worked. Eight years had passed and I was not only still being held liable for a debt that I knew I did not owe, but the debt had now grown 6 fold.

The whole situation looked about as bleak as it ever could have. In the natural, it just seemed like this case would never go away. If paying $5,000 was hard to do, and if paying $12,000 was totally unreasonable, what sense could I ever make of paying over $29,000? It just seemed like I was fighting a battle that I could not win. And, now one that I didn't even come close to having enough money to buy my way out of.

Upon feeling the sting and shock of this latest setback, and given the now heightened threat of arrest, all I could think to do was retreat and keep a low profile.

As I faded back into the shadows to avoid the increased threats that now hung even more prominently over my head, the urge was as strong as ever to accept as fact that my life was now forever. ruined by the mistake of accepting government aid – aid that I had never wanted in the first place.

At this moment it was hard to escape the fact that this case just wasn't going in my favor. At this moment I would also have to say that I had as hard a time as I have ever had *delaying judgment* and believing that the *Creator* could see me through.

At this moment it was very hard for me to trust in the power of *FAITH (APPLIED)*. But at that moment, when I had just finished reading that letter, that is exactly what I knew I had to do. As a matter of fact, it was about all I could do.

So often when we are trying to work our way through a matter in faith we look to receive a sign that our stand of faith won't be in vain. We certainly don't want to look up and see ourselves moving backwards.

But the truth is that if we did have a sign, if we did only experience forward steps, we really wouldn't need faith. If everything about our process were pointing toward our eventual victory, we wouldn't need to trust in faith or the *Creator* to see us through.

Delayed judgment activated the miracle-making power of the universe with a single word

For me, at this moment things couldn't have been any darker. And, it was precisely at this dark moment that the dawn finally began to break on this crisis. The events that sprang from my last efforts to free myself by seeking a reduced payoff amount had only resulted in me being saddled with more debt and forced into virtual hiding to avoid being thrown in jail.

But just as the year had begun with the delivery of news that could have dropped me into the depths of despair, the year would end with the revelation of a single word that gave me the hope that a brighter day was finally on the horizon.

Over the previous eight years I had tried without success to explain my story, that I was married to and residing with the woman and child that they claimed to be representing. But it seemed as though no one heard me – no matter how loud or adamant I was about these facts. Most of the people that I consulted on the matter thought that for me to get free I would have to buy that freedom.

It was a suggestion that I had flat out rejected from the first time that I heard it. But even I started to think that maybe this is what it would take and once I had finally bought into this notion, I petitioned the agency handling my case in an effort to lessen the cost of settling the matter without success.

Now the end was in sight and it had nothing to do with getting a lower settlement amount. And, just as I had always suspected, getting past this nightmare didn't entail me paying a ransom in exchange for my freedom.

Now, just like back on July 30th, 1995, it seemed as if I had passed some invisible test, like I was being asked a final time to stand firm for what I believed. As soon as I did, it seems like the **Creator** moved in a supernatural way to deliver me from my bondage.

He did it by way of a single word whispered from that little voice in my head. He did it just when I was starting to think that faith might not see me through this time. He did it by placing before me one word and then encouraging me to move immediately to search to see if *L.A. County Child Support Enforcement* offered any form of that word to people in my position. That word was ***AMNESTY!***

I had certainly heard of the concept before. There were amnesty programs for people who couldn't pay their traffic tickets or fines. There were amnesty programs for people who couldn't meet their tax obligations. But I had never heard of such a program for those people caught under the weight of a child support enforcement case.

Now at this dark hour, the spirit of **God** was leading me to investigate whether or not this type of program could be used to free me and my family from the erroneous label that had smothered us financially for eight long years. Unlike the days of old when I would be slow to follow the urgings of the spirit, I moved quickly to determine if there was any merit to what I felt had been whispered to me.

Thank ***God*** that this moment was taking place in the age of the internet. Perhaps of even greater importance, thankfully by this time the search capabilities of Google in particular had grown tremendously – as did my knowledge of how to search the internet in the right way to find obscure information. Without these three key elements there likely would have been no way for me to conduct the necessary research to uncover information that it turns out this agency was hiding in plain sight.

As it turned out, the spirit had led me in the right direction, as the same agency that I had been fighting for more than eight years did have an amnesty program. In all of my communications with them, in all of the court filings that had gone back and forth between me and them, no one had ever mentioned that such a program even existed. Instead, all they tried to do was to get me to pay up.

I'm not sure if the program was in existence the entire time that I was fighting for my freedom, or if it was something that had just begun to be available. What I did know is that it was there now and because of it, I could finally see the end ahead for me. Maybe this was exactly what I had ***delayed judgment*** for. I immediately moved to work this new angle in hopes of finally finding my freedom.

The Compromise of Arrears Program (COAP)

At the time of its release, *the Compromise of Arrears Program* was a temporary program that was designed to help those who owed back child support to the government to settle that debt. As I experienced it, it allowed the government to admit no wrong doing and free me from the case. I would later learn that what it did more than anything was give *L.A. County Child Support Enforcement* a mechanism to free me within the framework of the system that they had used to dog me for nearly a decade.

However, true to the nature of how this battle had played out for the previous eight years, when I first approached them about this program, they quickly showed me that it wasn't going to be a magic bullet. For starters, while the very existence of the program raised a level of hope and optimism within me, I also felt a bit cautious about approaching these folks.

Before becoming aware of this new development, I was still keeping a low profile. I had seen stories previous to this moment where the government or law enforcement would use the lure of something positive to smoke out people in hiding, then arrest them when they show up to collect.

I had also previously seen cases where they would use the positive lure to get people to expose their hidden assets and then seize them once they were exposed. So I was cautiously optimistic at best, and to say that I was very much on guard would be accurate.

At the time that I was approaching *L.A. County Child Support Enforcement* to inquire about the program I was living one way on paper and a whole other way in reality. As tough as it was to do, we were managing to maintain some symbolism of a quality of life. Namely, we weren't living in a ghetto or in dire poverty, at least not by outward appearance.

Just as I had imagined, qualifying for this program would mean having my assets screened and *L.A. County Child Support Enforcement* immediately used my reality at that moment, notably my address to decline my application. Apparently there were certain zip codes that didn't qualify and as far as they were concerned, broke people didn't live where we were living at the time.

The lady that was assigned to my case was nice and she told me that she sympathized with me. This was the first time that anyone from *L.A. County Child Support Enforcement* had expressed anything like understanding for my plight. She even told me that she understood why I desired to raise my sons in a safe community. But at the end of this first approach, she let me know that she still couldn't free me.

The experience showed me that the program was meant to help those who had been made poor by all of the enforcement tactics that had been heaped upon them, and still by my outward appearance, I wasn't one of them. Yet in reality that was exactly who I was, and my family, the family that they claimed to be collecting for had even suffered greatly as a consequence.

So now I had found a new tool to try and seek my freedom and here I was once again on the losing end of efforts that were supposed to produce the results that I desperately wanted – freedom from *L.A. County Child Support Enforcement.*

And, once again I could have thought that I would never get that freedom. But somehow this time I knew deep within that the end to this nightmare would soon be in sight if I could just manage to ***delay judgment*** for a little while longer.

Freedom arrives through the same door that brought financial bondage

Fast forward to 2009. By now I had been fighting *L.A. County Child Support Enforcement* for ten years to free myself from the bogus claim that I was a deadbeat dad without success. In this time my family had been forced to live through and suffer through a myriad of trying situations.

Everything from job and income issues, to housing issues and the threat of homelessness. As a couple we still lacked any form of a real support system and couldn't return to or count on family in any meaningful way. In fact, if time or desire permitted, I could chronicle several examples of the abuses that we encountered when we would try to call upon family members for help.

And, these abuses seemed to be reserved just for us (likely even me), as we would watch other family members get all the help and support that they needed in their times of need or wanted in times of plain want. This even though their times of need were completely self-induced. This even though their times of want were pure greed.

This even though many of these family members would abuse the generosity and the very person extending it. This even though many of these people had never made an effort to pay off the tab from their last bailout or handout – all things we (I) had never done, nor been given a chance to do before.

In our case, at this moment, we were completely broke on paper. And after eight years of fighting this battle I was being told that my debt had grown from $5,000 to more than $29,000. Just at this dark moment I first learned of the *Compromise of Arrears Program* and over a two year period of time I had made two unsuccessful attempts at qualifying for the program.

Now ten years had clipped off and at just this moment, I was starting again to think that maybe freedom just wasn't in the cards for me. Before throwing in the towel I decided to make one more attempt to seek out the legal advice that would help me to get free.

By the grace of the **Creator**, I was fortunate enough to not only find someone to give me advice, but a person who after hearing the details of my story, decided to help me pro-bono.

In this gentleman, I found the exact advice needed to finally yield the results that the **Creator** must have had in mind when he first whispered the word **AMNESTY** to me.

No sooner than I finished explaining that I had twice tried to qualify for the *COAP* only to be turned away, he added the final piece to the puzzle that was needed to start the wheels turning and give me what I had been seeking from day one.

After hearing the whole story, he simply said,

"If L.A. County Child Support Enforcement wouldn't free you because they don't believe you are broke and on paper you are broke, you should use your real financial status to give them what they want."

I don't know why I had never thought about it this way. The truth was that they had made it virtually impossible for me to gain real meaningful employment. They had also taken away the professional licenses that would have allowed me to employ myself. They were raiding my bank account on a regular basis and seizing whatever little money they found there.

On more than one occasion, they had even left me owing the bank as a result of their actions. Lastly, they had an order that allowed them to seize my income tax returns if I filed. In all of these actions, they had not only made me broke on paper, they had also made me broke in reality.

The fact that I was managing to provide anything for my family at all, with all of this going on and going against me was a sheer testament to my own will and hustle. Given these facts it was clear that they should be confronted with the truth of my diminished financial reality and they should be forced to use this new reality to reconsider my application for *AMNESTY*.

It was also a fact that at that precise moment my family had been made homeless by virtue of my deminished financial reality. We had been forced once again to take up residence in a hotel until we could find a new home that we could afford to move into.

Our new legal advisor explained to me that this too was a misfortune that needed to be used to our advantage. At his advice it was this temporary circumstance that we needed to use to once again apply for what has come to be a shining symbol of destitution – public assistance.

As I have already explained, in the past I would never have cared to seek public assistance. I thought it was beneath my dignity. But this time I was all for it.

Over the previous 10 years *L.A. County Child Support Enforcement* had taken so much from me. In falsely labeling me as a deadbeat father, they had taken my ability to work, my economic comfort and the great lifestyle that I had begun to build for my family. Now to my way of thinking, if they weren't going to allow me to take care of my family, then they should have to.

This time too we didn't make the mistake we made the first time that we went to the government seeking aid for the birth of our son. This time we went in and applied as a family, meaning that if we were approved, there wouldn't be anyone for them to erroneously hold liable for the help that we received.

Given the financial position that these people had put us in, we were immediately approved. Now in the eyes of the government, because we qualified for public assistance, I was officially considered broke.

With this designation now official, I could then turn back to *L.A. County Child Support Enforcement* to make one last attempt at clearing my name. I submitted a new application for the *Compromise of Arrears Program* that included a new financial statement that had been updated to reflect the fact that my family was now back on public assistance.

Before I put the form in the envelope I wrote a note on the bottom that read,

"Am I broke enough for you now?"

I wasn't sure whether or not this added comment would be taken the wrong way, but I wanted to eliminate any chance of someone opening this envelope and treating this new application like any of the other applications that cross their desk. I guess you can say that I wanted to add some shock value to this application to insure that it actually got read.

I will never be able to know whether it was this comment or simply the application itself, but after what seemed like an eternity, when the reply came back to me it came back saying that this nightmare was finally over.

While I wasn't free at just that moment, the letter let me know that in a very short period of time, I would be. Just like the lawyer had suggested, in showing them just how broke they had made me, the gate was finally opening for me to go free.

I had always known that **when God works a problem out for you, he works it out way better than you could have ever worked it out**. I had been endeavoring to clear my name for 10 years now and finally with a whisper from **God** it was done. Even better, now this moment was ending with the entire case being dropped and without me paying a single dime of the ransom money that they had been seeking.

In the end, I was right that I didn't have to pay a debt that I didn't owe. I had endured a great deal over this time. But it was a matter of principle. Had I paid any of that money I would have never saw it again. In fact, I have to believe that perhaps I would never have been granted amnesty if I was meeting this obligation.

When my freedom finally came, it came in the form of a process that had me listed as that same non-custodial parent who wasn't paying for the care and keeping of his wife and son. Only now it gave my wife the power to release me from this obligation, and with her release, the burden of all the years of missed principle and interest payments that had built up would simply be forgiven. With her release, the more than

$29,000 in debt that had been wrongly forced upon me would now simply go away.

They essentially sent two letters to the same address. One letter was addressed to me, letting me know that my request for acceptance in the *L.A. County Compromise of Arrears Program* had been approved by the agency, pending spousal approval.

My wife was granted the power to give approval to my freedom because in their eyes, or maybe I should say by their structure, we had now reconciled. We had reconciled even though we had never broken up. They were the only ones refusing to acknowledge this truth over all these years. Now through the framework of the *COAP* they were finally recognizing what I had been saying from day one.

In the other letter, the one that was addressed to my wife, they let her know that the agency had approved my application for acceptance into the *COAP*, and they let her know that all of the power now rested in her hands. They let her know that the freedom that I had long sought was now simply subject to her approval.

Each letter put a 90-day time frame for the final action. If my wife didn't reply, I would be freed in 90 days. If she objected, all she had to do was complete a form saying as much and my (our) nightmare would continue. Thankfully she was still my wife and I was in good standing with her.

I can only imagine where I would be today if I was really the deadbeat husband and father that they tried to say I was all along. As my fate was in her hands, she could have easily did me in with the stroke of a pen.

In another twist that was so typical of the absurdity of this whole case, it was revealed during this final **process** that they even had my wife listed as the spouse of a man who was failing to pay his child support obligations. They eventually sent her a letter warning her that she could be held responsible for this obligation.

The letter went on to warn her that all of the same punitive financial sanctions that had been leveled against me could be used in an effort to force her to pay herself. You can't make this stuff up. When this letter came, we read it with pure amazement.

It had taken me 10 long years of *delayed judgment*, *FAITH (APPLIED)* and effort to get to the day where I could finally proclaim that I was not the person that I had been portrayed as and have the freedom to match that statement.

I had gone into this knowing that sometimes the results that we seek will only manifest as a result of a process, and not by way of an event, but I would have never thought that it would have taken so long to overturn this bogus case and win my freedom.

I knew going into this that you have got to be willing to see a faith project through. I knew that you must be capable of believing over time and in the face of seemingly lingering obstacles, and when the results that you seek are not immediate.

I knew the power of *FAITH (APPLIED)*. I also knew that sometimes you will only find what you seek if you have the wisdom to just *delay judging* where you are in the moment. I knew that only then can you see the miracle-making power of the universe come to your aid.

However this battle had just about brought me to the brink of questioning all of this wisdom. But all of my faith was renewed after the 90-day period ended and my freedom papers showed up in my mailbox.

On that day, by the power of *Delayed Judgment*, the *Creator* had finally honored my faith and freed me on my terms. I was finally free to rebuild my life and I was easily one of the happiest men on the planet.

Delaying judgment allowed me to rise up, walk and overcome Multiple Myeloma

In going to war against the cancer that attacked my body, the *Creator* could not have blessed me with a greater weapon to take into battle than the wisdom to *delay judgment*.

I can now say this with all certainty because there was so much in the way of negative information and heavy considerations that could have wiped me out and rendered me a goner if I had just allowed myself to think deeply on these matters and judge them as they came to me. I would have been doomed if I had allowed myself to judge where I was or the diagnosis that I had been hit with; or the fact that, at that moment, my mobility had been taken away from me.

Or, for what it was worth, I would have been doomed if I had allowed myself to judge the serious treatments and medicines that were now being doled out to me; or even worse, contemplated the reality of my newly uncertain future.

If I thought about the true weight of all of these things, even for one moment, I don't think that there is any way that I would have made it through to where I am now. If it were not for having the ability to ***delay judgment***, I am sure that there is no way that I could have survived.

When you even think about it logically, the very thought of overcoming a serious disease like cancer demands that you ***delay*** the act of ***judging*** your fight over the short run. When you think of all of the treatments and medicines that you have to endure.

When you think of all of the test and scans that you have to go through and the fact that you are virtually in a constant state of suspended outcomes – constantly awaiting answers to some potentially life altering question, you will realize that there is no way to get through it all unless you have the ability to put off answering most of these questions that are swirling around you for a later time.

The simple truth is sometimes you have to put off these questions until a time when you have more and better information to give a valid answer. At times you are waiting to see how your body is reacting to the treatments and medicines. At other times you are waiting for the results of the test and scans that must be run to tell you where you are in your process of treatment and recovery.

Above all of this, you are waiting to see if your treatment protocol is having an effect on the disease, waiting to see if you are being healed. Inside of that reality there is a ton of room for your mind to get away from you and for you to get down and depressed.

While these emotions are perfectly understandable, and while even I had a few days where that spirit visited me, they are of no value to you in your fight for healing. It should even go without saying that these emotions often run counter to ***FAITH (APPLIED)***.

Realize some questions don't deserve your judgment

The simple truth is that in the midst of your faith project some questions don't deserve your judgment. I'll go even further and say that some questions don't even need to be answered if we are going to win in our faith project.

In the same way, there are also some emotions that we don't need if we are going to come out victorious in the end. I remember trying to help my friend *Earnest Peacock III* see this truth when he was trying to wrap his mind around the fact that his body had been attacked by cancer.

He was stuck on the fact that he had always tried to do right by his health and his body. He couldn't understand or accept the fact that even though he had lived a disciplined life where he ate the right foods and worked out to keep his body fit, and didn't smoke or drink, cancer still entered into his life. And, as the realness of this sickness sank in to him, he seriously took to questioning, *"how and why him?"*

For most people these certainly seem like valid questions. They definitely seem to flow out of understandable emotions. But just because they are valid, just because they flow from rightful emotions doesn't mean that you and I should indulge them. And, if we indulge them, that doesn't mean that we are going to profit in any real meaningful way in our fight for healing. As a matter of fact, entertaining these types of questions will usually have the exact opposite effect.

You see, not **delaying judgment** and allowing these kinds of negative emotions to run wild is not only debilitating, but if left unchecked, this spirit will only serve to immobilize you and render you helpless in your fight for healing.

Fortunately for me, I understood this truth both instinctively and from the very outset of my battle. Fortunately I realized this when my own doctor tried to encourage me to let the negative emotions flow.

Fortunately I knew that some of the questions that he thought I should have asked at that moment didn't deserve an answer and that it was better to **delay judgment** on these weighty matters.

And, luckily for me I knew that this was better than allowing myself to become overwhelmed with questions that could only serve to weaken my resolve to fight on to victory and ruin my confidence in the power of *FAITH (APPLIED)*.

Sadly, most people fail to see it this way when they are confronted by a serious illness or any other situation in life when they are thrown a challenge that is bigger than they believe they can handle. I have seen more than a few people do it when they were confronted with a challenge similar to the one that I had to battle.

Fortunately for me, by the time this illness came upon me, I already knew better and I already had the habit of *delaying judgment* when I found myself confronted by a challenging circumstance.

Now that I have overcome this disease and my life has been extended, I can say with all confidence that the whole process of beating a serious disease requires you to *delay judgment* in regards to every question or matter that runs counter to the outcome that you are seeking.

To get through all of the treatments, medicines, test and scans – to get through all of the questions and doubts that will surely race through your mind, if you expect to come out successful you are left no choice but to *delay judgment*.

From my experience, before you can get a report that says that things are working out for you, you must *delay judging* whether or not things are working out for you. If you can't do this, you'd simply drive yourself crazy, sink yourself into a pit of despair and ultimately give up.

I have also found that applying the power of faith in your everyday life, or to confront a challenge or go after that goal that you are striving for works the same way. You simply must be able to postpone answering any questions regarding where you are at a given moment or where you are prior to the end of your battle and give your actions and efforts the time that they need to bear the fruit that you are hoping for.

Delaying judgment on the questions that stood to hinder me in my quest to restore my health and mobility

Once I had made it to *Long Beach Memorial Hospital*, from the first moment that I was officially diagnosed with *Multiple Myeloma*, it seemed that there was no shortage of moments where I had to use the principle of **Delayed Judgment**.

As I have previously stated, the doctors that were awaiting my arrival and charged with restoring me to health were very aggressive. And from the moment that I arrived they got right to work with presenting me with the different testing options that I would have to submit myself to if I wanted to get to the bottom of what was going on with me.

It surprised me to learn that many people fight even going through with the testing that has to be run to diagnose their illness. I admit that some of these test were scary all by themselves, and most, had an element of pain that had to be endured. But still I could not imagine not going through them to get a clear picture of what was going on in my body.

Next, once the doctors had run their test and determined what was ailing me, I then was presented with a host of both the medicines and treatment options that I would have to consider taking in my quest to get well.

With regard to each of these medicines and treatments, like we so often see and hear on the television these days, each one of these options came with their own set of issues in the form of potential side effects that stood to wreak just as much havoc as the cancer itself. Before anything could be done to me or administered to me, I had to contemplate whether or not I wanted to submit my body and health to these potentially destructive substances.

Many times, if I had really stopped to judge the matter, I was literally having to choose between the lesser of two potential evils. To say the least, many times, the description of the potential side effects that I was having to confront was just as frightening as the cancer, if not more so.

Accordingly, one of the first areas that I encountered that was ripe with the potential to rob me of my faith, was this area of deciding what treatments and medicines to submit to.

As such, this is one of the first places that I seriously had to *delay judgment*.

On a daily basis, my doctors were presenting me with multiple lengthy legal disclosures that I had to read and consent forms that I had to sign off on. Eventually I found myself having to put off thinking about the heavy information that was contained in these documents.

For that matter, I also had to *delay judging* whether or not I would ultimately experience any of the negative effects that these disclosures were speaking of by taking the treatments and medicines that were being used in an effort to save my life.

Of a particularly great concern was the question of what if the procedures and medicines did their work and defeated the cancer, but the side effects left my overall health and body the worse for it. As it was presented to me, that was a real possibility.

It goes without saying that many people confronted with battling a serious disease don't make it past these considerations. Without the ability to lay these questions aside and quiet my mind, without the wisdom to *delay judgment*, I likely would have been one of those people.

I have no problem seeing that there is no way I could have gotten through all of this, and there is no way that I could have come to the place where I am now if I stopped to consider everything that was potentially involved. Without the ability to *delay judgment* there is no way I could have trusted the process or the doctors enough to relax and receive what these medicines and procedures have now brought to me in a spirit of positive expectancy.

On a separate note, while these heavy questions were raging, for my doctors, there were also the concerns that went along with being in the hospital. I would have never guessed it, but as it turns out, a hospital is the worst place to be for a person trying to defeat a disease like cancer.

With all of the doctors and all of the medicine that are there, I would have thought that nothing could harm you while you were in the hospital. I would have thought that a hospital would be the cleanest and most germ-free place a sick person could be.

My doctor eventually made it clear to me that just the opposite was true of all of these thoughts. And given my compromised immune system, a hospital was the last place that he would have liked for me to be over the long haul. In the end, this was even more heavy stuff to contemplate and more potentially unsettling considerations that I had to *delay judgment* on.

Meanwhile, on a minor note for me there was a concern over the fires that I knew were brewing on the home front. They were there when I first fell ill and a part of me felt that my wife and sons still needed me to be there to fight for them. As much as this should have been the furthest thing from my worries, for a time I couldn't help but to think about these matters.

I would eventually learn that though barely men, my sons stepped up nicely to help and support their Mom in my absence. But for a time, this too was stuff that I felt I had to give consideration to and yet another of the reasons why I had to employ the wisdom of *Delayed Judgment* to get through this crisis.

Delaying judgment on the greatest question of them all

Still bigger than all of these concerns, was the question of whether or not all of this effort was worth it, especially in view of the fact that I still couldn't get out of the bed. Not to mention the fact that I was still dealing with great pain on a 24/7 basis.

In fact, they were pumping me with a pain medication that was seven times the strength of morphine just to keep me comfortable. If I had stopped to judge from this vantage point, it would have appeared that I was perhaps fighting an unwinnable battle against cancer.

Most people think of *faith-based healing* as an event when in reality, as I just experienced it, it's most often a process. That is certainly what it was in my case. But I didn't know that that is what my expectations needed to be at that moment. If I didn't have the wisdom and strength to *delay judgment* it would have been very easy to just give up and except defeat as my fate.

Then there was the issue of my lost mobility. Even before my doctor confirmed as much, it was never lost on me that most people battling a disease like cancer are never confronted with a loss of their physical mobility, especially not at the very outset of their battle.

In fact, my doctors didn't even believe that I was dealing with a mobility challenge when they first started treating me. They simply thought that I was having some type of psychological blockage.

It wasn't until a round of detailed imaging studies of my back and spine was ordered that the truth that I couldn't stand or walk was acknowledged. And, I would eventually learn that once they got this information, my chances of returning to mobility were listed as improbable.

I would later learn that it was this development that led several of these doctors to write me off as a goner. It was also around this time that a few of these so-called professionals were excused from my environment when they revealed their pessimism to my wife and I.

I would also ultimately learn that these were the same doctors that tried to talk the lead doctor out of doing what he could to try and save me. With all of this going on behind the scene, if I didn't have the ability to *delay judgment*, he would have never saw the day when his efforts paid off.

On that day he got to take a picture of me standing and walking. He then emailed that picture accompanied by his extended middle finger to the negative colleagues who had tried to tell him that he was wasting his time treating me.

During all of this, it would have been very easy for me to question whether or not I was even being healed. After all, when you are going through a battle with a major disease, when you are taking all of the treatments and medicines and when you are dealing with the uncertainty of the moment, that is the overriding question,

"Is this even working? Am I actually being healed?"

At times, while you are going through the process of seeking healing there is no way for you to answer these questions definitively. You simply must trust that you are going to come out good on the other side.

From my experience, without the ability to *delay judgment*, it is next to impossible for most people to possess that level of trust. And, without trust, trust in the doctors and their process, trust in the procedures and medicines, trust in the *Creator*, there is just no way to get through the process that is healing by the power of faith, period.

Fortunately for me, thanks in large part to my having the *God* given wisdom to *delay judgment*, I had the trust that allowed me to get through the process and receive my healing.

Delay your judgment but never delay your response

To the undiscerned, this act of *delaying judgment* seems like the height of passivity. Perhaps you too might consider an act where you do nothing to speak to the seemingly logical questions and raging concerns, or the doubts that arise as doing nothing about your situation.

Some people think that they have to speak to everything and everyone that demands their attention as they work towards handling a challenge or achieving a goal. Most people certainly think that they have to answer every question that comes to their own mind as they work to handle a challenge or achieve a goal.

Perhaps you too have been brought up to think that way. But just because you aren't using your mental and verbal energy to judge your situation doesn't mean that you aren't doing something about meeting your challenge or hitting your goal.

Instead, the truth is that there is a power that comes from learning how to not judge – to just stay quiet and give your spirit a chance to connect with the universe. There it can draw on a power that is bigger than you and your limited resourcefulness.

In using these powerful *FAITH (APPLIED)* principles, specifically the principle of *Delaying Judgment*, in saying nothing, I have witnessed the existence of this power time and time again.

There was a season in my life before cancer struck me down where I got knocked down so many times I could have easily started to think that being down was my ultimate fate, felt sorry for myself and just stayed down. But instead I got right up each time I was knocked down. And, in looking back now I realize that it was this season that developed the toughness within me that enabled me to withstand the challenge of a serious disease like cancer.

I now know that this is where my faith was ignited, strengthened and readied for greater battles. This is where I learned how to fight back when life throws you a circumstance that isn't to your liking.

From a professional standpoint, this is also where the **Creator** gave me the business and selling skills and lessons that would allow me to build the level of professional and financial success that he had purposed in my heart years earlier.

Without the wisdom to **delay judgment**, I just don't believe that I would have been front and center to receive all of this good, especially when I consider the fact that I know so many other people who have seemingly had the exact opposite reality.

In stark contrast to my experience in life, these people had what appeared to be an easy ride. It is like they were allowed to sleep-in when the lessons of life were being passed out. It was like they were getting to play while I had to work for any and everything that I got out of life.

While I was forced to have an ongoing relationship with principles like **delayed judgment** and the **FAITH (APPLIED)** philosophy, and all of its other nuances, these folks didn't seem to have a need for any of this stuff. I even had to suffer through occasions when some of the fools in my life told me that I needed to be more like these people.

But fortunately for me I always knew that I just needed to be myself. As life would turn out, each of these people were eventually visited by the storms of life. And, when the storms of life came their way, most of them just washed out.

When they were knocked down, many of them didn't even get up once. Instead, of **delaying judgment** and working through their challenges, they looked into their moment of challenge and saw the worst and accepted defeat.

Today to a person, most of these people are still down and I am still standing, in spite of having had to overcome many more challenges and ones greater than the ones that took them out. And, in spite of having far fewer resources and sources of help and support than they had.

From this vantage point life ultimately taught me that adversity was my friend. Even though it didn't feel like it when I was going through it and even though I didn't like it, it was giving me an invaluable gift.

Adversity was giving me a tool and a weapon that would serve me in all aspects of my life and ultimately allow me to beat down cancer. That tool and weapon was the wisdom of **FAITH (APPLIED)**.

I realize now that there was no other way to get it on the level that I get it than via the fire of trying circumstances. In the sense that adversity held my feet to the fire, it left me no other choice but to learn the lessons of how to apply faith.

If you are blessed *(Yes, blessed)* enough to be challenged by the **Creator**, rejoice and know that this adversity is there to make you better. If you will allow the moment of crisis to, it will strengthen your faith and prepare you to handle whatever this life can throw your way. For that reason, know that adversity is your friend.

Now I should point out that I am not talking here about you going through adversity for adversity sake. Even in my case, many of the trying moments that I went through were self-induced. As such, although he used them for my growth, I don't feel that they were ordered up by **God**, and on some level, I know that these moments didn't have to be.

In reality these were times where my (our) own ignorance or disobedience to the guidance of the **Creator** were the cause of the problem. And yes, you can still learn something from this type of moment. For sure this was a time when I needed to grow up and get in line with where it was clear that **God** wanted me to go.

Certainly we all can have that moment; whether we are talking about the common sense things of **God** or the things that he has purposed in our heart that is just for us. But what I am calling adversity here is those circumstances that arise from situations and places beyond your control.

In all of the point stories that I have shared with you throughout this work, the trying circumstances that were spoken of emanated from some place that was beyond my control. Many of these challenges came out of nowhere and demanded a response from me. Most often they also demanded that I *delayed judging* me or them in an effort to get by them.

Also I am not talking about being an adversity junkie. There are plenty of people who live great lives that aren't filled with crisis and calamity. Perhaps these are the people who are just obedient. They obey their parents, their teachers, their coaches and most importantly, they obey their **Creator**.

I am also not talking about taking delight in having something to bitch and moan about. We have all known those people who seem to get their kicks out of bragging about the adversity that they are battling. Don't let that describe you.

To that end, remember when you are going through adversity you don't have to camp out. You should always seek to get through it ASAP. Remember, I never had fun dealing with any of the challenges that were thrown my way, ever.

Even now that I am aware of the power of **FAITH (APPLIED)**, even now that I am aware that adversity is my friend, dealing with challenge is not high on my list of fun things to do. If anything this new awareness helps me to stay calm as I go through it, but I still want to get through it as quickly as possible.

I have heard it said that the **Creator** will only continually take you through a thing when you are failing to get the lesson that it is there to bring. I have to say that I can definitely see that, as even in my life a challenge stopped visiting me when I got the lesson that it was sent to teach me.

Finally, please always remember that *delaying judgment* doesn't mean delaying your response to a challenge or delaying your efforts to go after a goal. It doesn't mean being weak or passive and checking out from the situation.

You and I can't delay time or the inevitable loss that will be ours if we do nothing to respond to a challenge that has been thrown our way. Likewise, you and I can't delay time or the inevitable failure that will be ours if we do nothing to go realize a goal or dream that we have set out before ourselves.

And, in *delaying judgment* you are not looking to put off the need to rise to the occasion and meet the challenge or goal that is in front of you. To the contrary, you are actually seeking to save your mental energy and free yourself to take a position of strength and action.

On July 30th, 1995, it was my ability to *delay judgment* that kept me from allowing that little negative inner voice to talk me out of going for the $1,000 bonus that had been placed before me. And, at the end of the day, this single principle probably played the greatest role in helping me to defy the odds and walk away with that bonus.

In July of 2012, in the face of all of the heavy and potentially negative information that was flowing to me, it was that same ability to *delay judgment* that allowed me to keep my mind quiet, submit myself to the needed medicines and procedures and once again defy huge odds and obtain a victory over cancer.

Once again, this single principle likely played the biggest role in creating the victory that I am now enjoying. That is the power of learning how to *delay judgment*, and that is why you must get this power working in your life and your faith projects.

Let's now look at the eighth and final principle that we need to learn if we're going to activate the miracle-making power of the universe:

Work up to and through the deadline

Fight on until you have your goal realizing that often times every minute counts. Delivery often comes in the 11th or the 12th hour and success is usually buried just beyond the point of your frustration. Hanging in there mentally, emotionally and physically right up to and through the deadline is often the key to getting your goal. So work on hanging in through the end while staying in prayer and remaining positive, without getting doubtful, negative or frustrated in the process. Above all, no matter what the score, no matter what your feelings, just keep working until the final tick of the clock.

In spite of my best efforts on July 30th, 1995, it was looking like I wouldn't be able to produce the results that I sought within the 8 hour work shift that I was scheduled. As a matter of fact, when the last 20 minutes of the day came, I was barely half way to my goal of $8,000 in sales for the day.

To make matters worse, as I have already stated, that little negative inner voice was bombarding me with a quit message that was hard to resist. Again, these thoughts had been coming at me all day, but now they were both greater in frequency and stronger in their appeal.

After all, it would be easy to argue that I had given it my best effort. I had worked a more focused and activity driven shift than perhaps I had ever worked. On top of that, while the amount of traffic that flowed into the store had been up and down all day, it had now diminished considerably from its peak. Even worse, the amount of traffic flowing into my actual department was considerably less.

When judging by these developments alone, it would have been more than logical to question my ability to produce another $4,000 in sales when it took me 7 hours and 40 minutes to get the $4,000 that I currently had. Thankfully our faith is not ruled by human logic.

By this time, virtually all of the store's personnel had shifted their attention to cleaning mode and were looking forward to heading home very shortly. Being a Sunday and given that no one could leave until the store was ready for the next business day, there was a big push to get this task done right at closing.

As for me, I was still in selling mode. Far from being concerned with going home, my focus was still on trying to earn the $1,000 bonus that had been sat out before us by management. To this day I can't explain how or why it was so, but for some reason I still thought I had a chance at hitting my goal so I kept both my mind and my body engaged in that task.

As such, some of the members of the *loser clique* that I had avoided all day grew angry with me for what they saw as my unwillingness to help out. To their view of things I was simply being lazy and shunning my part of our shared responsibility to maintain the department.

To understand the full significance of the challenge brought by this group, it might be worthwhile to remember that these people did not particularly care for me and they weren't going for the goal anyway – thus they couldn't have cared less that it was important to me. If anything, in an effort to exert pressure to get me to abandon my push to achieve this goal, they took their complaints to management in the hopes that I would finally be forced to give up and fold in with everyone else.

So when the clock struck 6:40 pm, I stood alone – still working and hoping to make sales and achieve the goal of the $1,000 bonus. And as the clock struck this time, that little voice inside my head gave me a final faith check, as a couple of thoughts flashed to my mind asking,

> *"Are you ready to give up? You have given this a great effort, but now **you only have 20 minutes** and you are still more than half way away from your target.
> Do you still believe you can achieve this goal?"*

Fielding these questions felt like an out of body experience, as it really did feel as if they were being asked by someone outside of me. In being asked these questions, I felt like something was asking me to state what I believed for one last time.

The voice acknowledged that I had put up a good fight. But at the end of the exchange, it made a point blank attempt to get me to question my ability to achieve the goal that I was endeavoring to achieve, and ultimately, my faith itself.

As logical as the argument was, as much as it would have made sense for me to give up right then and throw in the towel, something told me not to do it. As much as this perhaps should have been the moment for me to give up and join in on the store clean up duties that were now underway, I took it instead as the moment that I had to make a final decision. A decision of whether to release my faith and let up or to continue standing in faith and **work up to and through the deadline** that was set out before me.

I was now deep into the 12th hour of this goal. I had quietly and humbly been working in faith all day hoping to achieve my goal and it still had not come to pass. For this reason all by itself it would have been more than a logical choice for me to call this day a wrap and fold in with everyone else in preparing to go home.

To most people, it would have made perfect sense for me to let up and forgo working that final 20 minutes. After all, I hadn't taken any kind of break or stopped to eat anything all day. I was on duty and gave my best effort for every busy moment of the day and I had only managed to produce half of the results that I needed.

Now that it had slowed down and there were only 20 minutes left, no one could fault me for finally accepting that the goal wasn't going to come to pass. If I had chosen to take a moment to rest or grab a bite to eat, no one could have said that I had made a wrong decision.

All of these factors flashed quickly through my mind as I contemplated what I should do. And then, just as quickly as all of these thoughts flashed through my mind, I made my decision – I decided to **delay judgment** and keep going.

I took a deep breath, relaxed, cleared my mind of all the negative thoughts that had just rushed me, I went to the computer and looked at what I had done and restated what I still needed to do – then I recommitted to **work up to and through** the closing of the store.

To my way of thinking, I had already stood in faith on this goal for 7 hours and 40 minutes, now something from within told me that I might as well finish the job by standing in faith for the final 20 minutes. From all that I can tell in looking back on it now, this was likely the exact moment that the miracle-making power of the universe was summoned to my aid.

As it would happen, as rapidly as this series of thoughts had flowed through my mind and I had made the decision to keep standing in faith and working to achieve my goal, it appeared that the universe opened up to me and delivered up the final component to the success of the faith project that I had been working on all day.

Working up to and through the deadline delivered up a true miracle

It would seem that no sooner than I made the choice to stand in my faith and work up to the final moment the store would be open that the source of my victory appeared and a true miracle unfolded right before my eyes.

This miracle appeared in the form of a gentleman who, as improbable as it was, had a desire to buy the exact amount of goods that I needed to sale to reach my goal – the very thought of which seems almost unreal, even to this day.

As much as I was committed to standing in faith, when I looked at that computer to assess what still needed to be done, I'm not sure that I believed that I could actually do it. Thus the moment that was unfolding could have easily been seen as too good to be true.

But as this gentleman proceeded to describe to me what he had a need for, it occurred to me that it was very real. It also occurred to me that the implications of what was unfolding were almost too powerful to contemplate.

After all, to look at this unfolding moment from a logical point of view, I had labored for 29 days to get to my first $8,000 in sales for the month. In accepting the one day challenge to go after the $1,000 bonus, I had labored for a focused 7 hours and 40 minutes to secure another $4,000 in sales for the month. All total, 175 full working hours had gone into generating roughly $12,000 in sales for the month.

To even look at it more closely, 10,540 minutes had gone into bringing in the $12,000 that I had already secured. Using this math, that would mean that on average more than 3,500 minutes had gone into securing each $4,000 in sales for the month.

Now, after making a decision to stand in faith, the final $4,000 that I needed had materialized out of nowhere with only 20 minutes left on the clock. Not to mention the fact that by this time there was zero traffic flowing through the store. This gentleman was it.

What were the odds that he would come into my department to buy something? What were the odds that what he wanted to buy was a big television and big ticket purchase by itself? What were the odds that he would want to buy two of them?

I have never been so unspiritual as to think that what was unfolding before me was a matter of coincidence or luck. I have never been so naïve as to think that it was a matter of accident or chance. Nor have I ever been vain enough to believe that it was me who made this moment happen.

I knew from the very first time that I contemplated what had unfolded in this moment that there was a power much greater than any power that I might have had that caused this miraculous event to transpire.

What was also clear to me from that first moment of contemplation was the fact that I had set this miracle in motion the moment that I chose to stand in faith and ***work up to and through the deadline*** on this day. That was the role that I played in this miracle and I now know that it is the same role that the ***Creator*** ask you and I to play in every moment where we need faith to produce a miracle.

That is a choice and an action that you and I can perfectly control no matter what the circumstances or the backdrop of our faith endeavor. In fact, no matter what is going on in the moment, this is a simple act that we can do to demonstrate our faith in ourselves and the trust that we have for the ***Creator***. It is literally a way in which we can put works behind our faith.

When you understand the truth that success in a faith project often only comes after the 11th or 12th hour, you will see the power that you unleash when you decide to **work up to and through the deadline**.

By the time this moment would finish playing out, this gentleman had bought his two televisions, I had miraculously achieved the goal of earning the $1,000 bonus, the store was closed and we were well into the 13th hour. I had just witnessed the power of **FAITH (APPLIED)** for the first time.

Up to this point, it had been a fact of my daily life that in the push to overcome a tough challenge or achieve a big goal, that success had usually eluded me. But now I had witnessed the power of the universe to use my commitment to stand in **FAITH (APPLIED)** and deliver success against what appeared to be impossible odds.

We see people use this power time and time again in the sports world. We see people use this power time and time again in the business world. Yet many of us never realize the fullness of what we are seeing or that we have access to this same power to use in our everyday lives and affairs.

July 30th, 1995 was the first time that I became fully aware of the power of **FAITH (APPLIED)** and the ability that I had to find success via this power, by among other things, **working up to and through the deadline** of a challenging moment or in pursuit of a goal.

I guess that perhaps it was the first time that I fought long enough to see faith pull me through. But to be sure it wasn't the last time I used this power or witnessed its powerful truth.

Working up to and through the deadline – The very heart of Persistence

On any day prior to July 30th, 1995, I was the guy who would usually ask to go home early if things even looked slow, leaving whatever good fortunes that may have showed up in the late going to whomever was willing to wait around to receive them.

If I did stick around through the end of the shift, I would check out both mentally and physically well before the end of the day. You would almost never find me making an effort to help customers and close sales when the clock struck quitting time.

Having the faith to persist or having the discipline to *work up to and through the deadline* wasn't among my working habits. Like most others, I would be easily stopped by doubt. Like most others, I tended to have the need to see some physical sign that my efforts were going to pay off before I could muster any will to work a full day.

Like most others, the hardest thing for me to do was to fight on and work in the face of an uncertain end to my efforts. Or even worse, to fight on and keep working when I was losing in the late going, or when perhaps it appeared as though I had no real chance of winning.

On this day however, it was as if the wisdom to set aside these customs came through loud and clear and it came directly to and through my spirit. The wisdom that was imparted to me led me to *work up to and through the deadline* in an effort to secure the prize of the $1,000 bonus.

The sad truth is that many of us never learn the wisdom of setting aside such customs. We never develop the discipline to use every second available to us, to *work up to and through* the final tick of the clock of our challenge in pursuit of the deliverance that we need. And, yet, there are many areas of life where having this discipline is a staple of success.

In my own faith walk, I have seen this truth time and time again. I have used it to supplant defeat with victory on more occasions than I have time to list here.

On more than a few of those occasions, I have literally snatched my victory out of the jaws of what looked like certain defeat and I can tell you that there is no greater thrill. I can also tell you that there is no way to experience that thrill without developing the mental and physical discipline to *work up to and through the deadline*.

It should really go without saying that to exercise the power of *FAITH (APPLIED)* one must employ the power known as *Persistence*. From my experience, there is no success, by way of faith or any other means for the person who cannot survive an initial denial of success or early failure.

I have had many challenging moments where my sought after deliverance only came after I had not only withstood the initial denial of success, but a series of denials or frankly, after all hope of success appeared to be lost.

In each of these cases, there was plenty of time on the clock to battle with. But it didn't appear that I was having any success finding what I needed for victory. For most of us, these are the kinds of moments where it is all too easy to just throw in the towel and give up.

The last thing that most of us think about doing in this moment is being persistent. Even though we look out at the clock and it still shows that we have time to fight, we allow ourselves to throw the towel in and accept the fate of losing.

In these moments we go from using the time to work towards hitting our faith goal, to watching time tick down to our doom. If only we would have just kept pushing. If only we would have just knocked on another door. If only we had just asked another person to help us.

If only we would have known the power of **working up to and through the deadline**, we might have found the victory that we were looking for. If only we had employed a little persistence, the power of **FAITH (APPLIED)** could have come to our aid and gave us the miracle outcome or the successful goal completion that we were looking for.

Over the years I have been on both sides of this equation. But thankfully I have now developed the habit of fighting on no matter what the time reads on the clock. Today I have the habit of simply knocking on another door, or simply seeking out another source for whatever it is that I need to bring me victory until I have that victory firmly in hand. Because of this, I can tell you that there is no way to succeed without it.

My past experiences have clearly shown me that if you and I have the persistence to keep moving until we get what we are seeking, we will get it. **Working up to and through the deadline**, is the very heart of *Persistence*. Wrapped up in the discipline of **working up to and through the deadline** is the ability to convert the initial denials of success, failures and all other denials of success into victories.

So often we give up on ourselves well before the game is over. We hear a string of **"NO's"** or we get a **"NO"** from a supposed authority figure and we just stop fighting.

So what there is plenty of time left on the clock, because we rationalize that time is running out and there is no way for us to get what we want, it is easy for us to just accept failure as being inevitable.

I used to be one of these people as well. I used to so compartmentalize my challenges and goals that I thought that every little aspect had to play out in a sequential fashion.

For example, if I had a goal to come up with $500 in 5 hours, I would think that I needed to get $100 each hour or there was no way to succeed. I would literally throw in the towel if I failed to keep the sequence of things on track, believing that the whole thing was doomed to ultimate failure and that that outcome fell out of my control when the sequence was broken. I have also met my fair share of supposed leaders who foolishly thought and taught this same ignorant, faithless point of view.

Looking back on that thinking now, I can see how false and limiting it was. In fact, comparing it to my record of victories and my experience with using *FAITH (APPLIED)*, it is nowhere near realistic or representative of how faith works. Even the events of July 30th, 1995 defied the logic of this thinking.

In reality, these kinds of rules and feelings are just our attempt to feel a sense of certainty about the endeavor that we are engaged in and they have nothing to do with *FAITH (APPLIED)*. These are our time rules and time constraints.

The simple truth is that the *Creator* and faith power are not bound by our dictates of time. And walking by faith, walking with the *Creator* means letting go of our rigid time rules. It means giving up our ideas about how our victory must or will play out.

Using *FAITH (APPLIED)* to fight your battles means understanding that it is not your job to worry about the clock. In the realm of faith, time will always be the concern of the *Creator*. Thus standing in faith means trusting that there is more than enough time for us to get what we want or need.

Working up to and through the deadline reveals that you always have way more time than you think

Most of us never seem to see the truth of how the **Creator's** time works or the truth that there is always time to get what we need if we will only stand in faith. One of the most powerful lessons that I have learned by applying this principle of **working up to and through the deadline** is that,

"You always have way more time than you think."

Many times when we are challenged or when we are engaged in working to bring some goal to pass we can make the mistake of thinking that we are working against the most unforgiving time constraints. Many times circumstances will try to fool you and I into believing as much.

In those moments, it would appear that the time deadlines that we face are always hard and firm. But in reality, in most areas of life, time is a more fluid concept than we have been led to believe it is. Many times, just thinking that our time is running out will allow the temptation to give up to set in and make it easy for us to quit on our faith project and throw in the towel.

In the end, it is this quitting that actually becomes our undoing. If only we had fought on to the end of the project, we might have found the rescue from the challenge or the goal accomplishment that we were looking for.

Through no fault of the **Creator**, I used to seriously struggle with this malady. In spite of what I knew were strong urgings of reassurance from the **Creator**, I just couldn't get myself to see the truth of the need to **work up to and through the deadline** when I was confronted by a challenge.

I'd be engaged in trying to put down some crisis and the **Creator** would be sending me strong urgings that I had the time I needed to succeed and trying to reassure me that I should keep working toward my goal in spite of the clock. But I wouldn't be able to get myself to accept these urgings and the messages of reassurance. In turn I couldn't get myself to relax and just keep moving.

Instead, at the end of the day I would give up and accept failure as my fate. When everything would be said and done, I would end up watching the moment play out and yield way more time than I thought that I had to succeed – time that would have been enough to achieve the goal I had sought, if only I had kept working to the end.

When all was said and done, I would always end up saying to myself, *"If only I had known I had that much time, I would have did this or that and I would have won."*

Working up to and through the deadline aligns you with the Creator's time

Over the years since first learning these principles I have seen all too many times that victory by way of faith often comes in the 11th or the 12th hour. We have all heard it said that the **Creator** doesn't move on our time. He moves on his time.

By our time we always want our deliverance to come yesterday. The last thing that we want to hear is that we will have to wait for the hand of the **Creator** to move. In fact, I believe that much of why most people don't like relying on faith is because they don't like the feeling of uncertainty that we have to endure when depending on the **Creator**.

We all have heard that we must learn to have patience. This is an absolute must when we are using **FAITH (APPLIED)** and relying on the **Creator** to move on our behalf.

This is so because the **Creator** operates in Faith's real time, not the time of our worries. We always want things done now. We don't want to go through the heat of the moment.

Many of us will try to avoid living by faith because we don't want the feeling of uncertainty that we all have to be willing to work through. Most of us can get ourselves to work hard if we could do so while feeling certain of our success. But we have a hard time, if not even an impossible time of working in the face of what might appear to be a losing cause. These kinds of concerns are often the seat of our impatience.

But the truth is that the **Creator** is not moved to action by our lack of patience. He is not moved by our desire to see faith come through in our *"Yesterday Time."*

But if we learn how to use **FAITH (APPLIED)** and trust in his time, our victory will always come through on time. The actor *Mike Epps* put it comically in the movie *Lottery Ticket* when he delivered the line,

> **"God** *might not be there when you want him,*
> *but he is always there when you want him!"*

The role that we play in moving the hand of the **Creator** and activating the miracle-making power of the universe is in using all of the time available to us by **working up to and through the deadline**.

The "Merry Chris" Story: The year that working up to and through the deadline saved Christmas!

One of the most touching stories that I can share with you to demonstrate the power of learning to **work up to and through the deadline** took place when my kids were still little guys. The event took place at Christmas back in 1997. Back then these little guys were 6 and 2½ years old. As you can imagine, at those young ages Christmas was a real big deal to them, just like it is to all children.

Normally, a 2½ year old child probably wouldn't have really understood it all or expected too much in the way of gifts. But, being in the 1st grade, our older son had his school activities and school friends to help him get totally excited about the coming joy that this special day of gifts would bring. It was that boundless excitement that he in turn infected his baby brother with for the holiday.

Once again the times could probably not have been worse. As we were so often in our early years together we were struggling just to stay afloat, although at this moment for an entirely different set of reasons.

Our car had been on its last leg for months now and had just finally gone out on us for good. Because my job required me to move around a large part of the city to be effective, both my sales and income were down sharply.

In fact, my boss was not even aware that I was having car trouble. If he had known, I probably would have lost my job altogether. As Christmas approached, we did well enough just to pay the rent and the rest of the bills.

In addition, we obviously needed to find a way to put together some resources to get another car. Plus in my line of work, another challenge that crops up at this time of the year is that of being able to cut through holiday mode and find new clients and new sales.

It is generally a fact that most of us begin to shut down in the holiday season. Other than our normal course of bills and responsibilities, we put off making appointments with people trying to sale us things unrelated to the holidays.

We put off making decisions regarding getting involved with things that have nothing to do with the holidays. Likewise, we put off committing financial resources to things that have nothing to do with our normal bills or holiday spending.

This can also be true in the business community. Companies will use the excuse of the ending year to put off doing anything until after the New Year. So to arrive in December and need to achieve a successful selling month can be a bit of an uphill battle. And that is exactly how I arrived in December, literally.

With this backdrop, I'm sure that you can just about picture how the month was going. To say it was slow would be a complete understatement. Between my car situation and the *"holiday mode"* of thinking that we all go into, the prospects of pulling out a good month, one good enough to meet our responsibilities and have a decent Christmas were looking bleak.

It didn't look like we'd be able to buy our kids any gifts, much less the ones they were requesting. And, did I mention that it was a particularly rainy Southern California December? This further hampered my ability to move around to try and conduct business.

There is nothing worse than calling on a prospective client soaking wet – something about dripping all over their place of business has a way of making would-be clients want nothing more from you than for you to get out of their office.

In my case, this was made all the more worse by the fact that I had walked a hole into the bottom of my only pair of work shoes – so that my shoes would take on water as I walked around. It would then drain and distribute this water in the offices that I visited.

As the time ticked down on this month, things just were not coming together. I had literally gotten down to the last week before Christmas and still no sales had materialized that would allow me to meet all of our needs.

On the home front, my older son had been released from school for winter break. Now that he was home all day, every day, he spent his time firing up himself and his baby brother about the joy that they would soon experience on Christmas morning.

They were both all abuzz making list, cutting pictures out of the newspaper, (I blame that darn *Toys 'R' Us* paper). And, they were talking me and their mom's head off with all of their excitement. They could hardly sleep at night for counting down the days. Little did they know things were not looking good for us as Christmas got closer and closer.

As I hit the field each day, I did my best to keep working in the face of my discouragement and all the things that should have stopped me from even trying to succeed here. But as the clock ticked down, that was getting tougher and tougher. Especially given my car situation, the odds were seriously stacked against me.

Eventually the point came where all of my efforts to find some new clients for the month had led me to just two potential leads. Most likely these were people that I had started talking to in a prior month. Now all of the effort that I had put into these two people was to culminate in this Christmas selling season.

One was a Doctor who owned a practice that had a few offices. The other was a lady that worked out of a home office, when that was not really *en vogue*. And, to this day, I don't really know what she did.

From a financial standpoint, the doctor was clearly more established and financially successful than this lady. He was even easier to talk to, as she seemed to be a bit off. I had been running back and forth to their places of business and calling them on the phone all throughout the month with no success.

Before long my wife started taking notice of the fact that our holiday hinged upon one of these people doing business with me. She started weighing in on which one she thought would be the best option for me to try to work if I were to succeed.

Of course, she chose the doctor and flat out told me not to waste my time on the lady and her home business. She knew nothing about the fact that success usually comes from the source that you least expect.

With the circumstances that were confronting me and with all of the negative that was going on around me, I came real close to throwing in the towel. But then I got the ultimate jolt of faith from the most unlikely person – my 2½ year old son.

Like any other 2½ year old, he was barely talking at the time, but his brother had him so jacked up with all of this Christmas stuff that he was as cute as a button. He walked around daily with a Santa hat on his big head and just embodied the spirit of the holidays.

On this particularly ugly day, when I had been out battling the weather, trying to find a buyer and having no luck, I returned home pretty much defeated. The clock was just about out of time for this year and if something did not come through at that moment, Christmas would be totally lost.

As I sat on the couch starting to feel sorry for myself, this little guy came up to me and said the words that would lift my spirits and inject me with the faith power that would save Christmas. He simply said,

"Merry Chris...!"

In his best 2½ year old vocabulary, he said just what I needed to hear. Those big eyes looking up at me from under that Santa hat and that little voice saying those words fired off within me the thought that I had to pull this out.

In that moment, I told myself that I was going to make this happen, period and end of story. I got up off of that couch and that is exactly what I did.

First I called on the doctor again. I did my presentation all over, gave him all of the reasons why he should accept my proposal and buy right then. Once again, he put off making a buying decision. Among other things, he cited the upcoming holiday as his reason to wait for the moment.

I tried to overcome the objections that he offered up for not buying, but it was just to no avail. So instead of wasting what little time I had, I left there. I did so with just one more prospect for getting a deal done, the lady who worked out of her home.

The bus ride from the doctor's office to her home was about 5 miles or so. As I mentioned earlier, we were having some real rough weather at that time and it was raining cats and dogs that day.

There were puddles everywhere and my shoes took on a great deal of water. To make matters worse, she had hard wood floors, meaning there would be no way for me to conceal the puddles that I'd likely bring into her home.

I went to her home not even knowing whether or not she'd be there. I didn't want to call ahead and give her advance warning that I was looking to come by and try to sell her and have her tell me *"NO"* over the phone.

All the way over I fretted about getting there and finding her to be gone. Upon my arrival, I was relieved to find her there. Her assistant let me in and led me through the house to the back where the prospective client was decorating her own Christmas tree.

As I walked through the house, I couldn't help but feel self-conscious about the loud squeak coming from my rain soaked shoes and the puddles that I knew they were leaving behind.

Once I got to where she was, I immediately went into my previous proposal. I went over all of the benefits that I felt she would receive by buying my machine and covered all of the reasons why I felt she needed to do it right at that moment.

She asked me a few questions about my proposal, which I carefully answered. Then, I presented her with a little test to see if she might be willing to go forward with my proposal.

Once she took the small step forward that I put in front of her, I felt more emboldened to ask her for the sale – a direct question to which she said, *"Yes!"* And with that, despite dragging all the way down to the 11th hour, Christmas was one step closer to being saved.

Now all there was left to do was get the deal approved and get paid. It is worth noting that the doctor who should have been the one to do the deal, didn't. And, the lady who shouldn't have been the one to do the deal, did it and became the miracle that saved Christmas for two very excited little guys. It's also worth noting that had I not **worked up to and through the deadline,** I would have never got to see this miracle come true.

While this isn't a story where life or death hinged upon faith being successfully applied, I don't think that any incident in my life better illustrates the importance of learning to **"Work Up To and Through the Deadline!"**

Just like on the day that these 8 principles were first shown to me, there was simply no substitute for seeing the task through to the very last minute possible. Just like then, the 12th hour was the very hour of success.

For most of us, there is a lot of frustration in working up to the final minute of a project without any sign of or guarantee of success. Yet, we simply must learn to get over it.

I have seen so many of these moments that I have come to realize that,

> *"Success is often buried on the other*
> *side of your frustration."*

Back then I would allow myself to get emotionally spent while working a project like this. The danger in that level of frustration is that it can very easily cause one to give up altogether.

On most occasions, I had it that bad. I was so bad, that one of my goals today is to stop allowing myself to get so frustrated so easily. So I know the truth that I am speaking here.

Count down to a Christmas miracle: Our craziest and happiest Christmas Eve ever!

To tell you how this story turned out, it literally came down to a miraculous Christmas Eve affair. Once I got her commitment to do the deal, now I had to perform the real tasks that made the deal real.

My boss, *Mr. Ray Sterling* was kind enough to make a special arrangement with me whereby he would advance me half of my commissions upfront on the condition that I got the financing closed and booked and the equipment installed in the customer's place of business beforehand. And, in performing these tasks, I was up against that same *"holiday mode"* thinking that was so much of a hindrance to finding a client that would sign in the first place.

For starters, our financing houses that we got our clients financed through were all 3 hours ahead on the east coast. Also, it was Christmas Eve and these banks and leasing companies were all planning to close up early so working with them on this day meant that I had to climb out of bed extra early if I expected to get a deal in place that day.

For that matter, our own warehouse and delivery staff was closing early as well. So I would be working against a short clock throughout this entire process. Here again I found myself once again having to use the concept of **working up to and through the deadline**.

Given my car situation, I had to orchestrate all of this from my home. As such, I had to have a good amount of trust that the people back at the office actually understood how important this all was and that they were doing everything within their power to get it done, just like I was.

To complete this process and turn this miraculous sale into cash dollars in my pocket, I had to first get the financing in place. If I couldn't get the deal financed, all my work to get the lady to agree would have been a big waste of time.

Next, because prepping for delivery of a new machine is a bit of an involved process, while I was working on the financing, I needed the delivery team to start prepping for the delivery before the confirmation of the financing had actually come through – something that our boss seldom allowed them to do because it caused problems if the deal fell through. Fortunately for me, on this day they went along with my demands.

Once the financing was done, I had to get the equipment delivered and installed, and have the client and her staff trained on how to use the equipment. Then I had to orchestrate a three way phone call between the client and the funding firm where the terms of the funding would be confirmed and agreed to by both parties.

All of this had to be completed with enough time to spare for our own payroll manager to draw up a check for me and get it signed by my boss before he left for the company Christmas party. Essentially, given that it was Christmas Eve, I had a half of the normal work day to get all of these tasks done and to say that I used up all of the time allotted and finished with no time to spare would be another understatement.

Once all of that was done, the challenge was far from over. While I stood one big step closer to my goal, I still had plenty to overcome to pull our Christmas together.

Even though it took a fair amount of effort and a few nervous moments, I had managed to fight the holiday clock and I was able to successfully get the financing in place in time to have our delivery team make this deal their last delivery of Christmas Eve.

Against incredible odds, I had gotten the things done that put a check in my pocket on Christmas Eve. But there was still much work to do. Now to complete this miraculous Christmas comeback, I still had to get that check, get it cashed and become *Santa*, and all with no car.

The first of the challenges that came with this set of tasks was getting to the company Christmas party to get the check. The problem was that I had totally misunderstood where the event was to be held.

The place where I thought it was to be held would have been a very simple bus ride from my house and I was all jazzed up about how quickly and easily we'd be able to get there. But in calling the bus company to get route information, they informed me that I had the wrong location in mind for the place where I actually had to go. Big problem!

The right place was in a totally different direction and it sat at the top of a big mountain. As you might guess, there was no bus service to the top of that mountain. When all was done, the bus dropped us off at the base of the mountain and to get to the top, we needed to climb.

So there we were, my wife and I in dress clothes and dress shoes, climbing this very steep mountain to save Christmas for our two sons. Remember I said that pulling this Christmas miracle out was an uphill climb? I meant that literally.

As I am sure you can imagine, it took us a lot of time and effort to get up that hill, but given the importance of the task, we managed to get it done. By the time we got there however, the party was all but over. Everyone had already eaten and they were just sitting around chatting and making merry.

Once we arrived my boss made arrangements for us to get our dinners so at least we got to eat. But no sooner than we finished eating everyone began to part ways. We had barely had a chance to recover from climbing the hill and now it was time to climb back down.

All of the staff in our office lived in the opposite direction from us. But fortunately, one of my superiors was going down the hill in the direction that we needed to go. So she gave us a ride down to the base of the mountain – to the bus stop that we needed to get to.

Now with the check in our hands, we needed to cash it and get to the places where we could shop for the toys and dinner items to bring our Christmas to life. Here again the challenge of it being Christmas Eve came into play, as the place where we needed to go to cash the check was a good ways from where we were and would be closing early as well.

If any of the buses that we had to take to get there were to run late, we could easily miss it and end up with no cash. Thankfully, all ran well and we made it with a few moments to spare.

From there, with cash now in hand, we were able to upgrade our mode of transportation and grab a taxi to the toy store to do our shopping. Back then stores still had respect for their employees so even *Toys"R"Us* would be closing early. So once again we were up against a soon to be expiring clock.

We made it with barely an hour to spare; not a lot of time when the store is crazy crowded and you are trying to pick gifts out of picked over goods. But all in all, we were thankful to be there with those problems. It certainly beat having to disappoint our little guys.

From there, we had to hop back on the bus and get back home, which wasn't exactly close to where we were at the time. By now, even the buses had gone into *"holiday mode"* and switched to a less frequent running schedule, making our ride home take even longer than normal.

And still, after taking this longer than normal ride, once we arrived home, we still had to get down to our local grocery store and get a tree and the dinner – not to mention, find something for the kids to eat that night.

By now this had been a very long day for me and I could not help but to start feeling a bit exhausted. But picturing the joy of the coming Christmas morning on their faces gave me a boost of energy and made it all worth it.

The truth is that we will do more for others than we will for ourselves and we proved this truth on this miraculous day. The next morning we awoke to easily the two happiest kids on the planet. All we heard was the sound of wrapping paper being ripped off with sheer force and excitement.

When we finally made it into the family room we were greeted by the two brightest and cheeriest faces that we had ever saw. As our little guys played happily with the toys that they believed that Santa had brought them, they couldn't stop telling us how this was the best Christmas ever and thanking us for making sure that Santa stopped by their way.

We weren't so sure that they didn't know that they were looking at *Mr. and Mrs. Claus*. But we were just happy to see them happy, and relieved that they didn't have to awake to a morning of disappointment and lack. Just preventing this made all of the effort that we had to put out to achieve this victory more than worth it.

I had to go through what it took to find a buyer for the deal that I needed to put together, get the deal funded, delivered and installed. My wife and I then had to get ourselves clear across town, trek up a mountain to get my pay advance, get back down that mountain to find a place to cash the check and get across town to get to a toy store to play *Santa*. Only then could we arrive back home and make this Christmas miracle a reality for two boys that had no idea that a miracle was even unfolding.

We had to do all of this without a car, on Christmas Eve. And, this was at a time when we didn't have all of the conveniences like direct-deposited payroll, cell phones, Uber, the internet and home delivery or stores that stay open right up to the holiday like we have today.

With all that had to be accomplished to make this day a reality, there is no way that I could have even thought about succeeding if I didn't have the mental, emotional and physical instinct to see this objective through to the end. I would have never won without having the willingness to *work up to and through the deadline*.

Most people would have probably called this too much hassle and thrown in the towel very early on in the process. But there is just no way to achieve victory in a faith project if you have the habit of caving at moments like this.

From my experience, there is just no way to move the hand of the *Creator* and activate the miracle-making power of the universe without the discipline to *work up to and through the deadline*.

Once my little guy uttered those two little words *"Merry Chris"* failure wasn't an option for me, period and by *working up to and through the deadline* I was able to produce a Christmas miracle that my family will never forget.

Working up to and through the deadline helped me to move past three common stumbling blocks to overcome Multiple Myeloma

By the time my battle with cancer came along, I had been so conditioned with the habit of *working up to and through the deadline* and I had seen so many 11th and 12th hour victories that I knew to never give up on my ability to win against the odds.

This was one of the things that gave me the confidence that I could fight for my healing and restoration no matter what the medical report or the doctors said. It was one of the things that kept me positive in the face of what many others would have seen as a very dark moment.

For most people, just receiving a diagnosis of cancer would have been too much to bear. The diagnosis alone would have been seen as a certain and final defeat. Yet I knew from the experiences of my 11th and 12th hour victories that no diagnosis should ever be thought of as a certain and final defeat as long as you have breath in your body and a fighting spirit.

I knew that the challenge is never over no matter what the odds and that there is always a way to win if you have the power of **FAITH (APPLIED)** on your side – even in a moment as trying as that of battling a major disease. I also knew that that power can only be activated fully when you and I are willing to **work up to and through the deadline**.

I took just that spirit with me into my battle with *Multiple Myeloma*. And, as it turned out, no other element of this **FAITH (APPLIED)** philosophy could have been more important to my healing than this principle.

I couldn't have known it going in, but having this one principle on my side saved me from becoming a victim of a set of unforeseen obstacles that keep many people from witnessing the healing power of the universe. I couldn't have known it going in, but there are three major stumbling blocks that often make losers of all those who show up to battle with the wrong expectations.

In fact, without this principle on my side, I would have been no match for these impediments to *faith-based healing*. Would you like to know what these three stumbling blocks are, so that you too can use the discipline of **working up to and through the deadline** to blow them out of the water?

Let's look at the first obstacle that keeps most people from seeing the power of *faith-based healing*:

Stumbling Block #1 – Failing to realize that you have to beat both the illness and the aftermath of the illness to achieve true healing and restoration.

When this health challenge first begin, I thought that all I had to do was beat the disease. I could have never imagined that for me, at that stage in the healing process, the real fight would just be beginning.

Neither could I have ever imagined that overcoming this disease would mean possibly having to work for the rest of my life to recover the good health that I once possessed. Or, that ***working up to and through the deadline*** would mean being committed to doing whatever it takes to get back into good health – and seeing the project of attaining this level of health through with the rest of my days on this earth.

At the start of my battle, I thought that at the most I would need to take and endure some harsh medicines, or a multi-drug treatment regimen. Or, perhaps I would have to endure some rounds of radiation therapy or a surgery or two. I thought that once I had successfully done these things, I would be able to resume my normal life as if nothing had even happened.

While I did have to endure some of the things that I had imagined would be needed for my healing, I couldn't have been more wrong in the assumption that these things alone would equal the sum of my battle.

It seemed like no sooner than I started taking the medicines and medical procedures that the doctors said would heal me, I quickly got the results that we were looking for. But as much of a relief as it was to hear these results, the fact was that my body was not even close to being restored to the level of health that I had enjoyed prior to being stricken with cancer.

In fact, I found myself with the cancer in remission, but my body much worse off from the battle. Plus, I started noticing that there was a whole new set of issues taking a hold of my body.

I very quickly realized that while I was beating the cancer, there was an aftermath to all of the medicines and procedures that was setting up to be a health challenge in its own right.

From this I learned quickly that when it comes to fighting a serious disease,

"You not only have to overcome the disease, but you then have to overcome the effects of the medicines and procedures that were used to heal you."

To put it another way, I learned that to achieve true restoration, you will have to overcome the aftermath of the disease as well.

I also learned that in this case, the deadline that you are facing could be ongoing for as long as you are still on this planet and that only a person battling through this situation could ever know that.

Having this awareness can make all of the difference in the world for someone who is battling a serious disease. Without it, or at the very least, a willingness to **work up to and through the deadline** in the fight for healing, people can tend to go into the battle with the wrong expectations of the healing process.

Maybe just like I did, they seemingly beat the disease quickly but become discouraged when the reality of the aftermath sets in on them. Maybe they look at this aftermath and think that they aren't beating the disease after all.

From this place, perhaps they stopped taking the medicines or stopped going through with the treatments and procedures that will heal them because they consider the situation hopeless in light of the new challenges that are coming their way.

I have seen personal friends lose their fight with cancer because they held the wrong expectations about the battle that they were engaged in. Perhaps if they had the expectation that they would have to battle both the disease and the aftermath of the disease they would have prepared themselves mentally and emotionally for that fight.

Perhaps if they had done this they would have stayed engaged in the healing process long enough to win and receive the healing and restoration that they were hoping for. It has been my experience that without having this awareness, the only power that can see you through is a commitment to **work up to and through the end** of your fight for healing.

Thankfully for me, I made that commitment to myself from the outset of my battle. I committed to fight on and see this battle through until I have the victory that I am seeking as my living reality.

Looking back now, in the face of the ignorance that I had regarding this first stumbling block, there is no way that I could ever successfully received my restoration from cancer without the discipline to **work up to and through the deadline**. That's why I know that you must have this principle working in your life if you are serious about beating a serious disease like cancer.

Let's look at the second obstacle that keeps most people from seeing the power of *faith-based healing*:

Stumbling Block #2 – Failing to realize that healing is a process, not an event.

Having the awareness to **work up to and through the deadline** is especially vital when you realize the truth that **healing usually comes by way of a process, not an event**.

One of the things that I quickly learned in my push to overcome the cancer that attacked my body was that my healing wasn't going to be an instantaneous happening, but rather more of a progressive endeavor; and a slow one at that.

When it comes to what is commonly thought of as *faith-based healing*, it seems that there are two very distinct schools of thought. It shouldn't be a surprise to hear that on the one side, many people don't believe in the power of faith as an agent that can heal their body. This is especially true when they are confronted by a serious disease.

These are the people who see what is commonly called *faith-based healing* as the stuff of quacks or religious fanatics. I'm sure that it's not news to you that this is the attitude that most people have when they think of *faith-based healing*.

These are the people who think of the doctor as the only one with the power to heal, or as the author and the finisher and the authority of human healing. Sadly, these people fail to realize just how often the doctors that they put their trust in fail to live up to the confidence that they put in them.

Still sadder, they don't realize that there are a ton of doctors who never even try. That was not only my experience when I found myself fighting for my life, it was also the experience of several other people that I know who have had to go through a similar situation.

As a matter of fact, I have literally known more than a handful of friends and family members who lost a battle with a serious illness while in the care of an unprofessional and callous doctor.

For these people, it's only when their doctor gives up on them, or when traditional medicine in general fails them – or they are challenged by an illness for which modern medicine is thought to be no match that they begin to look to *faith-based healing* for a miracle.

Even when these people give consideration to the thought of finding healing through faith, because they are coming in a moment of desperation, they have a hard time wrapping their minds around the notion of truly believing in and relying on faith power to heal them. This is especially true given that faith is a force that we cannot weigh and measure – a power that we cannot see, feel, touch or hear.

Given these facts, and given that these people often come to this moment expecting a miraculous event, when their complete healing and restoration doesn't appear to be taking place in an instant, most think that no miracle is forthcoming.

As a result they walk away from the healing process. In the end, they simply give up on the healing process before faith power has had a chance to work things out in their favor.

On the other side of the equation, there are those people who believe in *faith-based healing*, but they see it only as the stuff of miracles, and most often as an instantaneous event. Perhaps this is the image of *faith-based healing* that they have seen in religious circles.

To be sure, we've all seen these images and most of us have often thought of them as being fraudulent. And, even for those who believe that they are real, the challenge with this view is that when healing doesn't take place in an instant, they can start to believe that healing isn't taking place at all.

Out of this spirit, the tendency is to give up on the process and to not **work up to and through the deadline** to find the healing and restoration that is being sought.

So even this school of thought has a lot of its basis in wrong concepts. As such, approaching the subject of *faith-based healing* from either of these points of view could easily serve as a major source of confusion – confusion that will ultimately lead to you not trusting in the power of **FAITH (APPLIED)** to deliver the healing and physical restoration that you desire.

It could also be said that each of these schools of thought exist in the realm of traditional healing, i.e., you have those who don't believe in healing and you have those who believe that healing must be an instantaneous event.

Having now used the power of *FAITH (APPLIED)* to take on and overcome a very serious disease, I can tell you beyond a shadow of a doubt that healing is real. I can also tell you that the recovery that we are seeking takes time. And, I can tell you that *FAITH (APPLIED)* will deliver healing when you give it the time that it takes.

With this experience now under my belt, I can tell you with complete certainty that without having a true understanding of the fact that *healing is a process, not an event*, most people won't do what it takes to get through the healing process and receive their recovery.

If only they had the discipline to *work up to and through the deadline* of their healing process, they would be able to override their ignorance to this stumbling block and fully restore their body to the state of health and wellness that they once enjoyed. That's why I believe that making a commitment to work this principle is such an important part of overcoming illness.

Let's look at the third and final obstacle that keeps most people from seeing the power of *faith-based healing*:

Stumbling Block #3 – Failing to realize that when your health is taken away, you have to earn it back.

Of course, when you are confronted with something as life altering as a major illness, the tendency is to want to get right back up and pick up where you were seemingly moments ago.

Of course, just like my falling out, the event of falling ill seems as though it happens in a single event. It seems that you just instantaneously go from being healthy and vibrant to being sick and lifeless. From that frame of reference the natural impulse is to want to spring back to health in an instant, with no effort on your part – to literally, pick up where you left off before the challenge came your way.

But whether that's true or not, restoring your body to its former self is almost never that way. The simple fact of matter is that the body has to first be set up for healing, undergo the healing process, then we undergo the process of rehabilitating ourselves in the physical sense.

Much like when you break a bone, the doctor sets the bone and then nature takes its course in healing the bone and then you go to work through physical therapy to restore the bone back to its prior level of functionality.

You might not give it much thought, but that process of restoring your bone, likely also involved restoring the surrounding muscles and all of the other parts of your body that you favored while you were injured and was actually both a physical and a mental endeavor. Meaning you had to undertake both physical and mental efforts to earn back the physical mobility that you once enjoyed and the mental trust that you had in that mobility.

You may have had to work through some experience of limited mobility as you went through the rehabilitation process to get back to full mobility. You may have also had to work through some experience with pain as you went through the rehabilitation process to get back to being pain free. You usually will have had to go through all of these processes to earn back the health and wellness that you once enjoyed.

In my experience, it is the same way when you are trying to overcome a major illness. You have to get the medicines in you and go through the procedures that will set you up for healing and then give nature a chance to use these resources to restore you to health. Then you will have to go through the rehabilitation processes in order to get back to your former self.

There is often no way to find healing and restoration without going through this process. And, from my observation, many people have a hard time taking on this process in the right spirit. Too many allow the spirit of pity and thoughts of *"Why Me"* to rule their thinking.

Too many wish for the days when they were healthy and didn't have to go through any of the stuff that they are now faced with having to do to get their health back. Along the lines of the first stumbling block that we talked about, they are having a problem with the fact that they have to now beat the aftermath of their disease.

In my experience, just like with the other two stumbling blocks that we have already discussed here, ignorance on this truth that **when your health is taken away, you have to earn it back,** let alone the fact that you can earn it back, causes many people to give up on restoring their health.

In these cases, they come through the illness but end up accepting what should be the temporary impediments that it brought with it as permanent. Or even worse, give up on finding healing all together – confusing the slow progress of full restoration with no progress on the healing front.

I feel that it must be said that this can often be a classic, *"Glass half full or glass half empty"* issue. As those with a generally positive outlook on life will have an easier time keeping score by looking at the progress that they are making, as opposed to the slowness of that progress.

But bigger than even that maybe is the truth that having the wisdom to see the process through to the end is the best and easiest way to get through this entire process in the right spirit. Having the awareness to **work up to and through the deadline** is the surest way to follow that wisdom.

Perhaps in the spirit of the seventh principle of *FAITH (APPLIED)*, this is also a place where we should apply the wisdom to just **Delay Judgment** as we go through the process of healing and recovery. When you find yourself battling against a serious disease, perhaps this is the best way and the easiest way to insure that you maintain your focus on **working up to and through the deadline** as you go through the battle for your life and health.

Perhaps this is the best way to insure that you get past this stumbling block and earn back the health that you once enjoyed. Or, even take your health to a greater level than you ever had before. After I got clear on the truth of this stumbling block, that's the goal that I set for myself.

Working up to and through the deadline saved my life from Multiple Myeloma and then restored my mobility

Fortunately for me, I knew about these principles and the power of *FAITH (APPLIED)* before cancer came calling. Fortunately for me, having the discipline to **work up to and through the deadline** allowed me to accept that I had to **beat the illness and the aftermath of all the medicines and medical procedures** that gave me the victory over Multiple Myeloma.

Fortunately having this discipline also allowed me to accept the truth that my **healing was going to be a process, not an event**. And, fortunately having this discipline allowed me to accept the fact that given that *Multiple Myeloma* **had taken my mobility away, I would have to earn it back**.

Just accepting these truths helped me to avoid falling victim to the three common stumbling blocks that keep many people from coming back from a serious illness.

It also must be said again that when I made the declaration to myself that *"I was going to beat whatever the doctors were going to tell me I had been attacked by,"* I thought that all I had to do was beat the disease itself. And in that moment, I would have thought that the event of beating the disease represented the deadline that I would need to work up to and through.

But when it quickly became clear to me that my fight to return to full health and mobility was going to be a slow, drawn out process, I had to accept that the deadline that I am working up to and through was likely going to be a never ending one.

Today my push to restore my body to the full state of health I once had is still very much a work in progress. At times it even looks like some parts of my old health may never return. Still I am grateful for the parts of this fight that I am winning. I am grateful that the *Creator* has given me the opportunity to fight this fight.

There are so many others who never got the chance to fight – much less a prior gifting of the principles that would allow them to come out victorious. We all know people who have had this misfortune. I certainly do. Just thinking about these people makes me remember to count my blessings each and every day that I am alive to fight.

It is these people who give me the inspiration and courage to **work up to and through the deadline** and to push beyond the stumbling blocks that will take many people out when they find themselves confronted with a serious disease like *Multiple Myeloma.*

In my battle against *Multiple Myeloma* everything led here to the eighth and final principle of **FAITH (APPLIED)**. As I have now discovered, there is no other place where being willing to **work up to and through the deadline** has been more valuable than in my fight to beat cancer and restore my mobility. In the long run it is what will allow me to restore myself to the level of health and wellness that I enjoyed before being stricken with this disease.

In the face of the ignorance that I had regarding these three common stumbling blocks, there is no way that I would have successfully received my healing from cancer without this principle. That's why you must have it working in your life if you find yourself confronted with a similar situation.

Working up to and through the deadline is the hallmark of champions in the world of sports, in life and in the realm of FAITH (APPLIED)

In closing out this last principle, I feel that we can find no greater example of the power of **working up to and through the deadline** than the world of sports.

If there is one arena that seems to embody this principle this would clearly be it. In the sports world athletes are first taught the concept of playing, and **competing up to and through the final buzzer** at an early age.

If you are a fan of college football, you have no doubt witnessed the moment where players from both teams hold up four fingers as the game transitions into the fourth quarter. This act is meant to serve as a reminder to each player of the need to play and compete to the end of the contest.

No matter what the sport, the fact is that all athletes are expected to maintain this discipline of playing a complete game throughout their careers. Not only are they expected to maintain this discipline from a mental standpoint, but they are also expected to maintain the physical conditioning and stamina necessary to actually put this critical success principle into consistent action.

Athletes are expected to maintain this discipline for good reason, as many sporting contest are won in the latter stages of the game. And, before becoming champions, many teams and players will have to overcome both their underdog label and a tough opponent who has taken an early lead in the contest.

Most often these types of feats can only be accomplished by those who have the mental and physical ability to fight on in the face of what appears to be insurmountable odds and circumstances. Most often these types of feats can only be accomplished by a team that has the habit of competing up to and through the deadline.

In this world, there is even a certain amount of pride that comes from being the person or part of the team that possesses the winning quality of a *"No Quit Spirit."* And, in the same way, there is a special pride that comes from being the person that hits the game winner.

How many games are won by the homerun in the bottom of the ninth, or by the buzzer beater shot sank at the last second or by the touchdown ran in or the field goal successfully kicked as the game clock ticks to double zero? There is no way for these victories to happen if the players or teams that achieve them didn't have the habit of playing up to and through the deadline of the game.

It's through experiences like these, that by the time the average athlete reaches the college or professional ranks, she has been so well conditioned with this habit that she is virtually assured of success in whatever endeavors she turns her hands to. At the very least, because of this habit, the high level athlete has a true fighting chance at getting whatever she is competing for in life.

A true champion and conqueror must be able to play from behind and finish strong

As true as it is in sports, often times it is equally true in our everyday lives that before you or I can conquer the challenge that we are confronted with or achieve that coveted goal, we must learn how to play from behind.

In his prime, what made *Tiger Woods* so great was that he was not only trained and conditioned to perform under the pressure of unfavorable conditions, but he also had the discipline of competing up to and through the deadline of the contest.

It was said that he first received these disciplines from his father. Once he rose to dominance, he continued to use both disciplines to rack up an impressive record of come from behind victories. He often did it by keeping his cool when he found himself in a challenging contest and by competing to the very end.

Likewise, you and I should take both of these disciplines to heart when things go awry in our faith projects. At the least we should give some consideration to the fact that things don't always go the way that we want them to go at every moment. But that often doesn't mean that things don't turn around by the end of it all.

To be sure, having these types of discipline develops a special kind of mental toughness and an attitude of confidence that would allow us to easily believe that we can press on in the face of challenging circumstances, circumstances that would easily discourage most people.

Having this type of confidence would make it easy for one to *work up to and through the deadline* of a sports contest. Just as having this same type of confidence will allow you to *work up to and through the deadline* of a faith project, let alone the regular affairs of your daily life.

Also, when it comes to having the discipline to *work up to and through the deadline*, you should always be ready to finish strong. You should expect to play harder as you come to the end of a project. You should expect the curve ball or the monkey wrench to be thrown your way.

Sometimes life is like a video game, it gets harder as you come to the end of the game. This is when you must stand and *work up to and through the deadline.* Now I'm not suggesting that you go through your life looking for opposition, but don't be shocked when it shows up either.

A good friend once told me that before he starts out in pursuit of a goal, he gives consideration to the things that could go wrong and then makes plans to cover those contingencies. In the physical arena, this strategy is meant to prepare oneself to fight on in the event you encounter foreseen challenges on the road to the success that you are seeking.

In the faith arena, following the discipline of *working up to and through the deadline* will all but insure your success by giving you a way to fight on when you encounter those challenges that may be unforeseen.

In my experience, this along with having the discipline to finish strong in pursuit of your faith projects will help you to overcome any/all obstacles that stand to get in the way of you achieving success.

As I move to close this principle out I cannot stress enough how vital this single principle is to your success in all faith endeavors. I know this to be true because prior to July 30th, 1995, when it came to how I conducted myself in my personal and professional life, I was one of those people who would never *work up to and through the final tick of the clock*. And, I had a lack of winning results to show for it.

I would never allow myself to work past the point of frustration and discouragement, or in the face of seeming defeat. Because I never followed through in this way, I had no clue of the fact that success in the faith realm often comes in the 11th or 12th hour. Most of all, I had no knowledge of the power that each one of us has to tap into the miracle-making power of this universe and to make it deliver victory to us against all odds.

Before I finally got this truth I used to get so frustrated that I would give in and give up before this miracle-making power could come to my aid. In giving up I would prevent this power from ever having a chance to deliver the resources that

I now know were on the way to help me meet my challenges or achieve my goals.

I ultimately realized that the real challenge that I had was learning to trust in the power of *FAITH (APPLIED)*, trust the *Creator* and control my emotions – especially in those moments when it didn't feel like my efforts were having an effect on my situation, or would result in my success. It seems like the *Creator* took me back and forth through circumstances that gave me a chance to see this truth until I got it.

In so doing, I saw firsthand that when it comes to *FAITH (APPLIED)*, success usually comes in the 11th or 12th hour. And, I became thoroughly conditioned with the truth that *working up to and through the deadline* was the only way to achieve that success.

One of my goals now is to pursue every faith project without allowing myself to succumb to the emotions of frustration, doubt or fear. And, since seeing the power that *FAITH (APPLIED)* gave me to recover from cancer, my goal has been to trust the *Creator* absolutely with every aspect of my life by the power of *FAITH (APPLIED)*.

We just talked about how much we cheer for the athletic heroes who use this principle of *working up to and through the deadline* to achieve the impossible victory, how much more meaning and joy could we derive if the victories that we were cheering for were our own faith victories?

Could it be that the *Creator* and all the angels in heaven cheer us on in the same manner and take the same delight in our faith victories? I'd be willing to bet that they do.

We have now thoroughly looked at this final principle of *FAITH (APPLIED)*. All there is left to do now is for you to make a commitment and make sure that from this day forward, you always *work up to and through the deadline* of every faith project that you enter into, no matter whether it originates from a place of challenge or the pursuit of a coveted goal.

The great truth of FAITH (APPLIED): You Get What You Do!

As we close out this eighth and final principle of *FAITH (APPLIED)*, let me share what I have found to be one of the great truths of the *FAITH (APPLIED)* philosophy. They say that to have any real power, our faith must be expressed by more than our feelings. In fact they say that to have any real power, our faith must be expressed in our actions.

We have also all heard it said that, *"You get what you focus on."* They say that this is the law of attraction, one of the supreme laws of this universe.

I can't say for sure if any of these sayings are true. But I can say that when it comes to the power of *FAITH (APPLIED)* the following 5 word concept represents a great truth that you would be wise to recognize. Simply put,

"YOU GET WHAT YOU DO!"

When it comes to wielding the power of faith, I have learned firsthand that when all is said and done, the simple truth is that, *"You Get What You Do!"*

It really is no more complicated than that. Whenever you have a question as to why you didn't get what you were standing in faith for, you don't need to look further than the question of,

"Did you do what you were hoping to get?"
"Did you do your part to achieve the results you sought?"

If you didn't, you need to know that why you didn't do it doesn't matter. The simple fact is that more often than not, you can't get the results that you are seeking if you didn't do the things that needed to be done to get those results.

More often than not, that is simply the bottom line. Our desires and feelings just don't matter if we don't get that we have to do what we expect to get.

From my experience, when it comes to *FAITH (APPLIED)*, you don't get what you want or what you should get – you don't get what you need or what you cry for. *You get what you do!* That's one large part of the significance of you and I learning how to *work up to and through the deadline*.

It's also the ultimate significance of employing these 8 principles to improve our odds of success in our faith projects. At the end of the day, there are only 8 questions that matter. They are:

1. Did you *accept the challenge*?
2. Did you *set the goal* in the form of the task that needed to be done and move to successfully complete those tasks?
3. Did you *position yourself for success*?
4. Did you *avoid the loser clique*?
5. Did you *ask for the help and support that you needed to succeed*?
6. Did you *avoid wasting time on the people and situations that don't help you* get your goal?
7. Did you *delay judgment* to give yourself a chance to succeed?
8. Did you *work up to and through the deadline* to find the success that you were seeking?

All of these questions cut to the heart of the broader question of,

"Did you do what you were hoping to get?"

If you truly want to get the power of *FAITH (APPLIED)* flowing in your life – if you want the power to overcome your greatest challenges and achieve your most coveted goals and dreams, there are simply no more important questions than these to constantly ask yourself.

Focusing on these questions is the easiest way to insure that you are taking the mental, physical and spiritual actions necessary to get the most out of the wisdom of *FAITH (APPLIED)*.

I have had my time of thinking that I had to have the perfect inner world to make my goals and dreams come true. I have surely witnessed several self-help gurus and many a religious leader teach as much.

For years I fought the fight of trying to get my inner world perfect and struggled mightily with the concept. But ultimately I found out that even more important than what I was thinking and focusing on was the question of,

"What was I doing?"

Believe me, I get the correlation between thinking and actions, and how one's outer world is a manifestation of his/her inner world. But I have also witnessed the power of these *FAITH (APPLIED)* principles to deliver victory in spite of whether I had the perfect inner world in the moment or in my life in general.

I have witnessed firsthand, the power of these *FAITH (APPLIED)* principles to deliver victory against impossible odds when I simply, ***Did what I wanted to get!*** Most notably, being my victory over cancer.

Because of this and all of the other faith victories that I have witnessed before and after it, I have learned that this is a great truth of *FAITH (APPLIED)* that you and I would be wise to learn and observe. In the same way, we need to learn to ***work up to and through the deadline*** when we are looking to achieve success in a faith project.

So there you have the eighth and final principle of *FAITH (APPLIED)*. On July 30th, 1995 the *Creator* led me in the use of these 8 principles and while I didn't know them by name, the application of them gave me the $1,000 bonus that I so desperately needed at that moment.

Little did I know at the time, in giving me the wisdom that I came to realize was the formula for *FAITH (APPLIED)*, he was giving me a tool and a weapon that was of far greater value than that $1,000.

In the aftermath of that day's events, I was given the names of each principle and shown how by applying the same formula to the affairs of my life I could bring to my aid the force and power that will activate the miracle-making power of the universe – a force and power that would allow me to literally stand up to the great many challenges that would ultimately come my way.

Over the years that followed, I have seen how in a moment of challenge, using these 8 principles will unfailingly allow you to pull miracles from the universe. And, in pursuit of your goals and dreams, these 8 principles will literally allow you to turn on the creation force of the universe.

Just like this power did for me on July 30th, 1995 and numerous other times since, it will allow you to achieve results that would otherwise be unachievable. It will allow you to defy both the odds and the clock. It will bring to your aid a force and power that will help you to achieve results far beyond any that you could ever produce on your own.

As I said at the beginning of this work, as I became aware of the power of this wisdom, the power to command the force known as faith in my life, I couldn't help but to believe that the *Creator* was giving me this wisdom for a future date and event in my life, and for a much bigger purpose where having such wisdom would be crucial.

To date there has been no bigger purpose for me than saving my life from the deadly cancer that knocked me down on July 14th, 2012. There has been no bigger place where having the power of these *FAITH (APPLIED)* principles has mattered more than this fight.

When *Multiple Myeloma* entered into my life, the stage was set for this to be my biggest faith project. Everything that I have ever gone through before, and I suspect that everything that I will go through after this fight can only pale by comparison to the importance and magnitude of this battle.

Looking back on the parts of that fight that are already behind me, I can see that there is a ton of insight into the inner workings of *FAITH (APPLIED)* that can be gleaned from the story of this battle.

Just understanding how this disease first entered my life, what I have gone through since it arrived, and how I have now used these 8 principles to *activate the healing power of the universe* might be the perfect epilogue to this work.

This one story might be the greatest proof that I can offer you of the power of mastering this *FAITH (APPLIED)* wisdom and of why you should get the power of these principles flowing and working in your life now. So to close out this work, I will leave you with:

The Multiple Myeloma Incident

From the beginning of this work I have tried to give you a view through my eyes of the role that the wisdom of *FAITH (APPLIED)* has played in helping me to overcome some very trying situations in my life. I have tried to get you to experience this wisdom in the same way that I first experienced it, to experience its validity the same way that the *Creator* led me to experience it.

Through the point stories that I have shared here it has been my goal to give you a bird's eye view of the power that you and I have to fight the battles that confront us as we make our way through this life. In recounting these stories, I am proud of the fact that I can raise my hand up to *God* and state the fact that every word of each tale is true.

These stories were perfectly amazing on their own. Thus I have had no need to inflate my testimony or to embellish upon any aspect of these stories in any way. Therefore you can truly take heart and inspiration from these stories because they are 100% real.

As I look back over the words that have already hit the page, even I am amazed at the journey that has been my life. Until taking on the task of creating this work, I have never had the occasion to put these events side by side for me to see how they correlate.

In so doing I can now see how I have been shaped by these events and the role that *FAITH (APPLIED)* has played in my personal life journey. I am truly proud of the person that I have become as a result of this journey.

Until now I have never felt the need to relive these stories and I have certainly never felt a need to put them together side by side. But now having taken this action, I realize that I have been given another opportunity to see that *FAITH (APPLIED)* was truly wisdom given to me from the *Creator* and a chance to recognize yet again that He truly gave me this wisdom for a greater purpose.

Over the years I have experienced a great many challenges and struggles and I truly thought that I had seen it all. I have had to face down several trials that at their time, seemed to rock my life and my spirit to my very core.

In this time I had been through so many moments where it took the power of **FAITH (APPLIED)** to pull me through, that I could clearly see that the *Creator* was using these adversities to develop my faith muscle.

Even more specific, I felt that this wisdom was being thrust upon me for a time or an event in my life when having an unshakable faith would be of the utmost importance.

Over the years I had fought faith battles as a single man and I had fought faith battles as a husband and father. Over the years I have had battles that challenged my personal peace and comfort and I have had battles that threatened the comfort and security of my family. I have even had battles that threatened my very ability to keep my family together.

Both as a single man and a married man, I have had to stare down joblessness and lack and all the things that go along with having empty pockets. I have had to stare down housing challenges, both the challenges of keeping a roof over our heads and of keeping the vital necessities in place underneath the roof. I have also had the challenge of trying to get a roof back over our heads after having become homeless as a result of adverse financial conditions.

These moments pushed me far beyond any level of strength that I thought I had. In their time, just getting through these events required the use of a ton of faith, a faith that I didn't believe was in me. Without the *Creator* giving me the wisdom of **FAITH (APPLIED)** there was no way that I could have ever withstood those moments.

Yet as vital as this faith was to getting through those moments, somehow I still knew that these moments and the faith muscle that I was building in them were actually preparation for something much bigger. In the end, I could have never been more right.

Defeating cancer: My faith's greater purpose revealed

The greater purpose that I was being prepared for was finally revealed to me the day I fell ill with *Multiple Myeloma – a cancer of the bone marrow*. From where I sit now, it is easy to see that all of the faith battles that I had been forced to fight over the years were preparing me for this day.

Because of all of those battles, the new reality that was thrust upon me that day didn't hit me in the same way that it would have hit most people, or the way it perhaps would have hit me had I not had those fights.

As the events of that moment were beginning to play out, I quickly realized that as big and daunting as the previous challenges that I once had appeared to be in their moments, they were no comparison to the challenge that was now standing before me. And yet, because I had been through all of those challenges, the challenge that was standing before me was no match for the *"ME"* that was standing there at that moment.

As big as I thought these challenges were at their time, none of them, nor all of them combined could equal the mental and physical challenge that was presented to me on that day. And yet, because of the collective bigness of all of those challenges, the challenge that was standing before me could not equal the mental and physical strength of the *"ME"* that was standing there on that day.

It already seemed as if there was a season of my life where I was going from one trying moment to the next on a continuous basis. And now, on top of all of that, I had to take on cancer.

Yet because I had fought one challenge after another for years, the challenge that was standing before me was not treated any differently by the *"ME"* that was standing there on that day.

And it wasn't like these other trying moments had subsided and then the cancer came my way; not even. When this challenge came, it made its appearance just as I was getting back adjusted to life after my release from the *Child Support Enforcement* nightmare that had dogged me for a decade.

I had just recovered the final piece to the puzzle that I thought would allow me to begin rebuilding the career and financial well-being that that challenge had taken away from me. Within a week of that accomplishment, I was felled by *Multiple Myeloma*.

When this moment came, it was on top of other challenges that were already enough to deal with by themselves. Only with this challenge the stakes were much higher.

There is nothing more important than life itself, whether it's our own life or the life of a loved one. Now mines was on the line and I instinctively knew that overcoming this challenge would require a deliberate faith; a confident faith that I could count on.

As this moment began to play out, I took stock of the situation that was shaping up and realized that the challenges that I had gone through in the past were sent to give me that kind of faith. Only that kind of faith would be strong enough to give me the power to stand in the face of a challenge as serious as cancer. Only that kind of faith could give me the ability to activate the healing power of the universe.

July 14th, 2012

Looking back now, the moment that became the greatest faith battle of my life started at least a year prior to its arrival. As for the day itself, July 14th, 2012 began like most other days back then. I awoke with a laundry list of things to do before the day came to an end – the most important of which was to go pick up a car that I was buying from one of my good clients, *Miss Jewel Presley*.

My wife and I were going to go together and we decided to just take the bus up and drive the newly acquired car back. Little did we know as we started out for the day that the short bus ride that we had planned would be unlike any other bus ride that we had ever taken in our lives. Little did we know that before this ride would end, my life would both change forever and be saved by the experience.

To get to our destination we needed to take two short bus rides, starting out first on a bus that picked up right in front of our home. This bus was to take us to a local bus depot where we would take a connecting bus for another short ride across town to meet up with *Miss Presley*.

We were the kind of people who always had a car and almost never rode a bus to go anywhere. So for us, just being on the bus would almost be a little adventure – one in which we really didn't know quite what to expect. But given the short nature of each ride, we thought that this would be a quick, simple trip; a no hassle transaction that would be over and done with as quickly as it began.

In hindsight I can see how out of touch we were with the reality that was shaping up in my body. The night before had been a night where I had trouble sleeping. My back in particular had been hurting me all night.

I had had a hard time getting comfortable in the bed and had barely slept. I had been having this same challenge off and on for the better part of the prior year without really getting the significance of these signals from my body that something was going on.

Over that year, these symptoms were perfectly fleeting. I might have a rough night sleeping one night and be totally fine the next night. I might awake with discomfort in my body one morning and awake feeling perfectly okay the next morning.

Most often when I did have a rough night sleeping or awake to discomfort in my body, my body would seem to recover and all would seem fine by the time I needed to get going with my day. Many times I would simply go to the gym and do some cardio or take a soak in the Jacuzzi and my body would appear to loosen up, allowing me to go on with my day. Given this history I didn't think much of the night that I had just experienced.

But as I awoke on the morning of July 14th, 2012 I felt a tightness in my back and chest that just wouldn't let up. Given my past experiences, I wanted to get to the gym or at least, take a moment to soak in our Jacuzzi to try and loosen it up.

I thought these challenges were a simple matter of the bodily tension that I'd felt before or a simple misalignment of my posture, perhaps a simple consequence of my having slept wrong the night before. I thought that given the chance, my body would adjust itself and like all the other times, I'd be able to go on with my day like nothing of a serious nature was the matter.

For her part, my wife sensed that something much more was wrong. For starters, she noticed that I was laboring as I moved about and as I walked. She noticed that I didn't seem to be moving at my usual pace.

Normally I tended to move with far more swiftness than she did. But on this day, she noticed that she was easily out pacing me. She was so convinced that there was something going on with me that she suggested that we put off our car buying trip for another time when I was feeling better.

I thought seriously about taking this advice. But in the end, I was able to convince her that nothing too serious was going on. So with her blessing, as I always had done, I pushed us to just get moving in spite of how I was feeling, thinking that I would eventually feel better as the day progressed.

But the experience of seeing me in distress did alarm her so much so that she did warn me for the first time that I would be taken to ER for a thorough exam if I continued to experience either of these symptoms. But beyond that brief discussion, we were both so eager to get the car deal done that we both dropped the matter and pushed on to the bus stop to head for our destination.

A short bus ride with lifelong ramifications

MTA Line 108, the first of two buses that we needed to catch to go pick up our new car came right on time. Given the early hour that we were riding it and the fact that this was a weekend, there was hardly anybody on it. From all appearances this looked like it would be a quick and simple process.

We boarded the bus and my wife took her seat as I paid our fair for this short ride. She took a seat right near the front, right near the driver to prevent me from having to take too many steps to join her.

After paying I made my way to this seat and settled in for the ride, thinking all the while that this ride would not only be a normal ride, but that it would be over in no time flat. But we weren't a solid minute into our trip when the signs that this ride was to be anything but normal reared their head.

For starters, a symptom that had only recently began to give me grief came calling. This symptom was an extreme sensitivity to every little bump or dip along the roads that we traveled over.

It seemed as if this was a particularly rickety bus and this particular driver was speeding and driving it like a bat out of hell on her way to her destination. She couldn't have known that my body was having a tough time handling all of the dips and bumps that we were encountering.

She drove this bus in a manner that none of us would ever think of driving our personal car out of the fear that we would ruin our suspension and alignment. Before long I noticed that with every major bump or dip that this bus rode over my body received a flash of pain that felt like someone had just socked me in my chest. Each of these blows was very intense and distressing. In fact, they were such a shock to my body that I had a hard time keeping the evidence of this pain from showing on my face.

It seemed that each block that we traveled had its own punch for me and it wasn't long before my wife noticed that something was going wrong and began to question me about how I was doing. After about 13 blocks, as the first leg of our short ride was coming to an end, my body had had about all that it could take of this torture.

As we were pulling into the bus depot I was starting to think that I might not be able to make it for the entire trip that we had planned. I was also starting to think that perhaps I'd need to find a way to make it to seek the medical attention that I had been putting off right then and there.

Despite the experience I had just had, I still thought that I had a say in what was to come next and that this was a decision that I would get to make at the end of this ride. In typical male fashion, I thought that I could tough it out and get to my destination to complete my car purchase.

I reasoned to myself that I could go to the hospital to seek medical attention after this task was complete. But as I stood to exit the bus and decide what to do, my body stepped forward to jolt me with the truth of where I was in this moment.

The worse pain that I had ever experienced in my life

Just at the moment that I stood up, my body was hit with a wave of pain unlike anything that I had ever experienced in all of my life. I had had pain before, most notably toothache pain and as painful as that was, this pain was far worse.

It was more intense and longer lasting than any pain that I have ever had before and worse than anything that I should ever hope to experience again. It was the kind of pain that you wouldn't wish on your worst enemy. I have no way of knowing what the pains of child birth feel like. But if it is anything like this I feel sorry for each and every mother that has ever birthed a child.

This pain accompanied each movement of my body and rendered me immobile, to say the least. With each wave that hit my body I let out the biggest yell and scream that I could muster. Each of which scared my wife to no end.

This lady had never even seen me cry and here I now stood in the doorway of a city bus in obvious pain, screaming and yelling uncontrollably. In her shock she quickly jumped down from the bus and began calling 911 to summons aid for me.

As for the few people that were on the bus, they were equally alarmed. I'm sure that this was not the morning bus ride that they thought they'd be taking and yet here they were caught in the middle of the moment that cancer was rearing its ugly head in my life.

For her part, the bus driver too was alarmed. Once she realized that I needed help she immediately got on her radio to dispatch the local paramedics to the bus depot. To her credit she tried to be as reassuring as she had been helpful. She tried to calm me by talking to me about an incident that she had had where her body had broken down in pain.

She tried to comfort me by sharing how her case was merely a pinched nerve – she tried to reassure me that perhaps I was simply experiencing a similar issue and a quick trip to the ER would reveal that I'd be okay before I knew it. But as the waves of my pain kept coming, I wasn't so sure.

In my case, each time I tried to make a move to exit the bus, I was hit with a pain wave that just seemed more serious than a pinched nerve. In fact, before long it became clear that I couldn't even get myself off of the bus. She ultimately had to employ the handicap lift to get me down.

In my case, this pain was the most intense when I did anything to move my upper body or to do anything that took me from the basic standing position. If I tried to sit, if I tried to bend, if I tried to raise my legs in anyway, if I tried to step too fast that same wave of pain would come calling. It didn't take me long to realize that all I could do in this shape was to stand still and wait for help to reach me.

Fortunately the fire station was literally a block away so the wait for help wasn't a long one. When the paramedics arrived they found me standing there in a totally distressed state. I couldn't even sit down for them to check me out.

Because I couldn't move without triggering the waves of pain, I even had to stand up while they hooked up all of the various equipment that they needed to help them monitor both my vital signs and the state of my vital organs.

Once they got everything hooked up they were confronted with the challenge of getting me over to and on their rig. I couldn't step up to get on it and I couldn't position my body in a manner to get on the gurney where they could lift me onto the rig.

For all intent and purpose, I could not move. So there I was, stuck for another 20 minutes while they figured out how they could manage to get me onboard their vessel.

Eventually a solution was found in raising the gurney to a high sitting position and having me sit down instead of lie down. Moving into that position was challenging in its own right, but I was able to make it into that position without causing too much pain. Now on the gurney, the firemen were able to lift me onto their rig.

Once onboard, the next challenge was making sure that I wasn't having a heart attack. This determination would have implications on both what medications they could give me to try to ease the waves of pain that I was experiencing and what hospital they'd need to transport me to. Nothing could proceed until this question was answered.

The equipment that was used to make this determination was malfunctioning and without it they had no way of getting an accurate reading. Fortunately, one of the firemen came up with a work around that allowed him to get the system jump started.

As for me, while they were working to solve this problem, because of the position of my body, I was forced to sit through a protracted wave of the most excruciating pain. It was all but unbearable to have to sit through this pain and just when it really did become too much to take they got the info that they needed.

The good news that their test revealed at that moment was that I wasn't having a heart attack. I was now on my way to the hospital to see the doctor that I had been trying to avoid and they were finally able to begin administering the pain relief medication that I so desperately needed.

Marina del Rey Hospital, a place from my past

As the pain medication kicked in and began to do its work, I quickly found myself almost forgetting where I was just a few short moments earlier. Now I was no longer in pain. And, gone with that pain was a real sense of the reality that was unfolding before me.

Based upon all of the factors involved, most notably proximity and the fact that I wasn't having a heart attack, the decision was made to transport me to *Marina del Rey Hospital*. It was a small private hospital that I had been fond of for a long time.

It was a place that I had been tied to both personally and professionally for years. Plus I lived in the neighborhood, so it was a place that I knew very well – a place that I knew to be quaint, yet efficient, with a caring, hard-working staff. Best of all, because it sat in an affluent area, it was a hospital that had very little traffic and I knew that I could get great care without a lot of delay or hassle there.

I had been in this hospital at least a hundred times before this moment. But it was never as a patient. On a few of those occasions it was with my eldest son when he was suffering with a flare up of his asthma. On the other occasions, it was as a member of a small group of investment advisors who walked the halls and visited with both doctors and nurses helping them to plan for their retirement, ironically visiting some of the same departments that I was now going to be a patient in.

Being back here now as a patient was both surreal and a small world moment. I had watched patients come and go from this place for years never imagining that I would one day be one of them. I had talked to several of these doctors and nurses as they tried to work on their patients, giving almost no thought to the concerns of the patient seeking care for their health challenge.

Now the patient was me. Now I was getting the rare chance to see things from the patient's perspective – the perspective that I had in the past given no consideration to in my quest to earn a dollar. Now I was able to see things through the eyes of one of those people. I was able to see what really mattered for them in that moment.

In a true full circle moment, here I was at *Marina del Rey Hospital* and some of the same people that I had counseled for the better part of a decade were now being charged with giving me counsel with regard to what was taking place in my body.

Being in this familiar setting probably helped me to distract myself from seeing the full magnitude of the moment, as I spent a good amount of time socializing with familiar faces and down playing my situation. There too I had taken to that old male habit of trying to reassure these old clients and friends that I was fine. While all the while I had no clue about the real state of affairs taking place within my body.

I didn't yet know that just as I was declaring that all was well, doctors had found a tumor growing in my body, near my spine. I didn't yet know that just as I was declaring that I was starting to feel fine again, I couldn't sit up or get out of the bed. I didn't yet know that just as I was declaring that I'd be back on my feet in no time, I couldn't stand or walk.

I didn't yet know that just as I was declaring that nothing was going on, doctors felt that I was dealing with a life-threatening malady. I had no clue that they were beginning to suspect that I had cancer and that the only thing that they were unclear about was the degree to which the disease had progressed through my body.

In keeping with the typical male moment that I was having, while all of this was playing out I was so oblivious to what was going on both in my body and in the moment that the point came when I began to think that the moment had passed. Like the old times, I thought the pain was gone and I was feeling fine again.

In my state of delusion, I actually thought that I could walk out of that hospital and go home. I thought that I could simply take the matter up with the same doctor that I had been avoiding for the longest of time.

As I saw it, I'd be able to go about my day and our plans for the car purchase and keep the doctor's appointment that I had reluctantly planned for the following week. I had no clue that the feeling of fineness that I felt wasn't based upon the true feelings of my body, but rather it was the result of the high dosage of pain medication that they had started pumping into me from the first moment that the paramedics determined that I wasn't having a heart attack. I had no clue that I was far from fine and I would soon find out that I was still very much in pain.

At the end of the day, as familiar and comfortable as this environment was for me, it wasn't in the cards that I would be able to address the fullness of this matter at *Marina del Rey Hospital*. Because it was a small hospital, they didn't have the resources, equipment or the doctors needed to properly diagnose my situation; much less treat it.

So unbeknownst to me, while I was keeping myself distracted from my situation, efforts were being made behind the scenes to find a facility that had all of the things that would be needed to render the care that I would ultimately need to battle for my life.

"Did the doctors tell you what is going on with you?"

After a few days of effort, the point came when the nurse in charge of admissions found a facility that had all of the things that I needed. She approached my wife and I with what she thought would be received as welcomed news only to get the shock of her life when I shared my delusional views regarding my situation.

I started out by thanking her for all of the effort that she had put in on my behalf. I then proceeded to explain cockily that I was feeling much better and outline my plans to go home and take up the matter with my primary doctor. After all I reasoned to her, I had already set up an appointment prior to the events that had brought me into her hospital.

When I was finally done talking, I noticed that this lady's face had grown flush with a look of disbelief, the likes of which I had never seen before. With the experience that I now have I know that medical professionals deal with patients all the time who go into a state of denial in the midst of circumstances like the one that I was now in.

Still I am sure that I took the cake with my confident demeanor and with what was coming out of my mouth. The look of disbelief that she had on her face quickly gave way to a look of sheer panic – a look that both my wife and I could feel, as much as we could see.

From the earliest part of this exchange I sensed that the emotions that she was displaying weren't in any way based on concerns that she was having for her. Granted, this lady had spent the better part of 3 days of her professional life working to find the resources and services that I needed to even have a shot at fighting the cancer that was growing in my body.

And after all of that, here I was in my ignorant, deluded state of mind, appearing to show little appreciation for her efforts. Here I was telling her that I was prepared to set aside the resources that she had meticulously pieced together, opting instead to walk out of the hospital and leave the matter to be addressed at a later date and time.

As easily as any professional could have been offended by a fool rejecting their expertise and wasting their time, both my wife and I could tell that that wasn't what was driving this lady's emotions in that moment. Instead we could both sense that her concerns at that moment were clearly born out of a concern that if I didn't have enough sense to take the help that she was offering my condition wouldn't give me a second chance at the offer.

So after she came out of the literal twirl that all of my foolish talk sent her into, she slammed my chart on the bed next to me and let out a big, loud sigh. It was apparent that she really couldn't find the right words to say to me in that moment. So instead she ask me just one simple question,

"Did the doctors tell you what is going on with you?"

In truth, she really didn't have to say much. In spite of my level of delusion, her reaction, her facial expressions and her simple question said it all. And, they were also perhaps my first true glimpse that something serious was going on inside of my body.

As for the answer to her question, the truth was that the doctors hadn't told me anything. They were busy running their test but hadn't made their way back to my room to update me on any aspect of their findings. I guess they wanted to have a definitive answer before they worried me with details of an illness that they had yet to diagnose for sure.

I would also imagine that they didn't want to give a diagnosis when they didn't have the equipment or resources to let me know the extent to which the disease had attacked my body.

Looking back now it was certainly a blessing to encounter a set of doctors who thought that far before opening their mouths. To consider the agony that I would have gone through if I was given a bunch of dire information that was in some part based on professional speculation. It would have also been unbearable to be told that I had cancer, but there was no way for me to know to what extent I had the disease.

But the reaction of this nurse really did cause me to focus for a moment on the ramifications of the events that were set in motion by that bus ride and the situation that was now unfolding before me. It forced me to think thoughts that up to that time I had been doing a good job of distracting myself from thinking.

Now I started to think about what it was that the ER doctors weren't telling me. Now her simple question began to play over and over in my mind like a stuck record.

It was perhaps at this very moment that I first elevated this entire situation to the level of a faith project. At this moment my mind zeroed in on the fact that the results had not been revealed to me, and maybe that was for the reasons that I have already mentioned here. I also began to think about the fact that maybe that had been for reasons that were not so friendly to me.

As I began to think, maybe these doctors meant well, but knew something of a dire nature and didn't want to be the bearers of that bad news, especially since I wasn't going to receive any of my treatment at their facility. Maybe I was even worse off than they were prepared to tell me. Perhaps the disease had already ran its course through my body and I didn't have much more time for this world.

At that moment, my mind really could have easily gotten away from me. Like anyone who has gone through something like this knows, it is a lot to take in, and there is usually a ton of stuff to think about. And just like in my case, once the moment gets going, it is all coming at you with lightning like speed.

Luckily for me, at this very moment, my instinctive wisdom kicked in. In addition, it was at this very moment that I believe the *Creator* reminded me that I had been given the wisdom of *FAITH (APPLIED)* for just such a moment as this.

Once mindful of this fact, I took the first step in activating the healing power of the universe by ***accepting the challenge*** and making up my mind right then and there that,

> *"I would beat whatever they would eventually come back and tell me they found, period!"*

And with this decision, I was able to quiet my mind and place myself in a state of total peace with what was going on while the doctors finished running their test on me. Now I was ready to talk to the doctors that had been running test after test on me to gain an insight into their findings. For that matter, now I was ready to talk to any doctor about anything concerning the state of my health.

Now my wife could talk to me without me feeling the need to make the typical macho assertions that, *"I was okay."* Now I no longer needed to distract myself from dealing with what was going on in front of me and I was able to accept that something was definitely happening.

It was like the *Creator* knew that I needed to have my mind prepared before going any further into this moment, or even before going to the next hospital. Although, I still didn't allow myself to think about all of the details or dwell on things that I still didn't have all of the answers for, at least I was able to step into the reality of the moment and accept that there were matters that demanded my immediate and undivided attention. I was now ready to actually absorb what the doctors would ultimately come to share with me in a state of mind that was clear and calm.

It seemed like almost on cue, the head ER doctor came in to have a talk with me. I was sure that he would finally place a label on the package of symptoms that I had been experiencing for just about a year prior to that time. Plus, with all that I had gone through physically in the prior few days, the build-up was huge and I just knew that the moment had come when everything would be explained to me thoroughly.

However despite all of the build-up, when the moment arrived, the doctor really didn't say much or offer me anymore than to finally make it clear that something urgent was definitely going on inside of me. Thus in terms of its impact, the moment turned out to be rather uninformative and anticlimactic. And with that, just as fast as I had become its patient, the stage was set for me to head out of the doors of *Marina del Rey Hospital.*

The place had virtually been a worksite for me for the better part of a decade. Now in this trying moment, the place and the clients and friends that I had made there were a source of great comfort for me. But now my patient experience was ending and it was time for me to leave my little haven to find the answers to the question of what was ailing me, as well as the resources needed to heal it.

One dedicated nurse paved the way for me to overcome Multiple Myeloma

Having now had the chance to hear from the chief person that had been working to figure out why I had fallen out on that bus, the stage was now set for *Marina del Rey Hospital* to play a huge role in my subsequent healing and recovery from the cancer that I would eventually be diagnosed with.

The fact that this tiny hospital could play such a big part in my healing wasn't born out of the meeting that I had with the doctors there. Instead it was born out of the efforts the nurse who worked her butt off to find me the facility, the bed, the doctors and equipment to properly diagnose and treat the cancer that revealed itself on July 14th, 2012.

It was born out of the moment that she got me to awake from the state of denial and delusion that I had managed lose myself in while I was in the familiar confines of her hospital. It was born in the moment that she got me to finally focus on the serious situation that was taking shape and the very real fight that lay ahead of me.

Beyond her one simple, but powerful question, this nurse never found the words to speak back to the foolishness that was coming out of my mouth. And, after sitting through the awkward silence that her question commanded for a few moments, she simply excused herself from my room.

Not only was this exchange taking place at the end of a few days labor for her, but it was also occurring at the end of her work day. So as she turned to leave, in reality it wasn't just my room that she was parting way with, she would actually soon be leaving the entire building for the day. A fact that as simple as it sounds, was no small matter.

As I would later learn, an empty bed in any hospital is akin to precious real estate. To find such a bed in a place that had the doctors, equipment and resources that I needed, and that accepted my insurance was truly an aligning of the stars – a kind of miraculous event in its own right.

That is what this nurse had managed to piece together in my case, and as I would later learn, in a private room at a decent hospital to boot. This huge contribution to my ultimate healing and recovery is what I was threatening to blow off in my deluded view of where I was.

Surely that bed wasn't going to sit empty forever. Neither was that other hospital going to wait around for me to figure it out. For sure we weren't even the only ones vying for that bed.

Surely there were other agencies and patients seeking similar or even the exact same accommodations that we were looking for. It was simply a matter of supply and demand. I'd even bet that if the clock had swung by a few minutes in either direction, that bed, at that hospital doesn't exist.

But at that moment, as things stood, for no other reason than the hard efforts of this nurse, that bed had my name on it. But it was her staff and her department that still needed to work with their counterparts at the other hospital to actually put me in it. If she closed shop for the day before that task was complete, that bed surely would have quickly been snapped up by someone who wasn't stuck on stupid like I was.

Thankfully for me, it was at that moment that my wife became both my brain and my mouth, or as some would say, truly my better half. After setting me straight about the fact that I was going to accept the transfer and go to the other hospital, she ran down to this nurse's office to try and catch her to say *"Yes"* for me and get her to set the wheels in motion.

By the time she arrived at the office she had already left the building but because she was still on the property, her aid was able to page her. While she wouldn't turn around and come back, she did take a few moments to guide her aid through the process that they needed to undertake to transfer me from wherever she was on the grounds. And with that, they started the process of discharging me from their facility.

Thank goodness she did because what I didn't know while I was being difficult was that I was going to be discharged either way. Whether I would have ended up receiving care at another facility or somewhere else receiving no care was completely up to me. And, when I spoke of my desire to go home and worry about it later, I had made my decision as far as *Marina del Rey Hospital* and my insurer were concerned.

That's how close I came to screwing this all up. And that's what my wife saved me from by stepping in and making the decision for me when my own male stubbornness wouldn't allow me to. A lot of this truth I learned well after the fact and it all came as a shock to me to discover just how precarious my situation really was.

In recent times there have been several notable instances where hospitals have been caught discharging patients who were clearly in need of care into the streets because they had run out of options for treating them. Now here I was running the risk of putting myself in that kind of position by taking it for granted that I could play around with the help that was being offered to me.

In the end, even though it was a small facility, *Marina del Rey Hospital* played a big part in my faith victory and my healing and restoration from cancer. While I was there I barely came to appreciate the full seriousness of the moment that had taken place. I didn't realize the seriousness of the disease that had attacked my body. Nor did I truly grasp the full weight of the battle that lay ahead of me.

However it was at *Marina del Rey Hospital*, in the still early hours of this developing crisis that I took what I believe was the single most important step in the process of overcoming *Multiple Myeloma*. That step was to follow the urging of the **Spirit of God** and commit myself to using the 8 principles of **FAITH (APPLIED)** to meet the challenge that was laying out before me.

I believe that it was this commitment that set the healing power of the universe in motion and brought it to my aid to help me beat the cancer that had attacked my body.

As I left *Marina del Rey Hospital* I still had no definitive answer as to what was wrong with me. But, as it stood, I was on my way to a new hospital with the wisdom of **FAITH (APPLIED)** fully activated and with my mind right to begin the fight of my life. Of even greater importance, I was parting with one decision firmly made,

"I was going to beat whatever it was that the doctors would ultimately come back and tell me I had!"

Fate took me home to find healing and restoration

On July 17th, 2012, a private ambulance was summoned to transport me home to *Long Beach Memorial Hospital* so that doctors there could get to the bottom of why I had fallen out on that bus 3 days earlier.

The ride in the ambulance seemed just as bumpy as the bus ride that started this whole crisis in the first place, and just like on the bus, my body absorbed every single bump that we rolled over.

But unlike the bus ride that seemingly caused my fallout, perhaps because my body and spine had been secured, and I had been well sedated, the sensations of pain didn't hit me in the same way. Instead I felt a new reaction, a new sensation of pain that was milder in intensity, but a much scarier experience to go through.

This new symptom, or spasm, as it really should be labeled, would actually turn out to be a foreshadowing of a new reaction from my body that would soon become a huge problem for me. Because of this new development, the short trip up the freeway felt like it was much longer.

By now, my mobility had so diminished that the paramedics that were charged with transporting me had to do the work of being my body. In fact, I had so little control over my core that they literally had to move me from the bed that I was in when they entered my room to their gurney – and, then from their gurney to the bed at *Long Beach Memorial*.

A few short days ago I used to control my own body and do this work for myself. A few short days ago I used to stand up and walk whenever I had to move or get somewhere. But now, as a result of the life altering events of July 14th, 2012, I was flat on my back and totally helpless.

Maybe not coincidentally, it was like this ride, was a ride of truth for me. I don't know if perhaps it was because this was the first time that I had experienced any major movement since this crisis began, but it was on this ride that I realized the truth of the physical condition that this unfolding crisis had left me in. Or, maybe it was the first time that I allowed myself to accept this truth.

Which of these two it was I didn't know. But for the first time, what I did know or accept at this moment was that on top of the fact that I couldn't stand or walk, I was unable to move or lift the core of my body in any way.

To be clear, I wasn't paralyzed. I had complete feeling throughout my body. I just had absolutely no control over my core or upper body. And, if I tried to force my ability to move on my own, I would run the risk of causing myself pain. Needless to say, I was motivated to stay still as much as possible.

All I could do was look up – a new reality that made me feel totally disconnected from the world that I had last known just a few days earlier. Maybe this new condition was symbolic in some ways, especially given that I was now looking to the *Creator* and placing my faith in him for my healing and restoration.

I don't know what they would call the condition that my body was experiencing. But whatever it was called, I had lost the ability to move the main part of my body on my own, and for me, that felt a lot like what it must feel like to be paralyzed. It certainly felt as scary as what it must feel like to learn that you have been struck down by this fate for the first time.

Even though I still hadn't received an official diagnosis of what was ailing me, just realizing that the mobility that I had just a few days ago was gone was a lot to take in. To be sure, at this moment I definitely realized that I was facing a circumstance that was very likely the *"Greater Purpose"* for which the wisdom of *FAITH (APPLIED)* had been given to me to begin with.

Long Beach Memorial Hospital: A God sent chance for healing that I nearly squandered

My discharge from *Marina del Rey Hospital* didn't start until well after 9:00 pm and it was just about midnight when I finally arrived at the new hospital and was admitted to my room.

It was a private room on an upper floor and even though I couldn't get out of the bed and take it in, I could tell that it had a great view of the city below and perhaps even the ocean off in the distance.

As I settled into my new room, key members of my new care staff began to come in to both make themselves known to me and welcome me to *Long Beach Memorial Hospital*. Given the late hour, I was amazed that anyone would call upon me to welcome me and inquire as to whether I needed anything at the moment. I thanked each person and let them know that I was fine before excusing them from my room.

Just when I thought that I was alone to begin collecting my thoughts about this new place, a member from what they called, *"The Hospitality Team"* came in to request my breakfast order for the following morning. This inquiry took me totally by surprise and almost made me forget that I was in the hospital and not on one of my past hotel stays. It was a routine that would continue for the full duration of my stay there.

One of the people that also called upon me within the earliest moments of my arrival was the head of the nursing staff. After introducing himself and some of the key members of his staff, he informed me that there was a dream team of doctors assembled to care for me.

He let me know that each member of this team was expecting me and each would be in shortly to introduce themselves to me, as well. It was made clear that each had a date with me circled on their calendar and that that date had arrived.

If I didn't know any better, I would have thought that I was in one of the fancy hotels that circumstances had forced me to stay in when my family and I had been displaced in the past. I was now getting my first glimpse of what the nurse at *Marina del Rey Hospital* had arranged for me; and to think that I had risk blowing it off in my delusion and ignorance about the situation that was unfolding before me.

With these visits ended, I finally settled in for the night and tried to get some rest from what had been more than an eventful few days. Little did I know, what I had experienced at *Marina del Rey Hospital* was nothing compared to what I was about to experience at *Long Beach Memorial*. Little did I know that in pursuit of the healing and restoration that I said I would get *"no matter what I was ultimately diagnosed with,"* my days were about to get a whole lot more eventful.

Fighting cancer left no place for rest and leisure

Whereas I was able to lounge around and socialize at *Marina del Rey hospital*, it was clear from my very first morning at *Long Beach Memorial* that things would be different. In fact, it was clear from the very start that beating cancer here meant that this would be no place for rest and leisure.

It was barely the crack of dawn when the various members of the dream team of doctors that had been assembled to render care to me began to make their appearances. And, I quickly noticed that meeting with these medical professionals in real life was nothing like I had seen it portrayed on television.

In reality, aside from being introduced by name, each one of these doctors was referred to by the title of their specialty. In my case, there was an Internist who acted as a coordinator of my care. There was an Oncologist / Hematologist. There was a Neurologist. There was a Radiologist. There was a Radiation Oncologist. There was a Physical Therapist. And lastly, there was a Nutritionist.

Here I thought that I was coming to this hospital to see one doctor, but instead I got several of them. All of these specialized doctors, each with their own specific title made for a bit of confusion for a guy like me who hadn't dealt with a doctor in years.

Also, unlike the laid back doctors that I had been used to dealing with at *Marina del Rey Hospital*, each one of these doctors seemed to be itching to jump right into doing their part to get to the bottom of what was going on within my body.

As a matter of fact, the same thing could be said for the entire care staff at *Long Beach Memorial Hospital*. I had had very little sleep at *Marina del Rey Hospital*. I had just arrived at *Long Beach Memorial* around midnight, and I barely had any sleep when I was awakened at 6 am by a member of the nursing team requesting to draw some of my blood. As far as I was concerned, I hadn't even officially settled in and these folks were approaching me ready to get to work.

This was all in huge contrast to what my experience was prior to coming here. Before I could even gather my thoughts I found myself on this new program.

It was a program that I couldn't have known I was signing up for when I *accepted the challenge* to overcome the disease that had attacked my body. I would soon come to know this as my new daily routine, a routine that I would have to endure for the next 8 weeks.

This new program involved daily early morning blood test, body scans, test, chemotherapy and radiation treatments – more body scans and more test. All of these events would take place within about a 12 hour timeframe.

I had no clue that getting my healing and restoring my health would be so involved. But to rise up to meet the challenge that was now standing in front of me, I willingly submitted myself to this process.

Mr. Mandolph, I'm sorry to tell you but you have Multiple Myeloma

It wasn't long before the initial battery of test that saw my body poked, prodded and taxed, gave my doctors the information that they were looking for to diagnose exactly what was ailing me. The verdict was in and it was *Multiple Myeloma*. As I would later come to understand it, it's a cancer of the bone marrow – specifically, a problem with the plasma cells.

In coming to *Long Beach Memorial Hospital* I had no clue what was going on within me. As far as I was concerned, it still could have been an issue with my vascular system, heart or some other vital organ. Or, it could have been something related to my circulatory system, blood pressure or something along those lines. And, given the fact that I was a bit overweight, I even still thought it could have been an issue related to diabetes or something regarding my blood sugar.

What I never thought I would hear was that I had cancer. And, given how the diagnosis was delivered, I almost didn't hear cancer at all. That was because the doctor who first gave me this diagnosis, called it by its clinical name – *Multiple Myeloma*. The problem with that was that I had never heard of any such thing as *Multiple Myeloma*.

Thus, at that moment, hearing this diagnosis was just like meeting those doctors for the first time, as it was nothing like this kind of moment had always been portrayed on television or in the movies. In those portrayals, the doctor usually comes in and tells the patient in plain language that he has cancer. On the contrary, in the moment that I was experiencing, the word cancer was never used.

So to my ignorant ears, while the doctor was trying to let me know what it is that had been causing the problems that I had been suffering with for the past 12 months of my life, I didn't know what he was saying or how to react. Instead, all I heard him say was that while the disease wasn't curable, it was treatable. Beyond that, I didn't at all understand what I had just been diagnosed with.

I guess it really didn't matter that I didn't understand what I was hearing, or what the actual diagnosis was for that matter. It didn't matter because I had already made up my mind that *it wasn't defeating me*. And, since the general belief is that *"Ignorance is Bliss,"* perhaps I was even served by my ignorance at this moment.

I had already ***accepted the challenge*** of beating this disease and now in ignorance, maybe I found it a bit easier to maintain that belief. To my way of thinking, I couldn't fear or be overly concerned about an illness when I didn't even know what it was – a line of thought that I picked up on very fast.

I guess it could be said that I unconsciously chose to stay with this line of thought during most of the first year of my battle to overcome this disease, as I never asked the doctor to help me overcome my ignorance by explaining the details of this disease to me. Instead, I ultimately chose to focus my mind on the details of my plans to beat the disease.

As I instinctively saw it, this was far better than filling my mind with all of the details about how the disease could cause my demise, like most patients in my position would tend to do. Even at this early stage of my battle I knew that a decision like this could make the difference between finding the healing that I sought through *FAITH (APPLIED)* and not.

Eventually I did have enough sense to figure out that I was dealing with a form of cancer. But even then, I still didn't ask for specific details about what type of cancer it was, how it functioned or what type of life expectancy those who were confronted with it could look forward to.

As a matter of fact, the doctors and I never talked about what stage the cancer was in or how long of a life I could expect to live now that this cancer had entered my body. As far as I was concerned, those questions were not relevant to the decision that I had already made back at *Marina del Rey Hospital.*

Those questions only needed to be answered if you were going to lose to this cancer. As I reasoned, because I had already decided that I was going to beat it, those questions simply didn't apply to me.

Over the years I felt that I had been led through a series of trials and test that were orchestrated to lead me to master the wisdom of *FAITH (APPLIED)*. I had believed that this wisdom was passed to me for a *"Greater Purpose"* challenge that would ultimately show up in my life and require a great Faith to overcome. I was now engaged in confronting a crisis that by all appearance was easily that challenge. And I was now about to see if the wisdom of *FAITH (APPLIED)* would get me through it.

The power of FAITH (APPLIED) vs. the threat of Multiple Myeloma

Now with the diagnosis in, the doctors went to work on the medical front to craft a plan to do what they had been trained to do over many years to combat this disease. While for my part, having already made up my mind that I would beat this now named ailment, I went to work on the *FAITH (APPLIED)* front to carry out the plan that the *Creator* had given to me many years earlier to bring complete healing and restoration to my body.

While these doctors had received their medical training at some of the best educational institutions in the country, I had received my lessons in **FAITH (APPLIED)** from the best educational institution in the universe – UHK, *the University of Hard Knocks.*

Over the course of the weeks that followed, each one of these doctors had their say in outlining a treatment protocol that would give me the best chance to find the victory over cancer that I had pledged to beat before we met.

As they worked through their processes, I was tasked with considering and making a decision on everything from having surgeries to going through radiation; from submitting to various chemotherapies to doing nothing at all. I also had to weigh how aggressive or passive to be and whether it was worth risking my life and future health against the various side effects that would potentially come with the drugs and treatments.

Some of these side effects were life altering and potentially deadly in their own right. As the plan got laid out to me, all of this and more had to be seriously considered. And, all of this information was coming at me in a blur.

Adding to my challenge was the fact that I wasn't walking, a condition that brought with it a whole different set of issues for the doctors, and ultimately, for me to worry about.

There were potential side effects and ramifications of the treatments and drugs that I would be taking that were made all the more likely to occur by the fact that I was bedridden. This factor alone became the basis of many a concern and gave me a ton of stuff to consider as we worked toward my healing.

While the typical cancer patient would receive treatment on an outpatient basis and have the opportunity to use their home environment and make it the haven for healing that they need. I had to start my treatment as a patient in the hospital and deal with everything that it meant to be in the hospital. Knowing what I know now, a hospital is not the best place for setting up an expectation of healing, especially given my condition at the time.

Getting people, especially doctors to believe that a cancer patient can return to health when the cancer has seemingly already claimed his mobility is truly a hard sell.

In fact, I now know that all but one of my dream team of doctors had privately counted me out even as they were supposedly in the process of trying to bring about my healing. And, while they didn't speak their pessimism to me, I could feel it's presence in our interactions.

From a faith standpoint, it could have been very hard to believe that I would overcome this disease with these kinds of sentiments swirling around me. But that is exactly what I was confronted with doing if I was to see the power of *FAITH (APPLIED)* pull me through this challenging moment.

FAITH (APPLIED) consumed my mind when Multiple Myeloma overtook my body

As amazing as it seems now, even as this diagnosis was being presented to me, I still had no clue of just how bad a shape I was in and just how big of a faith battle overcoming *Multiple Myeloma* would be.

For one, I still couldn't get out of the bed and walk. Secondly, even in the bed I still couldn't move the core of my body. So whenever I needed to move around, I required the assistance of the nursing staff. Finally, I was still being heavily sedated for the great pain that I was still dealing with on an everyday basis – pain that I was still trying to avoid at all cost.

For their part, the doctors had a concern that too much movement from me put me at risk for further damage to my spine and could possibly result in me causing permanent paralysis. So they were constantly cautioning me against movement. They had further channeled their concern into the creation of a number of protective braces that I would have had to wear if I wanted to get up out of the bed for any reason.

This is the state of affairs that I found myself confronted with as I settled into the biggest faith fight of my life. And given this state of affairs, I couldn't have made a more important decision than the one I made when I decided that I would beat whatever the doctors were going to ultimately diagnose me with.

If I had waited to find out exactly what was going on with me before deciding whether I could beat it, the condition that I found myself in as I settled into *Long Beach Memorial Hospital* would have surely gotten the best of me.

Had I not already committed myself to fight for my healing and restoration before learning just how much of a fight lay ahead of me, I likely would have never found the belief and faith that I would ultimately need to fight. I couldn't have known all of the challenges that lie ahead for me – for my mind, body and spirit. But in the end it didn't matter because the 8 principles of **FAITH (APPLIED)** unleashed the healing power of the universe into my life and helped my body to make efficient work of mastering this disease.

In the end, it was mastered so effectively that my doctor has told me on numerous occasions that he still can't quite figure out how I did it. He has also told me that the doctors that had counted me out are having an even harder time wrapping their heads around my recovery – especially considering the condition that I was in when I first arrived at *Long Beach Memorial Hospital.*

FAITH (APPLIED) gave me the Confidence and Calm to get back on my feet and defeat Multiple Myeloma

There was a singular moment at *Long Beach Memorial Hospital* that epitomized the essence of what having the wisdom of **FAITH (APPLIED)** gave me to take into my battle with *Multiple Myeloma.*

This moment occurred just after I had received the official diagnosis that *Multiple Myeloma* was what was ailing me and serves as a shining symbol of the confidence and calm that the **Creator** has blessed me with as I have moved through this fight.

It should go without saying that receiving word that you have a life threatening illness like cancer is a hard pill to swallow. To be sure, the average person receiving such news from their doctor would immediately be hit by any number of negative emotions.

It's perfectly conceivable that doctors have to deal with each of these reactions many times throughout the course of their career. I would imagine that the average doctor is racked with feelings of dread anytime they are faced with having to carry out the unpleasant task of delivering this kind of news to a patient.

Looking back upon the experience of my doctor, *Dr. Sassan Farjami,* informing me of this news, it is safe to say now that he thought that I would react with one of the same negative emotions that he commonly witnessed. It would seem that the rightful reaction for a new cancer patient to have would be some form of a negative emotional outburst.

I would even go so far as to say that for most people, in most of the cases where a doctor is informing them for the first time that a serious, life-threatening illness has invaded their life, that would be the only plausible reaction. I'd imagine that that is the response that *Dr. Farjami* encounters more often than not.

But that wasn't my reaction at all. Again, I was perfectly ignorant to the fact *Multiple Myeloma* was a cancer. I was also totally oblivious to the full scope of my physical condition. I didn't yet realize that I couldn't get out of the bed or stand up, or walk for that matter.

Plus, as he gave me the diagnosis, in an obvious effort to soften the blow that he figured hearing the news that I had cancer would deliver to me, he chose to open up his comments by saying,

"Let me say upfront that while the condition that you now have isn't curable, it is highly treatable."

With my generally positive outlook, once I heard him speak these words I was perfectly reassured that I would be okay. It was more than enough to enable me to set my sights on finding the healing and restoration that I was seeking.

Again, I had already made up my mind that ***"I was going to beat whatever they came back and told me I had."*** I decided at that moment to use the power of *FAITH (APPLIED)* to overcome this disease and it didn't matter what the name of the disease was. When I made that decision, I meant it and I didn't need negative emotions for a disease that I was beating.

At that moment I had already used the power of *FAITH (APPLIED)* in several crises and I knew what the power of faith could do. In taking the matter on as a faith challenge, I would undoubtedly approach it with the same mentality that I had approached all of the other crises that I had stared down in the past. More importantly, because of all the crises that I had successfully stood against in the past, I couldn't help but to be filled with confidence and calm.

Having all of these positive attributes going for me I was able to wall my mind off from the common negative emotions that one might experience after being told that they had cancer.

As I saw it, I was going to win, and if I was going to win I didn't need negative emotions. For me at that moment, all of these factors led to a frame of mind where I didn't even know how to get down about the diagnosis.

A man of faith doesn't need negative emotions

Out of this frame of mind, as the treatment process got under way, I always found a way to be upbeat and positive. Eventually *Dr. Farjami* took note of my laid back attitude and cheerful demeanor. And I guess to him, my demeanor didn't seem to resemble the proper demeanor for a person who had just been diagnosed with cancer. I guess I should have had some form of negative reaction and in the days that had passed by, I hadn't expressed any of that kind of behavior.

I guess he had forgot about the moment when he asked me if I was a *Man of Faith*? Or, maybe he didn't realize that when I told him that I was, I wasn't just mouthing empty words. Maybe he didn't realize that wrapped up in my answer was all of the confidence and might that *FAITH (APPLIED)* had given me over the years.

Perhaps I hadn't made it clear that I had already made a firm decision to stand in faith and conquer the disease he was now diagnosing me with. Or, I didn't make it clear that because of my past faith victories, I knew that faith power was strong enough to get me through this challenge.

What he could never have known is that the emotions that he was seeing in me were rooted in the same attitude and demeanor that I had always maintained as I worked through past challenging moments. And, at this moment, I couldn't see any reason why I would or should treat his cancer diagnosis any different.

While this most definitely was the biggest faith battle that I had to face up to that time, I couldn't allow myself to feel any different about it than any of the other major crises that I had had to stare down in the past.

So at that moment, my attitude was confident and my demeanor was calm because I was looking to get past this disease and get back to my normal way of life as quickly as possible. While at that same moment, *Dr. Farjami* was watching and waiting for me to have the typical emotional breakdown that his patients had always had.

When that moment didn't show up it perplexed him so much so that he decided that I must be suffering from an even worse emotion – denial. He immediately stepped forward to try and diagnose whether I was now suffering from an emotional malady on top of the cancer that I now had.

"Mr. Mandolph, do you understand you have cancer?"

As a matter of routine, *Dr. Farjami* would come see me every morning to see how I was doing and update me on the schedule of test, treatments and procedures that he had planned for my day.

By his normal routine, he would come in around 7:00 am, spend a few moments examining me, quiz me about what symptoms I might be experiencing, give me my update and then leave me to the care of the nurses that would administer the various orders that he had just given.

By this routine, normally when he came in he was physically trying to get his work done as quickly as possible so that he could get to the next patient, in the long list of patients that he had to stop in on before heading back to his office for more patients.

By this routine, he would normally be out the door as fast as he had come in it. In the days since I had first arrived at *Long Beach Memorial* I had just about gotten this whole routine down pat and accepted it as the way my time in the hospital would go.

Even though I was stuck at this hospital, even though I was stuck in the bed and even though I was dealing with a serious situation, I too had a routine way that I liked to start my mornings. By my routine, aside from the official ways that I had to deal with the doctors and nurses, it wasn't my desire to spend my mornings dealing with them, or for that matter, the reality of *Multiple Myeloma*.

Whereas most people in my situation would have dialed in and clung to these medical professionals at this moment, I had never been an illness minded person and this illness didn't change that.

In this spirit, when any of my doctors came to see me, it was my custom to help them breeze through my room as quickly as possible. However on this particular day, when *Dr. Farjami* called on me, it quickly became clear that he wasn't in his usual hurry to leave and my efforts to move him along weren't working.

On this day, instead of coming right to my bedside, performing his routine exams and asking his customary questions, he came in and simply took a seat. I knew this moment was going to be different when he put my guardian *"Big Joe the Family Dog"* on his lap.

Big Joe is my youngest son's favorite stuffed animal. A child sized, standing doll that we call our family dog. On this morning, instead of moving to go over the schedule of activities that he had planned for me, he started our time together by asking to hear the story of *Big Joe*.

Normally we'd talk about subjects ranging from the status of test that he had recently run to informing me about test or procedures that were upcoming. Then as soon as these talks were done, he'd ask me if I needed anything and then he'd flow right out the door. But on this day, given that we spent the first 30 minutes of our time together talking about the story of a stuffed animal, he clearly wasn't seeking to simply flow through.

As we settled into the moment beyond our discussion of the story of *Big Joe*, I noticed that *Dr. Farjami* didn't do any of the things that I was accustomed to him doing. Instead what he did do was assume a posture that said, *"Let's chat."* In these simple actions, in this posture he set a tone that said that this moment was about to be different from any of the other mornings that we had had up to that point.

As our talk shifted from *Big Joe*, it quickly turned to me and the state of my mental and emotional well-being. Doctor opened up by letting me know that he had been watching me to see how I would react to the news of my diagnosis.

He let me know that most of his cancer patients had reacted to receiving the news of their diagnosis by having some form of an emotional melt down. He noted that from what he could see, I didn't seem to have a reaction.

He said that from what he could see by my demeanor, it was like I thought all was well. Seeing this demeanor had baffled him to the point where he felt that he should check in to see where my head was. He went on to ask a line of questions that were clearly put together to get what he thought was my real take on my situation.

Wrapped up in this line of questions was a clear indication that my doctor thought that I was either acting like all was well on the outside, yet feeling different on the inside. Or even perhaps worse, suppressing my true feelings altogether.

I tried to answer his questions to the best of my ability, but I guess he wasn't satisfied with my answers. Before I knew it, *Dr. Farjami* hit me with a question that was meant to cut to the chase and make sure that I was living in reality. At just that moment, he asked me point blank,

"Mr. Mandolph, do you understand you have cancer?"

With that question it was like he was trying to give me the diagnosis all over again. Only this time he didn't use the clinical label of *Multiple Myeloma*. This time he put the diagnosis in terms that anyone could easily understand.

It was enough to have to get through being told that your body had been attacked by a deadly disease and contemplate the fact that your life would likely never be the same the first time. Now here I was receiving that news for a second time.

However as challenging as that reality was, wrapped up in this moment was a chance for me to once and for all reaffirm what I believed this moment was about and how I felt it would end. Not to mention a chance for me to prove that my initial response had been real. Most importantly, it was a chance for me to explain my faith and to finally show *Dr. Farjami* how I saw the whole matter of this illness.

In all of these ways it was a chance for me to set the tone for the journey to healing that we were about to embark on. I instinctively knew that in helping me to fight this disease, he would ultimately have to take his cues from me. So taking this moment to try to help my doctor to understand my faith would be time well spent.

"Mr. Mandolph, it's okay to cry!"

From the beginning of the time that we have been working together, it seems like *Dr. Farjami* has had a time understanding my faith. I have tried to explain it to him. I have tried to explain that I have had other crises in my past – that I believed that my faith had been developed for this moment through those past moments of challenge. I have tried to explain that I do realize that this is the biggest crisis that I've had to use my faith for.

I've even tried to explain why I would not treat this crisis any different than any of the other crisis that I have had to use the power of faith to overcome in the past. I have tried to explain all of this throughout the time that *Dr. Farjami* has been treating me for *Multiple Myeloma.*

And, in response to the larger question that he was asking me at this moment, I tried to explain it all over again. But just as I could tell he didn't hear me in the past, at this moment he didn't hear me either.

As this moment and conversation took yet another turn, perhaps the real purpose of why *Dr. Farjami* was stopping in to talk to me on this day was revealed. It was not so much evident in the questions that followed as it was in what he proceeded to tell me next. At that moment, he looked me right in the eye and said,

> *"Mr. Mandolph, you have cancer and you don't have to keep up the strong front about it. It's okay to get angry!*

It's okay to get sad or question why is this happening to you!

Mr. Mandolph, it's okay for you to cry! That's what most people do when they receive a cancer diagnosis."

He obviously thought that I was feeling some of these emotions inside but maybe due to the shock of the situation, I was just keeping it in. I can understand his position. Again, it is a reaction that I am sure he sees all the time in working with patients that are being told that they are dealing with such a serious illnesses for the first time.

Maybe these people have an easy time of reacting that way in part because they allow themselves to take ownership of the cancer right away. In some ways I think doctor was hoping to get me to take ownership of his *Multiple Myeloma* diagnosis. Maybe he thought that I hadn't done so because I didn't hear him clearly the first time.

But, what he was failing to see was that I heard him when he gave me the diagnosis the first time. And he was definitely failing to understand the fact that just because I had been diagnosed with cancer, didn't mean that I would accept it as *"Mines"* – just because this disease had entered my body, didn't mean that I had to give it a permanent place in my life.

One of the things that I instinctively understood from day one was that this disease doesn't belong to me. As I have moved through the process of being treated for this disease I have never accepted any part of the process as *"Mines."* I have been more then careful not to allow anyone to get me to refer to the disease or any element of the treatment process as if it were *"Mines."*

From the very beginning of this process, many of the doctors and nurses have tried to get me to call this disease *"Mines."* As I have moved through the treatment process, I have had several of the professionals treating me refer to the medicines and procedures that they were administering as *"My medicines, my treatments."*

I can even remember a particular occasion when *Dr. Farjami* tried to get me to accept *Multiple Myeloma* as a condition that I now own and will own for the rest of my life. In that conversation he looked me right in the eye and said,

"Mr. Mandolph, I need you to realize that you now have this disease and you will likely be dealing with it and taking medicine for it for the rest of your life."

To him it appears that these labels seem both rightful and harmless. But to me they are far from either and I have always rejected any notion that this disease will be with me forever.

Fortunately for me, I knew that from a faith standpoint, there is much that can be conveyed in a label. If I could accept having *Multiple Myeloma* as *"Mines"* – as something that I owned and something that would be with me for the rest of my life, I could also likely accept not being healed and recovering from it.

Fortunately for me, I knew that that was what was at stake at this moment when *Dr. Farjami* approached me to talk about my emotional state. Fortunately, I knew that if I took ownership of this disease, that act would have likely become my undoing. It didn't matter if that ownership was taken under the guise of letting off some emotional steam. The end results would have likely been the same.

Standing in faith means that there is no steam to let off because the matter is resolved and the victory is already yours. So at this moment, I knew that I needed to put an end to the question of where my emotions were once and for all – it was time for me to speak up and declare my position on the matter of this illness. I knew that it was time for me to give *Dr. Farjami* a master course in *FAITH (APPLIED)* whether he was ready to receive it or not.

Tears are for those dying of cancer, not those who are defeating it

After hearing him out, I could appreciate the effort that he was making to check in on my emotional well-being and to console me at what he saw as a time of concern. He deserves a ton of credit for the fact that he was even paying attention to the emotional wellness of his patient.

I have known of several occasions where people that I know were under the care of a doctor who paid no attention to any aspect of their well-being, emotional or physical. In the end, this lack of caring on the part of their doctor usually proved fatal to their chances of overcoming the disease that they were fighting.

However, I still had to set him straight about my faith, the source of my confidence and calm. Not to mention the fact that I had to answer his request for me to show some negative emotion.

Given the sincerity of my faith, it wasn't hard for me to come up with an answer to the questions regarding my demeanor. I gave him the only answer that I could give at this moment. I said,

"Dr. Farjami, tears are for the dying, not the living."

At that moment, I declared once and for all that as far as I saw it,

"Negative emotions as a whole are for the person who believes that he is dying of cancer, not the person who knows that he is defeating it."

Furthermore, I let him know that in choosing to stand in faith and put my trust in the **Creator**, I was certain that I wouldn't be let down. I had never been let down before in a moment of crisis, and I knew that I wouldn't be let down now.

I didn't need negative emotions because I was certain from the first moment that I entered *Long Beach Memorial Hospital* that I was going to overcome the disease that brought me there. That is the same wisdom that I tried to share with my friend *Earnest Peacock III* when he was having trouble wrapping his mind around the fact that cancer had entered his life.

It is wisdom that I have found to exist in the make-up of every person that I have met or studied who has overcome a major illness. It was wisdom that I instinctively possessed the day that my doctor decided to step forward and give me permission to indulge myself in the dangerous sea of negative emotions. Looking back upon this moment now, I am grateful that the **Creator** blessed me with the words and wisdom to answer my doctors concerns.

This wisdom permeated everything in my approach to battling this disease. It set the tone for everything that I have done to find healing and to recover from *Multiple Myeloma*. It was the confidence that I had with me as I have taken in all of the medicines that I have had to consume and the procedures that I have had to endure.

It was the calm that was with me in my hospital room. It was the calm that was with me when I went home. It is the calm that is with me as I pen these words today.

FAITH (APPLIED) and the Creator are the true sources of my healing and restoration

With that said, our discussion was ended, this moment was over, *Dr. Farjami* excused himself and he left my room. We never had this type of talk again. As a matter of fact, after this moment our daily talks resumed both the brevity and tone that they once had.

To me, it has always been significant that this talk took place near the very beginning of the process of us working together for my healing and restoration.

For me, it gave me a clear glimpse of the lengths to which this doctor was willing to go to provide care for his patients. It showed me that he was truly paying attention to all of the aspects of the care that he was charged with delivering to his patients.

And, I believe for him, it gave him a perfect representation of who he was treating. It also set the tone for how we were to work together to return me to the health and wellness that I once enjoyed.

I feel the need to make it clear that I'm not trying to suggest that I have never had a down moment, a doubtful moment, or even that I have never shed tears over the fact that cancer entered into my life. That not only wouldn't be accurate, but I feel that to leave you with that impression might do more harm than good.

Let me assure you that I definitely have had a few occasions where facing the gravity of this situation made me get emotional and even tearful.

But what I can also say is that through this spirit and by the power of the wisdom of *FAITH (APPLIED)* I have always been able to quickly pull myself out of that moment. I have always been able to lift myself out of that dark emotional place and get back into a place of faith. And I know that that has been a large part of how I have been able to regain my mobility and overcome this disease.

I have been told that my recovery is not typical of a person battling a bone marrow cancer like *Multiple Myeloma*. This is even more apparent when you consider the condition that the disease had left my body in after that bus ride jarred the mass into my spine.

It's even more apparent when you consider the fact that I didn't have a bone marrow transplant and only required one round of radiation treatment and one round of chemotherapy to place the disease into a full state of remission.

I don't profess to be an expert on *faith-based healing* and I am certainly not a doctor. All I can do is tell you of my experience and how through the might of the *Creator*, the power of *FAITH (APPLIED)* has given me the healing that I was praying for.

Now as I sit here writing these words, the outcome of this battle, the healing I found is a case for the record books and I am beyond convinced that this moment played a pivotal role in me finding that healing.

Obviously my reaction to having my body attacked by *Multiple Myeloma* on July 14th, 2012 could have been totally different. And, if it had been, I believe that so to would have been the outcome of my fight to overcome this cancer.

8 Principles for activating the healing power of the universe

Today I have come back from the place where I couldn't get out of the bed, where I couldn't walk, where my body was racked with pain and where cancer was threatening my life.

I have come back to the place where I am out of the bed, back on my feet, back in control of the core of my body and where MRI and P.E.T. Scan after MRI and P.E.T. Scan, and blood test after blood test has found there to be no active cancer growing in my body.

Just reaching this place gives me the right to declare that I have defeated *Multiple Myeloma*. Just reaching this place gives me the right to say that **FAITH (APPLIED)** is the source of my healing and restoration. I know beyond all doubt that it was my application of these 8 principles that activated the healing power of the universe.

The healing power of the universe was activated when I *"Accepted the Challenge"* of beating the disease that attacked my body even before I knew it by the name *Multiple Myeloma*. It was activated when I refused to see this moment as a challenge that was too big for the faith that the **Creator** gave me – or cancer as a malady that was bigger than what He could do in my life to deliver healing and restoration.

The healing power of the universe was activated when I refused to settle for the state of immobility that *Multiple Myeloma* had placed my body in and chose to set my sights on *"Setting New Health Goals"* and plotting the **Four Fundamental Truths of My Recovery**.

The healing power of the universe was activated when I *"Positioned Myself for Healing"* by *leaving my comfort zone* and submitting myself to the serious medicines and the *aggressive* treatments that were needed to place the disease into remission – and, when I created an environment that was a haven for my healing and restoration.

The healing power of the universe was activated when I *"Avoided the Loser Clique"* of so-called medical professionals who made the mistake of counting me out and the ignorant friends / relatives who tried to bind me to their dumb views and expectations of my condition and recovery – views and expectations that would have brought harm to my mind, body and spirit had I tried to engage in keeping up with their ignorance.

The healing power of the universe was activated when I took a *"Leave No Stones Unturned"* approach to finding my healing. And, when I *"Asked Everyone Who Might Help" and explored all the options that were available* to help me return to health and wellness.

The healing power of the universe was activated when *"I Decided Not to Waste Time With Any Person or Situation That Wasn't Focused On My Goal"* of total recovery, nor on any medicine or procedure that wasn't helping me to get back to the health that I enjoyed before *Multiple Myeloma* crashed into my life.

The healing power of the universe was activated when I *"Delayed Judgment"* on all of the pressing and weighty matters that I had to consider as I moved through the treatment and recovery process – as well as the larger question of whether or not all of the treatments and procedures were actually having an effect on the cancer that they were intended to treat.

Finally, the healing power of the universe was activated when I pledged to commit the rest of my life to working to build a level of health far and away above the health that I possessed before *Multiple Myeloma* barged into my life.

I pledged then, as I do now to *"Work Up To and Through the Deadline"* of my time on this planet to regain all that I lost in the way of mobility and wellness in the aftermath of the events of July 14th, 2012.

In all of these ways, I used these 8 principles of **FAITH (APPLIED)** to activate the healing power of the universe and the **Creator** restored my mobility and cleansed my body of the cancer to the place where I can now boldly proclaim that the wisdom of **FAITH (APPLIED)** heals!!!

I can also now proclaim with all confidence that no matter what tomorrow holds there are two fundamental truths that are firmly established as I pen these words on this day, the first is that as I sit here today,

"I am healed from Multiple Myeloma"

Second, the day will come when I and each one of us will depart from this earth. When that day comes for me, it will in no way diminish the truth that on this day,

"By the grace of God, I am a Cancer Survivor!
For this gift I am forever gratefulto my Creator!!!"

8 steps for applying faith to the affairs of your life

So there you have it – **FAITH (APPLIED)**. I purposely titled the book the way I did because we have all heard that we need to, *"Have Faith."* In our times of challenge we have all heard that we need to, *"Keep the Faith."* But if you are like me, the question has always been, *"How?"*

Until the *Creator* gave me these principles, I had no answer to that question. I had no way of knowing how faith could be put to practical use in the affairs of my life. Like many, I thought that it was a matter of a feeling or an act of believing in something at a given moment.

But in a moment of challenge or when I was trying to attain some goal, when I did those things, when I tried to have what I thought were the right feelings or beliefs, I still failed. That all changed in the aftermath of July 30th, 1995. That's when the *Creator* gave me what I ultimately realized was this formula for **FAITH** in an *(APPLIED)* state!

I feel the need to call your attention to the fact that the key to understanding these principles is to realize what each one meant on the day that they were first given. That's why I started the explanation of each principle out by discussing the role it played in creating the miracle that took place on July 30th, 1995 – the day of *the Great TV Incident*.

I also feel the need to reiterate the fact that the real power of **FAITH** is that when these principles are **APPLIED** properly, there comes to your aid another power or force that can get those things done that you can't get done alone. That is what I will call the spiritual side of applying these 8 principles to the affairs of your life.

The practical side of applying them in the way that the *Creator* first presented them to me is that in doing so, you will literally be walking down whatever challenge that you are looking to overcome, or goal that you are seeking to bring to pass.

In both these ways, this **FAITH (APPLIED)** formula represents 8 proven steps for applying the universal force known as faith to the affairs and circumstances of your life. In my own life, time and again using these 8 principles allowed me to conquer the crises that my family and I were confronted with. Ultimately, it was these 8 principles that gave me the confidence and calm to come back from immobility and defeat cancer.

At the end of the day I don't know if I could have achieved these feats by my own might. But I do know that there is a spirit and power that was standing at the ready to involve itself in the affairs of my life so that I didn't have to.

Because of these facts, I know that when we align ourselves with these 8 principles, this power goes to work on our behalf to get done what we could likely never get done alone.

I know that this spirit and power can help us to tap into the higher abilities that we have inside of us; **it can literally see around the corner, move the mountain and align heaven and earth** to give us the victory over circumstances that we could never defeat otherwise.

I know that when we apply these 8 principles we activate the miracle-making power and the creation force of this universe – the same power that created everything that is. I also know that through the application of these 8 principles the aid of this power is yours and mines for the taking.

To use it we only need to know that it is there and learn how to hear the still, small voice that whispers its urgings and obey the guidance that they convey to us.

Looking back now, those urgings were there with me from a very early point in my life. They were there to guide me when I was a young father and husband struggling to find a career that would allow me to provide for my family.

They were there to guide me when the *Los Angeles Child Support Enforcement Department* wrongly tried to take away my career, my finances and my freedom. They were there to guide me when *Multiple Myeloma* barged its way into my life, snatched my mobility and threatened to take my very life.

The urgings of the spirit of the **Creator** were there in all of these moments of crisis to help guide me to victory. Thanks to these victories, I have learned to never doubt the instructions that it puts before me – no matter how off base those instructions may appear to be.

Thanks to these victories, I have also learned that this power is 1000% reliable. Based upon my experience, when these 8 principles of *FAITH* are properly and steadfastly *(APPLIED)*, they always lead to odds defying success.

Faith for the Greatest Purpose

I have now had the occasion to reconsider the question of the real purpose for why the *Creator* gave me the wisdom of *FAITH (APPLIED)*. As I have already mentioned, there was a time when I thought that it was to give me the faith to stand against *Multiple Myeloma*.

From the vantage point that I now have, with the victory over that crisis that I have now won, I have an unshakeable feeling that that crisis and every other crisis that I have faced leading up to this point was really sent so that I would have faith for an even bigger cause, or what I would call, the *"Greatest Purpose."*

From where I sit now, I can clearly see that this is the real reason why the *Creator* gifted me with the wisdom of *FAITH (APPLIED)*. I believe that this *"Greatest Purpose"* is to live the life that He created each of us to live. I believe that's a life filled with happiness, joy, peace and abundance – a life that's filled with health and wellness and one that's free of worry, lack and stress.

If I had to put it in a slogan, I believe that it's about living a *"Victorious life"* – a life where we use the wisdom and knowledge that we've been blessed with to pursue the interest and opportunities that we've been given. Then trust in our *God* given gifts and talents to deliver all the best that this life has to offer.

That is the *"Greatest Purpose"* that I believe the spirit of *God* is now urging me to use these principles for. I believe that when we embrace this *"Greatest Purpose"* and make it the focus of our faith journey, we will have the power to overcome any challenge. We will also have the power to order up anything that we could ever need or want from the universe, at will.

Throughout this work, in an effort to help you perfectly understand how to wield thie power of *FAITH (APPLIED)*, I have tried to show you what each principle meant on the first day that they were handed to me. I have tried to give you a clear understanding of the broader implications of each principle, and finally, I have tried to show the role that each principle played in helping me to overcome *Multiple Myeloma*.

It is my belief that in helping you to see the effect that these principles had from these 3 different vantage points, you will easily be able to see how that power can work across the full spectrum of your life. In helping you to gain a clear understanding of how this power led to victory in the affairs and circumstances of my life, it's my hope that you will be easily able to put this same power to use in the affairs and circumstances of your own life.

Having consciously used these principles to take on and gain victories in a broad range of challenges and goals, I can tell you that they have not failed me once. Whether I was chasing a goal that would have no real impact on my life or my back was up against the wall or my very existence was at stake, whenever I have *APPLIED* my *FAITH* through the use of these 8 principles, they have always pulled me through and I have always come out on top.

Through the application of the wisdom of *FAITH (APPLIED)*, the *Creator* has perfectly delivered miracles for me time and again. Now as a result, I can tell you that if you will trust Him and apply this same wisdom to the affairs of your life, He will reveal the same miracle-making power to you.

In fact, I know if you will trust Him and apply this wisdom, the day will come when you too will be able to look back over your life and see that *FAITH (APPLIED)!*

Your
Guiding
Principles

FAITH (APPLIED)

8 Steps for Activating the Miracle-Making Power of the Universe

In a moment of challenge, these 8 steps will allow you to activate the miracle-making power of the universe. In pursuit of your goals and dreams, these 8 steps will allow you to turn on the creative power of the universe.

Step 1: Accept the challenge

What is the challenge that you are confronted with in trying to meet this crisis or achieve your goal? Can you identify it? Is it one main barrier, or can it be broken up into multiple smaller parts? Whatever the case, even if you can't identify what it is, don't think about what sounds realistic or doable for you. Just accept the challenge as it is. Be open minded and believe that it can be done, that you can do it, and hold this in your mind and thoughts intensely from that point on. Most importantly, during the undertaking do not see or entertain, for even one second, any other outcome for yourself other than the one you desired when accepting the challenge. That is the starting point of **FAITH (APPLIED)***.*

Step 2: Set the goal and a firm deadline to do what must be done to achieve the challenge

What is the goal that you are confronted with in trying to meet this crisis or achieve your goal? Are you clear about what that goal is? Is it one main goal, or can it be broken up into multiple smaller goals? Is it laid out in the form of the tasks that must be achieved in order to get the goal? Is there a specific timeframe within which you need to achieve this goal? The circumstance driven goal will usually include a specific time table for which completion is required, and for that matter, a consequence for failing to achieve the desired result. If your goal does not have a specific timeframe for completion and consequence for failure, give it both of these. Then be prepared mentally to stick to them, no matter what the outcome.

Step 3: Position yourself for success

Leave your comfort zone and take up an aggressive posture where you can make the most attempts possible at getting your goal. From this position, actively pursue your goal through a focused work effort. If it is a multi-day goal, do something physical each day to get your goal. If it is a one day goal, do something each hour. Do this no matter what the outcome of your last action, or results of the previous day. Don't quit this process until you have the goal.

Step 4: Stay out of the loser clique

Avoid hanging with and socializing with losers who aren't trying to go for the goal anyway. Especially do not talk with them about the goal and take in their negative self-defeating views of, why me; I wouldn't do it, so you can't; fault finding; blame and responsibility shifting.

Step 5: Ask everyone who might help

Try every avenue there is to getting your goal. Don't assume where your results will come from. Just be in motion and try every source until you have your goal. Also, don't be afraid to go high in pursuit of your goal. Often we think that it is easier to achieve small things than big things. We think the doors in lowly places will open for us faster than the doors in high places. Or, we believe it is easier to make it among the unsuccessful or the poor than it is to make it among the rich and successful. Simply put, we think that we are sure to get our goal if we just aim low enough. And, on the contrary, we think there is no way we can get our goal from a higher place. The truth is just the opposite. Often, it can be easier to get what you seek from the higher place than the lower one. It is we who usually struggle to believe that we can go to, and get our goal from the higher places. Realize now that asking *everyone who might help means being open to all of your options – the high end ones, as well as the low end ones. You don't know who will help you or where your results will come from, so truly stay open to asking everyone and exploring every avenue – including those in, and of high places.*

Step 6: Don't waste time on people and situations that don't help you get your goal

Move on once you see that you will not get what you need from a person or situation, no matter who it is or how promising it looks. It's better to pursue the lowly that will help you than to waste time chasing or waiting around for the mighty or the promising who will not help you. Often times, in the time that it takes to get one waste of time person to come around or give you their final "NO" you could have gotten five other people to go your way.

Step 7: Delay Judgment

While keeping your mind fixed on your challenge and goal intensely throughout the day or the days allotted, don't let the clock, the calendar, your own doubtful thoughts or the doubts and/or words of others discourage you and/or make you judge or doubt whether you will get to your goal. Don't let the judgment of others become your own judgment. Also, don't let the fact that things don't seem to be moving in your favor, i.e., prospective helpers canceling meetings, deals not closing, money not coming in when you thought it would, a slow answer to a request for help or an application you have submitted cause you to doubt that you will get your goal. Exercise patience here. At this moment, just take a deep breath, relax, clear your mind of any negative, doubtful thoughts and restate what is done and what needs to be done. Put off thinking and/or judging beyond that and just keep moving as if things are going your way.

Step 8: Work up to and through the deadline

Fight on until you have your goal realizing that often times every minute counts. Delivery often comes in the 11th or the 12th hour and success is usually buried just beyond the point of your frustration. Hanging in there mentally, emotionally and physically right up to and through the deadline is often the key to getting your goal. So work on hanging in through the end while staying in prayer and remaining positive, without getting doubtful, negative or frustrated in the process. Above all, no matter what your feelings, just keep working until the final tick of the clock.

FAITH (APPLIED) Project Planner

Describe the outcome that you desire from this Challenge / Goal:

Do not see or entertain, any other outcome for you, for even a second of the challenge.

Don't think of what sounds realistic / doable. Just accept the challenge as it is. Accept that some things are impossible for men, but with God, all things are possible!!! What you can do by Faith (Applied) is not based upon your might, but rather the might / power of the Creator.

Project Start Date: _____

#1 Accept the Challenge	#2 Set the Goal	#3 Position for Success	#4 Avoid the Loser Clique	#5 Ask for the Help You Need	#6 Do Not Waste Time	#7 Delay Judgment	#8 Work to & thru the Deadline
My mind's made up to:	5 Tasks to my Success:	1ˢᵗ Comfort Zone to leave	5 People to Avoid:	5 High People to ASK:	5 Signs to Move On:	- Take a Deep Breath	Project Deadline:
	Task 1.	#1.	#1.	#1.	- Relax Your Body	
	Task 2.	2ⁿᵈ Comfort Zone to leave	#2.	#2.	- Clear Your Mind	
	Task 3.	#2.	#3.	#3.	- Delay all questions	
	Task 4.	3ʳᵈ Comfort Zone to leave	#4.	#4.	- Release all doubts!	What's Done Now?	#1.
	Task 5.	#3.	#5.	#5.	What's Done Now?	3 Post Deadline Tasks:	#2.
		#4.				To Be Done Now?	#3.
		#5.					
By His Might	Put It All In	Get in the Flow	Avoid the Faithless	Turn Every Stone	Go Past Non-Help	Don't Talk You Out	Fight Thru the End

If more space is needed, use a separate sheet of paper to record your answers.

A Personal Message for the Reader

Thank you for taking the time to read *FAITH (APPLIED)*. It's my hope that this wisdom will do for your life, all of the great things that using it has done for my life. This truly is powerful wisdom from above. But to be clear, it is not my claim that these principles alone are the source of the miracles that they make possible. Nor is it my claim that you or I are the source of the miracles that we might obtain through their use.

Hebrews 12:2 says that, Jesus Christ is the author and finisher of our faith. I must state emphatically that my faith is in my Lord and savior, Jesus Christ and the God that is his and our Creator.

Romans 12:3 says that, the Creator has given each one of us the measure of faith. If you have never established a personal relationship with your Creator, there is no greater way to get the power of *FAITH (APPLIED)* flowing in your life.

John 14:6 says that there is only one way to the Father. It is through a personal relationship with Jesus Christ. If you have never given your life to Jesus, no single act will ever do more for you in this life or in the after life to come. If you haven't yet established a relationship with Jesus, there is no better time than the present moment to do it!!!

Will you say this simple prayer?

Dear Jesus,

I know I'm a sinner and I need a savior. I believe You are the Son of God, that You died, paying the price for my sins, and rose again. I ask You to come into my life now. I now receive You as my Lord and Savior.

If you have said this simple prayer, know that you have now accepted Jesus as your Lord and Savior and all the angels in heaven are rejoicing! Let me both congratulate and welcome you to the Christian family! You have taken a powerful step to unleash the real and true power of *FAITH (APPLIED)* in your life.

Now get in a Christ-centered, Bible-based, Faith-centered church in your area. Most importantly, from this day forward know that God is real! God is still here! God is still involved in the lives of his children today! And, through *FAITH (APPLIED)*, God is still your personal miracle maker!

Brent Mandolph II

A book for cancer patients and loved ones:

I Beat cancer with FAITH & YOU Can Too!!!

In "I BEAT CANCER WITH FAITH & YOU CAN TOO!!!" I will share 5 working principles of the FAITH (APPLIED) wisdom that the Creator revealed to me 25 years ago – vital principles I used to activate the healing power of the universe and beat cancer.

Made in the USA
Middletown, DE
25 January 2023